RUSSIA-UKRAINE WAR

Strategic Conundrum

RUSSIA-UKRAINE WAR

Strategic Conundrum

Editors

Bharti Das

Uday Pratap Singh

PENTAGON PRESS LLP

First published in 2025 by
PENTAGON PRESS LLP
206, Peacock Lane, Shahpur Jat
New Delhi-110049, India
Contact: 011-26490600

Typeset in Palatino, 11 Point
Printed by Aegean Offset Printers, Noida

ISBN 978-81-971986-5-6 (HB)

www.pentagonpress.in

CONTENTS

FOREWORD

The unfolding of the Russia–Ukraine crisis has exponentially enhanced the interest in scholarly work focusing on its impact on other regions, where fissures might turn into fault lines, resulting in ballistic behaviour from the states. The War is yet to abate, and has taken the form of attrition, defying modern ways of doing swift strikes and achieving early success. It is in this context, this book, 'Russia-Ukraine War: Strategic Conundrum,' edited by Dr. Bharti Das and Dr. Uday Pratap Singh, provides a comprehensive analysis of this ongoing war and its far-reaching implications.

The contributors to this book are esteemed scholars and practitioners in the field of defence and strategic studies, bringing a wealth of knowledge and diverse perspectives to the subject. Their collective insights into the intricate layers of the war, examining it from multiple angles including India's strategic response, global, diplomatic and economic ramifications, and regional implications for South and Southeast Asia, Europe, the Gulf States, and the Indo-Pacific region.

The War, with the West playing a major role in the background, serves as a model for understanding and preparing for similar treatment in the case of India-China relations. India's learning curve should enhance its possibilities of dealing effectively with China, and the Russia–Ukraine crisis is one such experience. The notion of powerful states winning is dismantled with technological innovations and changing nature of warfare making it possible even for a middle power like Ukraine to brace and prepare for the impact of the relatively bigger Russia. The need is to let India socialise with these experiences to learn and better prepare itself for plausible contingencies in the future.

'Russia-Ukraine War: Strategic Conundrum' is an essential addition to the literature on contemporary international conflicts. It offers a rigorous analysis and a multifaceted approach to understanding one of the most significant political events of our time. The editors and contributors deserve commendation for their thorough research and profound insights, which will undoubtedly enrich the discourse on global security and diplomacy.

Dr. Bharti Das and Dr. Uday Pratap Singh, the editors of the book, have done remarkable work by analysing the Russia-Ukraine War that would help the students and scholars of international politics to study the scope of war and peace. The book is neither urged by an instinct nor is a result of a premeditated plan but is the product of serious fascinating efforts and provides a truly multifaceted account of Russia-Ukraine war and its consequences. I am happy to recommend the book to a wider readership.

Maj. Gen. RPS Bhadauria, VSM (Retd.)
Additional Director General,
Centre for Land Warfare Studies
New Delhi

PREFACE

In the annals of history, conflict has often acted as a catalyst for change, reshaping global dynamics and redefining the course of nations. The ongoing Russia-Ukraine war stands as a stark testament to this enduring truth, casting a shadow of uncertainty over international relations and stirring the conscience of nations worldwide. As the world watches with bated breath, the ramifications of this conflict extend far beyond the borders of the warring nations, permeating the geopolitical landscape with profound implications for global security. This book, titled "Russia-Ukraine War: Strategic Conundrum," embarks on a voyage of exploration into the heart of this seminal conflict, unraveling its multifaceted dimensions and discerning its implications for one of the world's largest democracies, India. Drawing upon the wisdom of scholars, diplomats, military strategists, and policymakers, this book endeavors to dissect the intricate strands of the crisis and illuminate the path forward for India in safeguarding its national interests amidst the shifting tides of international diplomacy.

In the unfolding drama of the Russia-Ukraine war, the character of war assumes myriad forms, from conventional battles on the plains of Eastern Europe to the shadowy realm of information warfare and hybrid tactics. The emergence of multiple domains of warfare, encompassing land, sea, air, cyberspace, and the information environment, heralds a new era of multi-domain operations, where conflicts are waged with lethal precision and hyperactive intensity. In this fluid landscape of geopolitical contestation, India finds itself at a crossroads, compelled to adapt its strategies to the imperatives of a rapidly changing world order.

The lessons of the Russia-Ukraine war offer profound insights for India's security calculus. The myth of war's obsolescence in an era of globalization stands shattered, as the specter of full-scale conflict looms large on the horizon. The strategic miscalculations and misjudgments that have characterized the early phases of the conflict underscore the imperative of astute military planning and agile decision-making in the face of uncertainty.

Moreover, the Russia-Ukraine war underscores the imperative of self-reliance in war sustenance, as nations grapple with the challenge of securing their supply chains and maintaining their technological edge in an era of heightened competition. India's journey towards self-reliance in defense production assumes newfound urgency in light of the lessons gleaned from the conflict, as the nation seeks to bolster its military capabilities and enhance its resilience in the face of emerging threats.

Yet, amidst the stark realities of conflict, there exists a glimmer of hope, a beacon of resilience that transcends the tumult of war. As the people of Ukraine stand united in the face of adversity, rallying against the forces of oppression with indomitable courage and fortitude, they offer a poignant reminder of the human spirit's capacity for resilience and renewal. In their struggle for freedom and dignity, we find inspiration and solidarity, reaffirming our shared humanity in the crucible of war. "Russia-Ukraine War: Strategic Conundrum" stands as a testament to the enduring quest for peace and security in a world fraught with peril and uncertainty. As India navigates the turbulent currents of international diplomacy, let us heed the lessons of history and chart a course guided by prudence, wisdom, and compassion. In the crucible of war, let us forge a future founded on the principles of justice, liberty, and fraternity, transcending the barriers of nation and creed to build a world where war is but a distant memory and peace reigns supreme.

Prof. Bharti Das

Dr. Uday Pratap Singh

CONTRIBUTORS

1. ***Dr. Shekhar Adhikari*** is a retired Professor and Former Head, Department of Defence and Strategic Studies, University of Allahabad, Prayagraj, Uttar Pradesh.
2. ***Maj. Gen. Manoj Kumar*** is a serving Major-General in the Indian Army at Selection Centre East, Prayagraj, Uttar Pradesh.
3. ***Dr. Sukanta Ghosh*** is an Assistant Professor, Department of Political Science, Cooch Behar College, West Bengal.
4. ***Neeraj Singh Manhas*** is a Special Advisor for South Asia at the Parley Policy Initiative, Republic of Korea.
5. ***Dhruv Ashok*** is a Research Fellow, Department of International Studies, Christ University, Bengaluru, Karnataka.
6. ***Abhigya Langeh*** is a Ph.D. scholar, Department of National Security Studies, Central University of Jammu, Jammu and Kashmir.
7. ***Dr. Bharti Das*** is a Professor and Head, Department of Defence and Strategic Studies, University of Allahabad, Prayagraj, Uttar Pradesh.
8. ***Dr. Dhirendra Dwivedi*** is a Professor in the Department of Defence and Strategic Studies, Iswar Saran PG College, University of Allahabad, Prayagraj, Uttar Pradesh.
9. ***Mayank Saraswat*** is a Ph.D. Scholar in the Department of Defence and Strategic Studies, Iswar Saran PG College, University of Allahabad, Prayagraj, Uttar Pradesh.
10. ***Dr. Raghvendra Pratap Singh*** is an Assistant Professor, Department of Defence and Strategic Studies, SPM Govt. PG College, University of Allahabad, Prayagraj, Uttar Pradesh.
11. ***Dr. Arvind Kumar Kushwaha*** is an Assistant Professor, Department of National Security Studies, Rajiv Gandhi University, Rono Hills, Arunachal Pradesh.

12. ***Dr. Mohammad Afsar Alam*** is an Associate Professor, Department of Geography, Jamia Millia Islamia, New Delhi.
13. ***Md. Abusaad*** is an Assistant Professor, Department of Economics, Lovely Professional University, Phagwara, Punjab.
14. ***Prachi Kushwaha*** is an Assistant Professor, Department of Defence & Strategic Studies, JN Smarak PG College, Siddhartha University, Maharajganj, Uttar Pradesh.
15. ***Jay Maniyar*** is a Research Fellow at Defence Research and Studies and a former Research Associate at National Maritime Foundation, New Delhi.
16. ***Col. Abhishek Yadav*** is a serving Army Officer and Ph.D. scholar in the Department of National Security Studies, Manipur University, Manipur.
17. ***Dr. Uday Pratap Singh*** is an Assistant Professor, Department of Defence and Strategic Studies, Iswar Saran PG College, University of Allahabad, Prayagraj, Uttar Pradesh.
18. ***Dr. Manvendra Kumar Verma*** is an Assistant Professor, Department of Defence and Strategic Studies, Iswar Saran PG College, University of Allahabad, Prayagraj, Uttar Pradesh.
19. ***Vishal Dixit*** is a Ph.D. scholar, Department of Defence & Strategic Studies, Iswar Saran PG College, University of Allahabad, Prayagraj, Uttar Pradesh.
20. ***Dr. Sreshtha Chakraborty*** is an Assistant Professor, Department of Political Science, Bennett University, Greater Noida, Uttar Pradesh.
21. ***Divya Rai*** is a Research Executive at National Maritime Foundation, New Delhi.
22. ***Lt. Col. Harikesh Pratap Singh*** is a serving Army officer and Ph.D. scholar in the Department of Defence & Strategic Studies, Meerut College, Meerut, Uttar Pradesh.
23. ***Tanvir Ahmed*** is a Ph.D. scholar, Academy of International Studies, Jamia Millia Islamia, New Delhi.

SECTION I

INDIA'S PERSPECTIVE AND STRATEGIC RESPONSE: RUSSIA-UKRAINE WAR

1

Russia-Ukraine War and the Indian Approach

Shekhar Adhikari

Introduction

India's approach to the Russian aggression in Ukraine has been notably distinct from that of the other major democracies. While Western nations have sought a more confrontational stance against Russia, India has opted for a constrained and nuanced diplomatic path. National interest is paramount for any country, and in India's case, its foreign and security policies are shaped by national objectives. India's goal has been to carve out an independent approach that balances the 'fractured world order,' a concept disrupted by recent developments in Eurasian politics. India's response to the Russian invasion stands out among the major democracies, including its strategic partner, the USA.[1] To India, the Western nations' actions seemed insufficiently concrete in their criticism of the Russian aggression in Ukraine.

At the Summit for Peace in Ukraine held in Switzerland on 15-16 June 2024, over 90 countries participated. Many signed a final communique advocating Kyiv's territorial sovereignty and demanding Russia's withdrawal. However, countries like India, Saudi Arabia, South Africa, and others refrained from signing the declaration, favouring dialogue and diplomacy instead. While the Western nations pushed for a consensus on ending the war, Russia dismissed the summit and proposed alternative solutions, demanding Ukrainian concessions. India, maintaining its strategic relationship with Russia and its dependency on Russian defence supplies, adopted a nuanced diplomatic stance. It abstained from condemning Russia directly but strongly advocated a peaceful resolution. Prime Minister Modi emphasized a dialogue during his meeting with President Zelenskyy at the G7 Summit 2024 held in Italy and supported sending a delegation to the Swiss talks. Modi reiterated India's commitment to a human-centric approach and strengthening bilateral ties with Ukraine.

Before further analyzing India's role in the Ukraine conflict, it is crucial to understand the developments that have transpired between Russia and Ukraine. The latter has played a dominant role in the global security order, and is now finding itself at the centre of renewed great power rivalry, a dynamic many strategic experts believe will influence international politics for years to come.

The Russian aggression in Ukraine in 2022 marked a dramatic escalation of a conflict that had been simmering for nine years. This aggression was a historic turning point for European security. Furthermore, Western aid to Ukraine has added complexity to the region's geopolitical landscape. This situation can be analyzed from two different angles. Firstly, Russian frustration in its prolonged and costly invasion has left President Putin without clear success, contrary to his past experiences in Chechnya, Georgia, and Crimea where he achieved quick victories. He miscalculated, expecting Ukraine to be another quick conquest. Secondly, the Western powers, in response to the Russian attack, have firmly supported Ukraine, with the European Union and NATO seeking to integrate Ukraine into their alliances, though this process remains contentious and unresolved.

Ukraine: A Geo-Political Flashpoint

During the Cold War, Ukraine was important to the then Soviet Union in the realm of realizing the Soviet global aspiration of becoming a superpower. Behind only Russia, it was the second most populous and powerful of the fifteen Soviet republics. Ukraine was rich in agricultural products, defence industries, strong military power including the Black Sea fleet and some nuclear weapons. Ukraine was so important to the Soviet Union that its decision to sever ties in 1991 proved to be a coup de grace for the ailing superpower.[2]

It becomes clear that politically Ukraine witnessed a major upheaval in the past. Russia has always considered Ukraine to be a part of its 'Motherland'. It has some meaning, considering Kievan Rus was imperial Russia's cultural foundation from the 9th to the 13th centuries. It was the Soviet Union that succeeded in the characterization of the socio-cultural ties that brought Ukraine under its dominance by the end of the first decade of the 20th century. Moreover, until 1917, when a short-lived autonomous government was established, Ukraine was a part of many empires, especially Russian empires. Under the banner of the Ukrainian Soviet Socialist Republic, Ukraine rejoined the Soviet Union in 1919. In spite of Russian influence over Ukraine for many years, its cultural leaders like the poet Taras Shevchenko pushed for a free Ukraine. Despite political differences, Ukraine had always been an important part of Russian history. Ukraine became an independent state after the disintegration of the Soviet Union.[3] Since then, relations between the two countries have been tense. The peninsula of Crimea and the city of Sevastopol were bones of contention. The problem of Russia's Black Sea naval fleet in Sevastopol was settled by the two countries when both agreed for a long-term lease on the naval facility.[4]

Until May 1997, Ukraine's control of Crimea and Russia not recognising it as a sovereign state remained the political dispute between them. But, in 1997, the Russian-Ukrainian Friendship Treaty was signed and Russia formally recognised Ukraine as an independent country. Steward saw this treaty as 'dropping the cloak of common history between king and ruled'[5] at the time. After independence, Ukraine has sought to forge its own path as an independent country while openly siding with Western institutions. However, Kyiv tried to balance its foreign relations and narrow down deep internal divisions. In Ukraine, two schools of thought emerged. First, Ukrainian nationalists living in the western parts of the country wanted integration with Europe; the second was the Russian-dominated community in the east which favoured closer relations with Russia.

In 2014, Ukraine became a hot spot of military rivalry when Russia forcibly took Crimea and began to arm separatist groups in the Donbas region in the south-east. Between 2014 and 2021, more than 14,000 people died in this region. It was the bloodiest struggle in Europe since the Balkan wars of the 1990s. It was also witnessed that for the first time since World War II had a European country annexed the territory of another. For many strategic experts, the rivalry caused a shift in the world security order. In other words, the world shifted from a US-dominated unipolar world to renewed competition between the great powers. In February 2022, Russia attacked Ukraine with the sole purpose of replacing the present government led by Volodymyr Zelenskyy with a pro-Soviet government there.

Russia's Interest in Ukraine

Russia has common social, cultural, economic, and political relations with Ukraine. More than this, Ukraine is key to Russia's identity. These are the following broad interests of Russia in Ukraine.

Social Relations

Ukraine and Russia have strong social and cultural ties that go back to centuries. Kyiv, the Ukraine capital, is often understood as the 'mother' of Russian cities. It was to Kyiv in the 8th and 9th centuries that Christianity was brought from Byzantium to the Slavic peoples. It was also Christianity that served as the anchor for Kievan Rus, the early Slavic state from which modern Russians, Ukrainians and Belarusians drew their lineage.[6] The former President of the Soviet Union, Nikita Khrushchev, was born and had grown up in Ukraine. In 1954, he gifted the Russian-dominated Crimean region to Ukraine.

Russian Diaspora

According to the 2001 census, almost eight million ethnic Russians were living in the south and east of Ukraine. The Russian government felt it was its duty to secure the life of the people as a pretext for its actions in Crimea and the Donbas regions in 2014.

Superpower Confrontation

After the Second World War, the world was divided into two halves. One was led by the USA and the other by the Soviet Union. This was a 'cold war' at its chilliest, marked by the hostile and primitive anti-Soviet doctrine of containment and the flexing of US nuclear strategic superiority.[7] The cold war lasted for almost 45 years. In 1990, one saw the disintegration of the Soviet Union. Many Russian analysts then viewed the divorce with Ukraine as a mistake of history that would pose a long threat to Russia's capability as a great power. Furthermore, it was seen by Russian analysts that Ukraine moving towards the West to normalize its relations would be a big hit to the Russian global image.

Crimea

In 1954, Nikita Khrushchev transferred Crimea from Russia to Ukraine to solidify the 'brotherly relations between the Russian and Ukrainian peoples.' After the demise of the Union, many Russian citizens in Russia and Crimea longed for a return of the peninsula. The city of Sevastopol is home port for the Russian Black Sea Fleet. It was the powerful maritime force in the region.

Trade

For a long time, Russia was the largest trading partner. But in recent years, the growing Chinese economic influence in Ukraine has replaced Russia as the largest trading partner. Prior to the Crimea invasion, Russia wanted Ukraine to join the Eurasian Economic Union (EAEU). Today, this economic forum includes such countries like Armenia, Belarus, Kazakhstan, and Kyrgyzstan.

Energy

Russia was a big market of national gas to the countries of Central and Eastern Europe for many decades. For the supply of gas to these countries, Russia had to rely on Ukrainian pipelines. For this, Ukraine was paid billions of dollars per year as transit fees. The flow of Russian gas through Ukraine was regular till February 2022. When the war started, this supply was discontinued and Russia had to search for an alternative. The supply of Russian gas was done through the Nord Stream-2 pipeline which passes under the Baltic Sea to Germany. But Germany too froze regulatory approval of the project after Russia's aggression in Ukraine.

Political Influence

Russia's foreign policy priorities lie in the complete political subordination of Ukraine to Russia. Earlier, both shared a common culture and Russia tried to bond Ukraine to a 'shared future with other post Soviet Republics'. Mikhail Zurabov, former Russian ambassador to Kyiv, had declared that Ukrainians and Russians are both citizens of the same country.[8] But modern Ukraine was witnessing a major cultural change that did not go down well with the Russian authorities. Perhaps, Ukraine's move to adopt Western culture became a bone of contention between Russia and Ukraine. Putin accused NATO and the European Union of manipulating Ukrainian national sentiment as part of their geo-political competition with Russia.[9]

Russia was keen to preserve its political influence in Ukraine throughout the former Soviet Union, particularly after its preferred candidate for Ukrainian President, Viktor Yanukovych, in 2004. Russia lost to a reformist competitor as part of the popular Orange Revolution movement. It was a shock to Russian interests in Ukraine which came after a similar electoral defeat for Russia in Georgia in 2003. It was known as the Rose Revolution and was followed by another named the Tulip Revolution in Kyrgyzstan in 2005. Yanukovych later become President of Ukraine in 2010 with Russian government support.[10]

Russia's Moves in Crimea and the Donbas Region in 2014

It was Ukraine's relations with the European Union that become a cause of tension in 2013-14. In late 2013, President Yanukovych was supported by the Russian government. On Russian behalf, Yanukovych had scrapped plans that could have formalized closer economic relations with the European Union. Russia, at the same time, pressurized Ukraine to join the Eurasian Economic Union. Many Ukrainian nationalists felt that this Yanukovych decision was a betrayal to the Ukraine cause. Further, they regarded Yanukovych's government as corrupt and inefficient and it gave rise to countrywide protests. This countrywide protest was known as Euromaidan. This protest forced Yanukovych to quit and Putin saw this move as a Western-backed fascist coup. It had endangered the ethnic Russian majority in Crimea. As a consequence, Putin planned a 'covert invasion' of Crimea and later he called it a 'rescue operation'. In 2014, while formalising the annexation of Crimea, Putin said that "there is a limit to everything and with Ukraine our Western partners have crossed the line".

A similar narrative was followed by Putin justifying his support for a separatist movement in south-eastern Ukraine. This was another region which was a home of ethnic Russians. He referred to this area as Novorossiya (New Russia). It was a term going back to 18th-century imperial Russia. It was believed that some armed provocateurs had played a crucial role in stirring the anti-Euromaidan separatist movements in the region into a rebellion. Unlike Crimea, Russia initially denied government involvement in the Donbas region but seeing the deteriorating relations with Ukraine, Russia launched a full-scale invasion of Ukraine in 2022.

Full-Scale Aggression in Ukraine in 2022

From 1991 to April 2008, Russia and Ukraine have coexisted more or less peacefully. In 2008, Vladimir Putin came to power and one saw dramatic changes in Russia's foreign and security policies toward the European Union and NATO. The reason was the expansion of NATO deep into the eastern parts of Europe. It covered almost all the client-states of the Warsaw Pact. In 2008, at the meeting held in Bucharest, NATO had declared that it would include Ukraine as its member. The announcement had annoyed Putin because he regarded it as a betrayal of trust by the West. In 1990, the USA and NATO gave a verbal assurance and there was no written guarantee that NATO would not move towards East Europe. It was not acceptable to Russia as NATO forces and possibly nuclear warheads would have been at its border.

Moreover, the then Vice-President of the USA, Joe Biden, favoured Ukraine's inclusion in NATO. In February 2014, the US State Department and the CIA managed to keep the pot boiling. It was reported that with the US funding there was a violent upheaval. The purpose was to overthrow the pro-Russian government in Ukraine.

At NATO's 2008 summit, President Putin warned a US diplomat that steps to bring Ukraine into the alliance "would be a hostile move towards Russia." Months later, Russia was involved in Georgia and Putin showed his military power to secure his country's interests. Despite being a non-member of NATO, Ukraine's relations improved with it. Ukraine held annual military exercises with NATO and in 2020 became one of six enhanced opportunity partners. It was a special status given to Ukraine which no other non-member of NATO had enjoyed.

In the weeks leading up to its invasion, Russia made various major security demands from the USA and NATO. They included ceasing expanding the alliance, seeking Russian consent for certain NATO deployments and removing US nuclear weapons from Europe. Alliance leaders responded that they were open to new diplomacy but were unwilling to discuss shutting NATO's doors to new members.[11] Thomas Graham told *Arms Control Today* in February 2022, "While in the United States we talk about a Ukraine crisis, but from the Russian perspective this is a crisis in European security architecture."

Perhaps, the most significant factor for Russian security was Putin's fear that Ukraine would develop into a modern, Western pattern of democracy. This would automatically undermine Putin's political influence in Ukraine and lessen the hope of recreating a Russian-led sphere of influence in Eastern Europe. Anne Applebaum writes in the *Atlantic* that Russia wants to destabilise and frighten Ukraine. The Russian government wants Ukrainian democracy to fail. It wants the Ukrainian economy to collapse and foreign investors to leave the country. Moreover, the Russian government wants Belarus, Kazakhstan and even Poland and Hungary to consider whether democracy will ever be successful in the long run.

Russia's Objectives in Ukraine

Russia is regarded as a 'revanchist power'. It aims to regain its former power and prestige. Putin's aim was to restore Russia as a great power in northern Eurasia. The ultimate goal is not "to recreate the Soviet Union but to make Russia great again".

Russia's seizure of Crimea in 2014 has put it in a comfortable zone in Black Sea. Now, Russia can project power deeper into the Middle East, the Mediterranean, and North Africa. Earlier in these regions, Russia had a limited role. Some strategic analysts believe that the Western powers failed to impose maximum costs on Russia in response to its annexation of Crimea. Putin's effort has paid off well as Russia can utilize its military power in obtaining his security policy objectives. Until its invasion in 2022, Russia's strategic gains in the Donbas region remained fragile. As such, by supporting the separatist movement in the region, Russia, had increased its bargaining power vis-a-vis Ukraine.

Putin also described Russians and Ukrainians as "one people" who occupy the "same spiritual and historical space".

Putin then changed his policy and tried to encircle Ukraine with tens of thousands of troops. In February 2022, when Putin ordered a full-scale invasion of Ukraine, Russia encircled Ukrainian territory from the south (Crimea), east (Russia), and north (Belarus). It was an effort to seize major cities and depose the present government. Putin's aim was to de-Nazify and demilitarize Ukrainian territories.

However, in the early period of the conflict, Ukraine put up a brave effort in resisting Russian attacks. Some defence analysts believed that Russian forces have suffered from poor logistics, bad military strategy, and low morale. But it was for a short duration. Putin realized his mistake and worked over those points where Russia was lagging. After some time, Putin gained much from his ongoing conflict and now Russia is in an advantageous position.

The United States of America and the European Union Policy in Ukraine

After the disintegration of the Soviet Union, the US government's utmost priority was to push Ukraine, Belarus, and Kazakhstan to surrender its nuclear weapons to Russia. At the same time, the USA went one step ahead to bolster the shaky democracy in Russia. It was felt that the US government should work on fostering geopolitical pluralism in the rest of the former Soviet Union rather than showing friendly gestures towards Russia.

Zbigniew Brzezinski, former U.S. National Security Adviser, writes in *Foreign Affairs* in early 1994 that a stable and strong Ukraine was necessary to counter Russia and he even mentioned that this should be the new grand strategy of the USA after 1991. It was also felt that even without Ukraine, Russia can cease to be an empire but with a subordinated Ukraine, Russia would automatically become an empire. After the publication of Brzezinski's article, the USA, Russia and Britain pledged to honour Ukraine's independence and sovereignty. In return, Ukraine should declare itself as a non-nuclear country.

Both the USA and the European Union are committed to the

restoration of Ukraine's territorial integrity and sovereignty. It has re-emerged as top US and European Union foreign policy objectives. These powers do not recognize Russia's claims to Crimea or to the Donbas region. Prior to the 2022 aggression, the USA and the European Union supported a settlement of the Donbas conflict. But it was a futile exercise. Following the 2022 aggression, the USA and NATO have taken various steps to increase military, economic, and humanitarian aid to Ukraine and put the most stringent economic sanctions on Russia. The USA gave Ukraine more than $ 1 billion in emergency security assistance in early 2022 and later increased it to several billion dollars in aid. The USA and NATO have trained Ukraine forces in recent years. They have provided and still provide such equipment like grenades, launchers, sniper rifles, radars, Stinger anti-aircraft, night vision gear, Javelin anti-tank missiles, and unmanned aerial systems (drones and patrol vessels).

Besides military assistance, harsh economic sanctions were imposed on Russia. They covered energy, finance, defence and the technological fields and targeted the assets of rich oligarchs. The USA and some European countries also banned some Russian banks from the Society for Worldwide Interbank Financial Telecommunication (SWIFT). Russia's vast foreign reserves were also made the target and even central banks were blacklisted. Furthermore, many Western companies have stopped operating in Russia. But all these efforts failed and did not deter war and work for peaceful solutions.

Ukrainian Government's Objective

In recent years, Russian aggression has paved the way for Ukraine's westward leanings. The Euromaidan gave Ukraine a billionaire businessman, Petro Poroshenko as its President. He wanted integration with the European Union and NATO. In 2019, Zelensky defeated Poroshenko because the latter failed to curb corruption and an oligarchic economy.

Before the 2022 conflict, polls were conducted and Ukrainians held mixed views of joining the European Union and NATO. In this survey, more than 50 per cent supported European Union membership and 40 to 50 per cent favoured the idea of joining NATO. After the aggression, a people's survey found that a large majority favoured armed resistance against Russia. The Ukrainian government also rejected Russia's claims to Crimea and the Donbas region. It also held the view that Ukraine should not give up future NATO membership to terminate the war.

India's Approach

India took its own time to analyze the current situation that erupted due to the Ukraine war. Initially, world leaders wanted to know the Indian government's stand. Right from the beginning till date, India's position has been a neutral one. The Indian Prime Minister, Narendra Modi, and Foreign Minister, S. Jaishankar, reacted to the Western allegation about India's role in war.

Narendra Modi discussed this issue at length and called for a high-level meeting to review India's security preparedness amid the ongoing conflict in Ukraine. Modi said India is relatively far from Ukraine in terms of geography but was more anxious over the impact of this war on India per se than any other country. It is not difficult to fathom why. This is flawlessly revealed in Prime Minister Narendra Modi's conversations with leaders of Russia, Ukraine, France, Poland, heads of governments of QUAD, and the President of the European Council.[12] The Indian Prime Minister laid emphasis on India's role as a peace-building nation in the midst of the Russia-Ukraine war and said India is the new hope for the world in this global crisis. From delivering vaccines and medicines to the world during the corona crisis, India is the new hope of the world today.[13] Today we want to take an oath to establish a new India, and we are working to do it. India has a new forward-looking identity while it maintains its age-old traditions.[14] Narendra Modi focused on a number of issues. He said that today's era is not an era of war. Every country is sovereign and should recognize the protection of territorial integrity. One should focus on development, and even in the case of crises, it should be settled by agreement and cooperation.

The Indian Foreign Minister, Jaishankar, also reacted to the Western allegation about India's role. He said that "one has to follow the path of diplomacy and, to do that, the fighting must stop." There are wider consequences of the war. There is no winner in this conflict and the immediate effect is on oil and food prices. He further mentioned the shock that the international order is experiencing due to the COVID-19 pandemic, Afghanistan and the Ukraine crises and the friction between the West and Russia, and the USA and China.

US President Joe Biden earlier applied pressure on India but did not want to cross the limit by telling India what to do and what not to do. According to the *Economist*, China sees Russia as a partner in dismantling the liberal world order by which the alliance can exploit the war in Ukraine. By doing so, it will hasten the decline of the West.[15] India is watching the Russia-Ukraine war and Biden is watching Modi. The USA began its 2+2 dialogue with India and India's support for Russia's war in Ukraine seems to have figured in both conversations.[16]

Safe Return of Indian Nationals

A tense situation arose in the conflict on 24 February 2022. The root causes for this are complex, going back to a range of issues including the security architecture, political governance, and inter-state politics. What is pertinent to note is that the hostilities placed the Indian community of 20,000-plus in direct danger. The challenge was to safeguard our citizens and ensure that they were not harmed in any way.[17]

Prime Minister Narendra Modi gave importance to the safety and security of the 20,000 Indian citizens. Most of them were students who had gone to Ukraine for study. These nationals were trapped dangerously in Ukraine. The Indian government wanted their safe return to India. On the directions of the Prime Minister, Operation Ganga was launched. It was one of the most challenging evacuation exercises during the ongoing conflict situation. The Indian community was dispersed across Ukraine, posing its own logistical challenges.

The exercise was taken at a time when military actions including airstrikes and shelling were underway. It involved movement in a war-torn situation in a large country spread over 1,000 km. It is required crossing border check points that were clogged by an estimated 26 lakh refugees. The Ministry of External Affairs of the Indian Government monitored the evacuation operations on a 24x7 basis.[18]

Steps were taken in advance of the actual conflict situation. As tensions increased, the Embassy of India in Ukraine had started registration of documents for Indian nationals in January 2022. As a result, around 20,000 Indian nationals registered with the Indian Embassy in Kyiv. Most of them were students and were spread across the country. More than half of them were in universities in Eastern Ukraine that borders Russia and was the epicentre of the conflict.

In view of the continued build-up of tensions in February, the Embassy issued an advisory on 15 February 2022 advising Indian nationals in Ukraine not to leave the country temporarily. It also advised them not to travel in Ukraine or to undertake non-essential movement. Further advisories were also issued on 20 and 22 February 2022 calling upon students to leave Ukraine. The Indian government consulted the Ukraine government to increase the number of direct flights. As a result, 4,000 Indian nationals were brought home from Ukraine by direct and indirect flights by 23 February 2022.[19]

The strategy for evacuation was to take out Indian nationals from the western neighbouring countries. These countries were Poland, Slovak Republic, Hungary, Romania, and Moldova. This was necessitated due to the closure of Ukraine air space on 24 February 2022. Constant intervention at border checkpoints helped to address the severe challenges posed by over-congestion. Their liaison with local governments and community organizations was responsible for the boarding, lodging, and medical attention of evacuees. They handled the complexity of flight operations on the ground so that their return home could be a smooth process.

Under Operation Ganga, 90 flights were operated out of which 76 were civilian and 14 were Indian Air Force flights. During this period, the Indian Prime Minister spoke to the Presidents of Russia and Ukraine on multiple occasions. Narendra Modi specifically took up the issue of the safe evacuation of Indian nationals, especially from Kharkiv and Sumy. Modi also spoke to the Prime Ministers of Romania, Slovak Republic, Hungary, and the President of Poland to seek their support for the facilitation of entry of Indian nationals to their countries. In the entire exercise there was only one casualty.

In line with the Indian principle of *Vasudhaiva Kutumbakam*, foreign nationals were also evacuated from conflict zones and brought to India. They included about 150 citizens of 18 countries.

Humanitarian Assistance

In response to the humanitarian crisis, India provided relief materials to Ukraine. India sent 90 tons of relief materials like medicines, blankets, tarpaulins, tents, sleeping mats, goggles, and surgical gloves.

At the Raisina Dialogue held in New Delhi, Jaishankar commented on the USA, NATO and the European Union stands on the conflict. He pointed to challenges in Asia and India's neighbourhood in Afghanistan and China and said it was a wakeup call for Europe to look into all these instances where problems have been happening.[20]

The European Commission's President, Ursula von der Leyen, described the killing of Bucha as a "severe violation of international law" and said the outcome of the war in Ukraine will not only determine the future of Europe but also "deeply affect the Indo-Pacific region and the rest of the world".[21] Did India ignore the Bucha killing? The External Affairs Minister made it quite clear that "India condemned the killing of civilians in the Ukraine town of Bucha and sought an independent investigation."[22] What happened then? Did the world leaders took serious note of the brutal killings in Bucha? These countries supported Ukraine with more lethal weapons instead of stopping the war.

Similarly when Norwegian Foreign Minister Annikin Huitfeldt raised a question on the current issue at the Raisina Dialogue, the External Affairs Minister categorically stated, "You talked about Ukraine. I remember that a year ago what happened in Afghanistan where the entire civil society was thrown under the bus by the world. We in Asia face our own sets of challenges which often have an impact on the ruled-based order."[23]

United Nations and India

United States President Joe Biden has appealed to the world leaders at the UN General Assembly on 19 September 2023 to stand with Ukraine against the Russian invaders. In his speech to the UN General Assembly, Joe Biden said, "Russia believes that the world will grow weary and allow it to brutalise Ukraine without consequence. If we allow Ukraine to be carved up, is the independence of any nation secure?"[24] Joe Biden drew applause when he said that the USA and its allies would stand with Ukraine's fight for freedom.

"Russia alone bears the responsibility for this war. Russia alone has the power to end this war immediately."[25] Joe Biden has managed to persuade US allies to support Ukraine, a leading component of US foreign policy. He argued that the world must send a clear signal to Russian President Putin that he will not be able to outlast the West. Republicans in the USA want the country to spend less money on the war. Former President Donald Trump has vowed to seek a quick end to the war if returned to power. Trump has voiced scepticism about Washington's engagement with traditional allies, including NATO.[26] In his speech, Biden said Russia's February invasion of Ukraine and occupation of territory violated the UN Charter of violating a country's sovereignty and territorial integrity. His remark echoed those of UN Secretary-General Antonio Guterres, who said Russia's invasion "has unleashed a nexus of horror."[27]

So as far India was concerned, members of the United Nations pressurized India to take a stand by criticizing the Russian action and calling it a violator of war. But India's position was a neutral one. On the other hand, the USA and the Western powers expected India to maintain a distance from Russia. Jaishankar has rebuffed the West over India's neutral stand. He said that Europe must learn to look beyond Ukraine at other dangerous spots in the world. He said that "there is no other choice between the path of diplomacy and dialogue. We have emphasised to all member-states of the UN that the global order is based on international law and respect for sovereignty and territorial integrity."[28]

The European Union leaders have been trying to arm-twist India to take a critical stance towards Russia. India did not budge which is for the good. It is evident that India could not take an anti-Russian stance because of past history where the then Soviet Union stood beside many crises that India faced. The Soviet Union has consistently used its veto power on the issue of Kashmir in the UN Security Council. When the Russian Foreign Minister visited India, Sergey Lavrov thanked India for its neutrality on the Ukraine Issue. The visit of Sergey Lavrov also showed that Russia was not isolated but had the support of India and China.

Oil Diplomacy

In spite of heavy economic sanctions imposed by the West on Russia, India's neutral stance has not affected its trade relations with Russia. It is not that India did not help Ukraine but that did not compel India to restrain itself from Russian purchases. The European Union and the USA had passed various resolutions from time to time to sanction Russian oil and to restrict Russian oil exports to 90 per cent by the end of 2022.

On being asked about the purchase of Russian oil and natural gas, Jaishankar replied, "Look I don't want to sound argumentative but the buying of Russian gas is not funding the war. Is it only Indian money and Russian oil coming to India that is funding the war and not Russia's gas going to Europe?" Sharply criticising European nations, Jaishankar said, "India's total purchases of Russian energy for the month was less than what Europe does in the afternoon?'[29]

Further, he said, "Look the whole narrative has gone up nine times; it has gone up from a very low base. If countries from Western Europe and the USA are so concerned, why don't they allow Venezuelan oil to come to the market?"[30]

However, the interesting fact is that neither pressure from the USA nor heavy European sanctions has made India roll back purchasing cheap crude oil. In June 2022, Russia's supplies of crude oil to India averaged 380,000 barrels a day. In other words, "India's Russia oil imports have jumped 50 times. It now accounts for 100 per cent of all imports."[31] Prior to it, it was merely 0.2 per cent. India's Reliance Industries and the Rosneft-backed Najara brought the maximum amount of crude oil. It enabled Russia to become India's second largest oil supplier, overtaking Saudi Arabia and is just behind Iraq. India took this opportunity at such a time when the global energy crisis was heading towards catastrophe.

Conclusion

The current Ukraine crisis has led to several deliberations about the relationship between the USA and Russia. Mearsheimer maintains his position that "the USA is at fault for provoking Putin." Actually, the trouble started in 2008 at the NATO summit in Bucharest where NATO came out with a statement that Ukraine and Georgia would soon be part of it. To Russia, it was an existential threat. As he further says "what has happened with the passage of time is that we have moved forward to include Ukraine in the West to make Ukraine a Western bulwark on Russia's border. Whatever is going on between the USA and Russia, it is great power rivalry. Trying to have control over Ukraine had made Putin more aggressive because the USA does not care much about what Russia thinks. If one tries to meddle in another country's affairs, that country will definitely retaliate. So was the case with Russia. Even Henry Kissinger, former US foreign secretary, remarked at the Davos forum that "these European countries, including the USA, may sacrifice Ukraine's interests at any time." The problem with the US government is how much military and economic support it can give Ukraine when the USA itself is facing serious challenges in the Indo-Pacific and West Asian regions. The question is whether the US support to Ukraine will be half-hearted as was seen in the case of the Vietnam and Afghanistan crises.

In every crisis, some are always gains. In the case of the Ukraine crisis that is the Indian Prime Minister, Narendra Modi. By refusing to condemn Russia and join Western-led sanctions, Modi has managed to raise India's global image. Each of the other major powers—the USA, Russia and China are intensely courting India to deny any kind of strategic advantage to their adversaries. India's aim is to carve out an independent great power role, hasten the transition to a multipolar world, and ultimately try its new emerging status to obtain a permanent UN seat.

Furthermore, how will the Ukraine conflict impact India's *Atmanirbhar Bharat*. Prime Minister Narendra Modi stressed the significance of self-reliance while talking about the war. If India wants to be an *Atmanirbhar* nation then it should maintain strategic autonomy by calculating India's interests in world politics. It was clear when India refused to side with the West; it also abstained from resolutions brought by Russia in the UN. India has always stood for an early end to the violence so that peace and stability can prevail in Ukraine as soon as possible.

REFERENCES

1. Ashley J. Tellis. 25 April 2022, https://carneigie endowementorganisation (2022/04) 25, what-is-our-interest-India-and- Ukraine-war-pub-869619
2. Jonathan Masters. 'Ukraine: Conflict at the Crossroads of Europe and Russia,' Council on Foreign Relations, last updated 1 April 2022.
3. T.B. Alabo, E.C. MacAlex-Achinulo. 'Russian-Ukraine Crisis and Regional Security,' *International Journal of Political Science*, vol. 8, issue 1, 2022, p. 21, www.arcjournals.org
4. Ibid.
5. D. Steward 'The Russian-Ukrainian Friendship Treaty and the search for regional stability in Eastern Europe,' Naval Postgraduate School.
6. Jonathan Masters. op. cit., 2.
7. B. S. Lambeth. 'Contemporary Soviet Military Policy' in R. Kokowiez and E.P. Mickiewier (eds.), *The Soviet Calculus of Nuclear War*, p. 12, 1972.
8. A. Bogomolov and Olytvynenko. 'A ghost in the mirror: Russian soft power in Ukraine, 2012, Russia and Eurasian Programme.
9. http://enkremlin.ru/events/ president/news/66181
10. Jonathan Masters. op. cit. 2.
11. Ibid.
12. www.first post.com. 8 March 2022, 'The Ukraine crisis: Why Prime Minister Narendra Modi's telephonic talks with Putin and Zelensky deserve effective applause.'
13. 'India is capable of ... Prime Minister Modi on India's role in Russia-Ukraine war,' *Hindustan Times*, Lucknow, 19 May 2022.
14. Ibid.
15. The print. in, 12 April 2022.
16. Ibid.
17. Suo moto statement by External Affairs Minister, Dr. S. Jaishankar, in the Rajya Sabha on the Situation on Ukraine, 15 March 2022, Ministry of External Affairs, Government of India.
18. Ibid.
19. Ibid.
20. 'Jaishankar ticks off Europe: Ukraine a wake-up call to look at problems in Asia,' *Indian Express*, New Delhi, 27 April 2022.
21. Ibid.
22. *Indian Express*, New Delhi, 4 June 2022.
23. See note 20.
24. 'At UN, Biden asks the world to stand with Ukraine,' *Times of India*, Allahabad, 20 September 2023.
25. Ibid.
26. Ibid.
27. Ibid.
28. https://www. The quint. Com>opinion.
29. See note 20.
30. Ibid.
31. Ibid.

2

Russia-Ukraine War: Emerging Dynamics of Warfare and Lessons Learnt

Manoj Kumar

Introduction

We all yearn for an ideal world free from war, but it is important to recall Plato's observation from the fourth century BCE: "Only the dead have seen the end of war." As the dynamics of state affairs evolve into a complex web of interdependence, cooperation, and competition, there is increasing pressure on states to adeptly utilize the tools of statecraft to achieve their political objectives. As a result, states develop comprehensive strategies to realize their national vision and goals, taking into account current political conditions.

Carl von Clausewitz defined "strategy" as "the use of the engagement to attain the object of war." While states may exhibit a degree of reluctance towards inherent hostility with other states, Clausewitz's principle that "war is a continuation of politics by other means" underscores his belief that war and politics are deeply intertwined. His concept of war as an extension of politics is linked to the secondary trinity of his time: the people, the military, and the government. For Clausewitz, the nation-state is defined by its ability to mobilize the resources and energy of its population to engage in warfare. His theory remains relevant today, as the nation-state continues to be the central unit of international politics.

Regarding war itself, it represents an act of violence within a conflict, while "warfare" refers to the various forms and types of war. War is "an act of violence intended to compel our opponent to fulfill our will." Through war, the goal is to influence the adversary's behavior to align with our objectives. War exhibits four enduring characteristics: a political dimension, a human dimension, the presence of uncertainty, and the nature of war as a contest of wills. Although war is an inherently irrational activity, it begins with a logical basis and generates additional rationales to sustain itself. While the fundamental nature of war remains constant, its character evolves.

The character of a war, or the nature of a particular type of war, is shaped by how violence is applied by the warring parties. This character is ultimately influenced by the complex interaction of three factors: passion, reason, and chance. As an instrument of policy, war is used by policymakers to achieve specific objectives. Reason tends to guide the application of violence in a measured, restricted, and purposeful manner. However, conflicts involving death and destruction often stir the passions of both decision-makers and the populace, which can lead to an escalation in violence and a broader scope of conflict. Chance also plays a significant role in how a war progresses, driven by unpredictable elements such as weather, leadership, morale, and sheer luck.

Violence is an intrinsic aspect of war, defining its very nature. The specific character of a war—whether it is guerrilla, limited, world, nuclear, hybrid, or otherwise—is determined by how this violence is applied. Ultimately, the manifestation of violence in any given conflict results from the intricate interplay of passion, reason, and chance.

Warfare occurs across multiple domains. At its core, a domain can be defined as a space where forces maneuver to produce effects. More comprehensively, a domain is "the sphere of influence in which activities, functions, and operations are conducted to accomplish missions and exert control over an opponent to achieve desired outcomes." Historically, when we were commissioned, warfare was primarily categorized into three domains: land, sea, and air, with each domain being predominantly controlled by a specific service. Cross-domain operations involved supporting or coordinating actions across these domains under the dominant service. The air-land battle concept and the Gulf War emphasized the importance of joint operations. Although nuclear warfare emerged, it was soon overshadowed by deterrence theories, and warfare remained relatively simple and conventional, albeit with a nuclear overlay.

The past few decades have witnessed a revolution in military affairs (RMA), characterized by the deployment of knowledge and information as tools of warfare. The RMA was marked by the information revolution, the rise of non-state actors, and the blurring of traditional frontlines. Hybrid warfare emerged through non-state actors, multinational corporations, radicalization, politicization, and the commercialization of the battlefield. The era saw the rise of knowledge economies, urbanization, and globalization, alongside the conceptualization of hard and soft power. This period highlighted the sobering reality that battlefield victories could sometimes lead to political defeats.

We now appear to be transitioning into an era of disruption in military affairs (DMA). Although the term DMA has yet to gain widespread acceptance, it has led to the expansion of warfare domains. While physical domains like land, sea, and air were once understood, new non-physical domains such as cyberspace, the information environment, and the electromagnetic spectrum have emerged, presenting new challenges and vulnerabilities. Consequently, we now contend with a multitude of domains—land, sea, air, deep sea, space, cyber, information, and nuclear—with new domains emerging almost regularly.

In today's fluid geopolitical landscape, there is neither complete peace nor total war. Conflicts of varying intensities are ongoing across different time zones, both day and night. Alongside state actors, non-state actors play a significant role, and the balance between hard and soft power is increasingly crucial. The rise of DMA has introduced the concept of multi-domain operations, where conflicts are complex, fought across both physical and virtual domains, and characterized by fluidity, dynamism, lethality, and hyperactivity. These conflicts produce effects that are often imaginative yet plausible, and frequently beyond conventional expectations. Multi-domain operations necessitate dominance across these domains to impose significant penalties on adversaries. The Chinese three-war strategy, encompassing public opinion warfare, influence operations, and legal warfare, has further complicated the landscape, making the study of war and warfare increasingly engaging.

The spectrum of warfare as exemplified by the Russia-Ukraine conflict offers a compelling case study and is highly relevant to India. Recently, a UK parliamentarian remarked, "The Train India Express has left the station and is now the fastest-running train in the world." This statement encapsulates India's dynamic progress and relevance on the global stage.

We, as the fastest emerging global power in multiple domains, need to see the unseen aspects of the Russia-Ukraine conflict so that we understand the emerging world better and set a course for ourselves. Some of views on the Russia-Ukraine conflict, albeit these are at best deductions which are not yet fully conclusive.

The Russia-Ukraine war has busted some age-old myths. Some of them are:

- No war shall be waged by the great powers and they shall have only interventions.
- Future wars shall be short and swift only. Let's remind ourselves that we have just completed one year of the Russia-Ukraine war and there is no end in sight.
- Dell theory of conflict prevention stipulates 'No two countries that are both part of a major global supply chain, like Dell's, will ever fight a war against each other as long as they are both part of the same global supply chain'.
- There is actually a difference between war estimation and war outcome. In the instant case, before the commencement of the war, Putin seemed to be winning when he was not fighting.

So far the war has not only caused massive destruction in the war zone, but also created a global crisis which has polarised the world, engineered an energy crisis, and caused an economic recession, that too immediately in the aftermath of the COVID crisis. It is almost a year since the Russian bombings pummelled Ukrainian cities, inflicted heavy civilian casualties which are growing by the day, and sparked an enormous refugee crisis. However, instead of forcing Ukraine to capitulate, the war has unified the Ukrainian people, unified the transatlantic alliance, unified European defences, and isolated Russia from the global economic system.

The biggest tragedy of the present war is that the global community missed the prediction and possible impacts of the war. Further, all kinds of deterrence methods failed to prevent the conflict. It also failed to anticipate the progress and outcome of the war. I wonder if it is all right to say that Russia is now fighting a campaign against the USA-led NATO with Ukraine only a proxy front.

The Russian strategy for the campaign can be ascribed to political and military aims. The political aim was to enforce a regime change by installing a pro-Russian government in Ukraine, demilitarize Ukraine, and block the expansion of NATO. While the military aim was to inflict a decisive military victory over Ukraine at the earliest and annex territories west of the Dnieper River. Also, it aimed to establish land connectivity with Crimea and permanently take over the strategic port of Sevastopol.

The special military operations on 24 February 2022 commenced with shaping operations followed by a barrage of long-range operational firing from Russian air and missile forces engaging high-value targets. These operations were accompanied by a near simultaneous launch of airborne land and sea-based operations. The air assault was followed by a ground offensive launched from multiple directions towards the capital city of Kyiv from Belarus. The first phase of the war was defined by rapid manoeuvre operations to outflank and seize key objectives with Kyiv as the initial key Russian military target.

Russia made the most progress in the south from occupied Crimea, reportedly imposing significant casualties on Ukrainian forces in the region. Russian forces advanced quickly towards Kherson and eventually turned toward the Ukrainian coastal city of Mariupol. In other regions, Russia made slow but initially steady progress, seeking to encircle rather than capture major urban centres such as Sumy, Kharkiv, and Chernihiv. Logistics issues and other factors soon stalled most Russian advances. The Russian forces ran into effective Ukrainian resistance from the invasion's outset.

Russia captured Lysychansk city in July, thereby getting the whole of Luhansk province coming under its control. It saw Russia gaining control of 25 per cent of Ukraine. However, heavy Russian losses forced it to halt the ground offensive to allow its troops to regroup and recover. The timing coincided with Ukraine beginning to receive advanced mid-range rocket systems such as high mobility artillery rocket systems (HIMARS) from the USA.

Ukraine, which has been planning this counter-offensive for months, saw this as a window of opportunity to move ahead with its plans. The initial counter-offensive was launched on 29 August to regain the territories of Kherson and Mykolaiv. Its forces have pushed back the Russian Army from almost the entire Kharkiv. As per Ukraine claims, it has retaken some 3,500 square miles of territory since its counter-offensive began earlier this year, including Izium and Kupiansk, two strategically important towns in the northeast that served as logistical hubs for the Russian forces.

The current Russian-Ukraine conflict has impacted the entire globe in some form or the other; it has impacted global energy supplies, created a food grain crisis and is leading the world into another economic recession. The US-led Western order has shaped a narrative that has portrayed Russia as the antagonist. The IW campaign has created a bias in across the social media. However, when it comes to geo-politics, the world is not buying the US narrative at face value. Russia continues to enjoy support in Asian and African countries. In fact, Russian oil imports have increased due to unprecedented global demand. All US efforts to isolate Russia in the global community have hit a road block with many nations supporting it in the UN. Nobody seems to be winning.

A study of each domain provides major lessons, whether they are air wars, naval wars, cyber and electro-spectrum wars, mechanised operations, space-based operations and, more importantly, information operations. However, some of the strategic and operational takeaways are as follows:

Firstly, conventional, full scale, long-duration war is a reality. The Russia-Ukraine war is a full spectrum conflict which has been ongoing for more than a year now. This war has shattered the myth that in the present global order of intertwined economies and international relations, full-spectrum conflict may not happen at all. The widely accepted belief of only grey zone assertions and short duration local conflicts has been proven wrong. There is a space for a conventional conflict and India should retain its focus on readiness of a smart, tech-enabled joint force while maintaining its competencies in the grey zone.

Secondly, an analysis of the initial phases of the Russian campaign suggests that a misjudged military aim was selected and incorrect CoG was identified though the same is debatable. The initial military aim, though not officially laid out, was most likely to capture Kyiv or Line of the Dnieper River and thereby lay down favourable terms to Ukraine on capture of the same. CoG probably was the regime or the will of the armed forces. However, the siege of Kyiv or even Kharkiv was not easy and the armed forces of the Russian Federation (AFRF) suffered early setbacks. The Ukrainian leadership has proved itself to be resolute and determined. After facing early setbacks, the military aim could have been revised and the efforts thereafter focused on the Donbas regions. The selection of a military aim and identification of correct CoG is a decisive factor in the outcome of the battle.

After the dissolution of the Soviet Union, Ukraine held about one third of the Soviet nuclear arsenal, the third largest in the world at the time, as well as significant means of its design and production. In 1994, Ukraine agreed to destroy the weapons, and to join the Treaty on the Non-Proliferation of nuclear weapons (NPT). Today, Russia is a major nuclear power possessing the largest nuclear arsenal in the world whereas Ukraine is a non-nuclear nation. Putin's nuclear signalling has been a major factor in preventing the West from intervening militarily, as also in retaining the levers of escalation dominance. On the other hand, security analysts also believe that had Ukraine been a nuclear-armed nation, the ongoing conflict would have been prevented. In the Indian context, nuclear deterrence is the most powerful war avoidance tool, particularly with our northern adversary.

Thirdly, Ukraine is not a formal member of NATO; however, it relied heavily on NATO's support for the conflict. Article 5 of the NATO charter obliges countries to come to the defence of a fellow NATO member if attacked, but since Ukraine is not a formal member, the other member-countries did not deploy any troops for the war. Massive support in the form of weapons and equipment was provided by all the member-nations, including some high technology modern weapon systems which caused some reverses for Russia. On the other hand, it was apparent that the aggressive stance adapted by Ukraine prior to the conflict was on the behest of NATO and it possibly believed that NATO forces/US Army would join the war in support of Ukraine. It is said that Ukraine is fighting NATO's war using its own army and NATO's modern weapons in Ukrainian territory, which is a very costly option for Ukraine. Overdependence or reliance on alliances and expecting foreign powers to intervene on one's behalf in a war would prove costly.

Fourthly, the Russia-Ukraine conflict is characterized by the participation of common citizens in disseminating videos, images, and information about the war on a real-time basis. This primarily presented the Ukrainian view to the world and highlighted either the Russian oppression or Ukrainian successes. The Western media, supported by various think tanks, also came together to portray Russia as an oppressor. The Ukrainian President, Mr. Zelensky, displayed a media-savvy attitude in swaying the world community in his favour. On the other hand, a complete silence of Russia proved detrimental in communicating its 'just war' cause to the world. A well-coordinated information operations structure is a must to shape world opinion, particularly of the neutral majority. Strategic messaging like the Russian nuclear alert followed by silence is also important to deter adversarial nations from interfering. Most important is control over foreign media and think tanks to present a favourable opinion through a third-party perspective which is much accepted by neutral observers.

Fifthly, self-reliance for war sustenance has emerged as an important lesson of the Russia-Ukraine conflict, particularly for India since it is not part of any military alliance and it has two belligerent neighbours. There are two issues to be addressed by India. First is to reduce its reliance on Russian equipment and broaden its military equipment base. Due to the ongoing conflict, there is a buzz that there is a criticality of spares. The second issue is that since India does not form part of any military alliance, equipment support from other countries during any future conflict is not guaranteed. Although Indian diplomacy has a strong standing overseas and in the past conflicts/heightened situations along the borders India has received substantial support from friendly countries, a similar support in future cannot be guaranteed. Hence, for India to emerge as a regional military power, it needs to develop its military production base and achieve self-reliance in terms of weapons and equipment. The present government has given a lot of impetus to this aspect. The *Atmanirbhar Bharat* programme is progressing in the right direction and it needs to continue till the self-reliance goal is achieved.

Sixthly, Russia spent around USD 62 bn on defence in 2021 compared to the just USD 6 bn defence spending of Ukraine. Russia outnumbered Ukraine in any comparison of force levels. Since Ukraine has sustained the war for more than nine months now, key enablers of its force structure merit analysis. It has emerged that nimble modern weapons provided to Ukraine by supporting nations were game-changers in the ongoing conflict. In the battle of Kyiv, Russian tanks, vehicles, helicopters, and fighters were destroyed by small and mobile Ukrainian defence units armed with weapons such as Stingers, Javelins and armed drones. The platform-heavy Russian force suffered setbacks against a smaller but agile force equipped with modern counter weapons. Similarly in the battle of Donbas, just four units of high mobility artillery rocket systems (HIMARS) provided by the USA caused heavy degradation of Russian resources using precision strikes. The future force structure may need to prioritise emerging technology over legacy platforms.

Seventhly, the USA, EU, and many other nations have imposed economic sanctions against Russia. Within a month of commencement of the conflict, Russia became the most sanctioned country. The aim of these sanctions was to cause a collapse of the Russian economy and force Russia to cease hostilities. There were some initial setbacks but the Russian currency bounced back within two months. Russia also imposed counter sanctions which affected the EU economy to some extent. Overall, these sanctions on Russia are likely to have long-lasting consequences on Russia's defence industrial base and access to advanced technology, which in turn, would degrade the Russian weapon industry's ability to produce and stockpile weapons to replace those that have been destroyed in the war. However, the moot question is that despite a large number of sanctions and counter sanctions, the war could not be deterred which was the ultimate aim of imposing the sanctions. We too could face similar sanctions in the eventuality of a future conflict; however, a nation must have the capabilities to absorb the economic shock and tech-starvation which would be the impact of such sanctions.

Conclusion

Debates concerning the future of warfare have persisted for as long as war itself. Currently, discussions about future conflicts often emphasize the transformative potential of emerging technologies such as artificial intelligence, space exploration, quantum computing, blockchain technologies, and robotics. Although drawing hasty or sweeping conclusions from the ongoing Ukraine-Russia war may be premature, there is undeniable evidence of a significant shift in the nature of warfare. New military technologies appear to be reshaping the balance between offense and defence.

Nevertheless, several key lessons have emerged that highlight the need for investment in advanced areas such as sensors, electronic warfare, digitization, satellite communications, and unmanned systems. These technologies should not only be leveraged for reconnaissance and surveillance but also for offensive operations. This does not entail abandoning legacy platforms but rather enhancing their lethality and effectiveness. Increasing missile forces may also be necessary to bolster offensive capabilities.

The concept of self-reliance, or *Atmanirbharta*, in sustaining military capabilities has become a crucial lesson from the Russia-Ukraine conflict, particularly for India, which is not part of any military alliance and faces two adversarial neighbors. The Indian armed forces must continuously evaluate the technological and doctrinal aspects of the Russia-Ukraine conflict to adequately prepare for future wars. The conflict has demonstrated that cognitive and cyber warfare, though important, are insufficient on their own to provide a strategic advantage. Instead, the Ukraine war has reaffirmed the enduring relevance of conventional warfare tactics and the principle that victories are ultimately achieved through ground forces.

3

India's Security Concerns in Light of the Russia-Ukraine War

Sukanta Ghosh

Introduction

In an increasingly interconnected world, the ripple effect of global conflicts extends far beyond the borders of the nations directly involved. One such conflict that has reverberated across the international stage is the Russia-Ukraine war. While the focal point of the war lies thousands of miles away from the Indian subcontinent, its implications have ignited a security imperative that demands India's careful consideration. The Russia-Ukraine war, characterized by complex geopolitical manoeuvring and shifting alliances, has captured the attention of global policymakers, analysts, and scholars. It has generated debates on the evolving nature of warfare, the enduring significance of national sovereignty, and the potential for great-power confrontation. Beyond the headlines and the frontlines, the conflict resonates deeply with India, a nation that grapples with its own unique set of challenges and opportunities.

India has consistently maintained its stance since Russia's invasion began in February 2022, refraining from criticizing Moscow while advocating an end to hostilities and a return to negotiations. This position underscores India's commitment to dialogue and diplomacy in resolving the conflict. The ongoing war's impact on global food, fuel, and fertilizer prices further accentuates the importance of India's role in advocating peace.

Ahead of Prime Minister Narendra Modi's trip to Italy for the G7 Summit outreach session, Foreign Secretary Vinay Kwatra reiterated India's stance on the Russia-Ukraine war. The summit, focused on artificial intelligence, energy, and Africa, will also include discussions on the Ukraine war in Modi's bilateral meetings. Modi's participation in the outreach session highlights India's proactive approach in addressing global challenges and underscores its significant role in the international community. Additionally, India will participate in the Ukraine peace summit in Switzerland, with the representative yet to be decided. This involvement further emphasizes India's commitment to contributing to global peace efforts.

This article delves into the multifaceted dimensions of the Russia-Ukraine war and its pivotal role in shaping India's security and foreign policy. It explores how a distant war shapes the contours of Indian diplomacy, defence strategies, and economic interests. As the world watches the conflict's ebb and flow, it is imperative to scrutinize how India navigates these tumultuous waters, for it stands at the crossroads of several intersecting and often conflicting interests. This study is not merely an analysis of global events; it is an inquiry into the very essence of India's role in a rapidly changing world. As a nation with a rich history of diplomatic finesse, strategic resilience, and economic aspirations, India's responses to the Russia-Ukraine war have profound implications, not just for its own security and foreign policy, but also for the evolving global order. With comprehensive research and analysis, this article seeks to illuminate the far-reaching implications of the war and the imperative it places upon India to adapt, engage, and redefine its place in the world.

Historical Context

To grasp the current significance of the Russia-Ukraine war for India, one must embark on a journey through history, examining India's relationships with both Russia and Ukraine. This historical backdrop provides insights into India's evolving diplomatic and strategic considerations in the context of the ongoing war.

India's Relations with Russia

India's historical association with Russia dates back to the mid-20th century when the two nations established diplomatic ties. A defining moment in this relationship was the Indo-Soviet Treaty of Peace, Friendship, and Cooperation signed in 1971. This treaty has been described as the 'bedrock' of the India-Russia relationship, underlining the deep-rooted political and military cooperation between the two nations [Nadkarni, 1995]. Over the decades, this partnership has extended into various sectors, particularly defence and nuclear cooperation. Russia has been a major supplier of defence equipment to India, with the Indian military relying heavily on Russian weaponry [Stein, 2023]. The Indo-Russian partnership has not only encompassed military aspects but also collaborations in areas such as space exploration and energy [Mathieu, 2008]. Furthermore, both countries have cooperated closely within international forums like BRICS (Brazil, Russia, India, China, South Africa) and the Shanghai Cooperation Organization (SCO), adding a layer of geopolitical significance to their relationship.

India's Relations with Ukraine

On the other hand, India's relationship with Ukraine is marked by historical connections that predate Ukraine's independence in 1991. During the Soviet era, India maintained diplomatic relations with the USSR, and it was only after Ukraine's independence that India established direct diplomatic ties with the newly-formed nation.

While the India-Ukraine relationship is not as extensive or entrenched as India's partnership with Russia, it has evolved over the years. India and Ukraine have collaborated in various sectors, including trade, technology, and education.

India has also shown interest in Ukraine's defence industry, exploring opportunities for cooperation [Junior & Branko, 2022]. In the light of these historical ties, the Russia-Ukraine war presents a complex web of considerations for India. The war places India in the delicate position of maintaining its relationship with Russia, while also acknowledging the political and strategic dynamics surrounding Ukraine's sovereignty and its relations with the West.

As this article unfolds, it will delve deeper into the contemporary challenges and opportunities that emerge from India's historical ties with Russia and Ukraine and how they shape India's response to the Russia-Ukraine war.

Impact on India's Security

The Russia-Ukraine war, while physically distant from the Indian subcontinent, has sent ripples that reach far beyond Europe. India, as a rising global power with multifaceted interests, is not immune to the security implications of this war. The impact on India's security can be examined through a nuanced lens that encompasses both direct threats and strategic considerations.

Direct Threats and Challenges

Deteriorating Stability in Eurasia: The war's potential to destabilize the Eurasian region is a significant concern for India. Instability in neighbouring regions has historically affected India's security environment. For instance, the Afghanistan crisis following the Soviet withdrawal in the 1980s had a profound impact on India's security situation [Tellis, 2022].

Uncertainty in Defence Procurement: India has been a long-standing buyer of Russian defence equipment. However, the war introduces a layer of uncertainty into the procurement process. Sanctions on Russian arms exports and concerns over reliability can impact India's defence preparedness. This uncertainty has driven India to diversify its sources of defence equipment, seeking partnerships with other countries to reduce over-dependence on Russia [Solanki, 2023].

Energy Security: India relies heavily on Russia as a key source of energy, particularly in the form of oil and gas imports. Disruptions in the energy supply chain due to the conflict can threaten India's energy security. The ongoing crisis underscores the importance of finding alternative energy sources and supply routes to mitigate these risks [Paul, 2023].

Increased Geopolitical Tensions: The global geopolitical tensions resulting from the conflict can indirectly affect India's security. India's diplomatic manoeuvring becomes more complex in a polarized world.

As a nation that values non-alignment and multi-alignment in its foreign policy, India faces the challenge of preserving its strategic autonomy while navigating the turbulent waters of international geopolitics [Sharma, 2022].

Strategic Opportunities and Considerations: Diversification of Defence Suppliers: The war has prompted India to diversify its sources of defence equipment. Reducing over-dependence on Russia is seen as a strategic imperative. India has actively sought partnerships with other major defence equipment suppliers, including the USA, France, and Israel. This diversification not only enhances India's defence capabilities but also strengthens its long-term security interests [Stein, 2023].

Balancing Act in Diplomacy: India's nuanced foreign policy aims to balance its relationships with both Russia and Ukraine. This approach allows India to maintain diplomatic channels with key players in the conflict and potentially contribute to conflict resolution. India's experience in non-alignment and conflict mediation serves as an asset.

Energy Alternatives: To mitigate energy security concerns, India is actively exploring alternative energy sources and suppliers. This shift not only reduces vulnerability but also aligns with India's renewable energy goals. Investments in domestic renewable energy projects and diversification of energy sources through partnerships with other countries contribute to long-term energy security.

Geostrategic Positioning: The conflict's global repercussions offer India opportunities to redefine its geostrategic position. India's diplomatic engagement in various international forums and contributions to peacekeeping efforts enhances its role on the world stage. As the conflict reshapes the global order, India seeks to carve a niche for itself, showcasing its diplomatic prowess and commitment to global peace and stability [Pant & Mishra, 2022].

Direct and Indirect Threats

The Russia-Ukraine war, though geographically distant, casts a shadow of influence on India's security landscape, creating a nuanced web of both direct and indirect threats. This section examines the multifaceted dimensions of these threats and their implications for India's national security.

Direct Threats:

1. Geopolitical Instability in Eurasia: A primary direct threat emanating from the Russia-Ukraine war is the potential to destabilize the Eurasian region. India's national security is intricately linked to regional stability. The conflict's potential to ignite tensions or conflicts among regional actors impacts India directly. In particular, India has longstanding ties with countries in Central Asia and the Middle East, and instability in these regions could have spillover effects on India's security [Antonov, 2022].

2. Uncertainty in Defence Procurement: India's defence procurement has, for decades, heavily relied on Russian arms and technology. The conflict introduces a layer of uncertainty in this relationship. With international sanctions on Russian arms exports, there are concerns about the reliability of defence supplies. Any disruptions in the procurement process can impact India's defence preparedness, creating a direct threat to its national security [Bedi, 2022].

Indirect Threats:

1. Energy Security: India's economic growth and development depend significantly on energy resources, and Russia has been a key source of oil and gas imports. The Russia-Ukraine war adds an element of vulnerability to India's energy security. Any disruptions in the energy supply chain due to the conflict can have cascading effects on India's economy and, by extension, on its national security [Kar, 2022].

2. Increased Geopolitical Tensions: The conflict has spurred heightened geopolitical tensions between the major powers, including the USA and Russia. As India's foreign policy emphasizes non-alignment and multi-alignment, it is indirectly affected by the polarized world order. India must carefully navigate these tensions to preserve its strategic autonomy while managing its international relationships, impacting the nation's security landscape indirectly [Kar, 2022].

Economic and Geopolitical Implications for India

Beyond security threats, the Russia-Ukraine war also reverberates in the economic and geopolitical domains, shaping India's strategic considerations and future path.

Economic Implications:

1. Energy Supply and Economic Consequences: As mentioned, India is a substantial consumer of Russian oil and gas. Any disruptions in the energy supply chain can lead to increased energy prices and inflation, potentially impacting India's economic stability. In the wake of the war, diversifying energy sources and supply routes has become a priority to mitigate such risks.

2. Trade Dynamics: The war indirectly affects India's trade dynamics. As Western nations impose sanctions on Russia, India must navigate its trade relationships carefully. Economic penalties against Russia can have ramifications for Indian exports and imports, influencing its trade balance and economic growth.

Geopolitical Implications:

1. Strategic Shift in Defence Procurement: The war accelerates India's strategic shift in defence procurement. India seeks to diversify its sources of defence equipment, reducing dependence on Russia. This diversification enhances India's long-term security interests and technological capabilities while also improving diplomatic leverage in negotiations with various arms suppliers [Pandit, 2022].

2. Diplomatic Engagement: India's diplomacy plays a critical role in addressing the geopolitical implications of the war. India's role as a non-permanent member of the United Nations Security Council offers opportunities for active diplomatic engagement. India has voiced its concerns about the crisis and called for a peaceful resolution, contributing to the international discourse on the matter. In conclusion, the Russia-Ukraine war presents a complex array of direct and indirect threats to India's security. Simultaneously, it influences India's economic and geopolitical positioning. India must deftly navigate these challenges to secure its interests and continue its ascent on the global stage.

India's Diplomatic Role: Examining Mediation Efforts and Effectiveness

India's diplomatic role in mediating the Russia-Ukraine war emerges as a critical aspect of this article, highlighting the nation's endeavours to influence regional and global diplomacy.

Mediation Efforts:

India's diplomatic overtures in mediating the Russia-Ukraine war are a testament to its nuanced foreign policy and diplomatic finesse. India, as a member of the United Nations Security Council and a nation with a rich history of diplomacy, has actively engaged in diplomatic efforts to mediate the conflict [*The Times of India*, 2023].

1. United Nations Security Council: As a non-permanent member of the United Nations Security Council (UNSC), India has a platform to engage in high-level diplomatic discourse. India's presence in the UNSC allows it to contribute to discussions on the conflict, express its concerns, and advocate for peaceful resolutions [Indian Council of World Affairs, 2023].

2. Bilateral Engagements: India has also conducted bilateral engagements with key stakeholders in the war, including Russia and Ukraine. These engagements serve as channels for India to convey its concerns and, where possible, promote dialogue and peaceful resolution. The practice of Track II diplomacy, where non-governmental organizations and experts facilitate discussions between conflicting parties, is also significant [*The Indian Express*, 2023].

Effectiveness of India's Diplomatic Role:

Assessing the effectiveness of India's diplomatic role in regional and global diplomacy vis-à-vis the Russia-Ukraine war is a complex undertaking, influenced by a multitude of factors.

1. **Regional Dynamics**: India's effectiveness in mediating the conflict is partially contingent upon the receptiveness of the parties involved. The Russia-Ukraine war is influenced by an array of complex regional dynamics, and India's influence may be limited by the broader geopolitical interests at play [Mohanasakthivel, 2022].

2. **Multilateral Approach**: India's approach to diplomacy tends to be multilateral, emphasizing a collaborative and non-confrontational stance. In the case of the Russia-Ukraine war, the ability to influence conflicting parties and major powers is mediated by these diplomatic principles. The conflict's resolution might require a stronger international consensus and collaborative efforts [United Nations press releases, 2023].
3. **Ensuring Regional Stability**: India's primary concern is maintaining regional stability and avoiding further escalation. Its efforts are directed at averting crises and ensuring peace, which contributes to the broader objectives of global diplomacy in conflict resolution. The effectiveness of these endeavours is difficult to gauge in the short term but can yield results over time [Rajagopalan, 2015].

Defence and Strategic Alliances: Adapting to the Changing Security Environment

India's defence and strategic alliances, crucial components of its national security, have been significantly influenced by the Russia-Ukraine war. This section delves into the assessment of India's defence and strategic alliances in the context of the war, along with an analysis of how India's defence policy has adapted to the evolving security environment.

Assessment of Defence and Strategic Alliances

1. India's Historic Ties with Russia: India's historical defence relationship with Russia dates back several decades. Russia has been a principal supplier of defence equipment to India, comprising a substantial portion of the Indian military's arsenal. The Russia-Ukraine war, however, has cast a shadow of uncertainty over this relationship. India must assess the potential implications of sanctions on Russian arms exports, both in terms of existing procurements and future agreements [Menon, 2023].

2. Diversification of Defence Suppliers: To mitigate the risks associated with overreliance on a single source of defence equipment, India has actively sought to diversify its defence suppliers. Strategic partnerships with the USA, France, and Israel, among others, have gained prominence. This diversification strategy not only bolsters India's technological capabilities but also enhances its bargaining power in defence negotiation [Pandit, 2022].

3. Defence Alliances and Strategic Partnerships: India's strategic alliances with countries such as the USA, Japan, and Australia are instrumental in bolstering its security posture. These partnerships, notably the Quadrilateral Security Dialogue (Quad), play a crucial role in maintaining regional security and countering potential threats. The evolving dynamics of these alliances are closely tied to the changing security environment influenced by the Russia-Ukraine war [Joshi, 2020].

Adaptation of Defence Policy

1. Modernization and Technological Advancements: The changing security landscape necessitates the modernization of India's armed forces. The conflict has emphasized the importance of adopting advanced technology and capabilities to respond to evolving threats. India's defence policy has shifted towards the development of indigenous defence technologies, fostering self-reliance, and enhancing its defence industry [Menon, 2021].

2. Preparedness for Hybrid Warfare: The Russia-Ukraine war has underscored the importance of being prepared for hybrid warfare, which combines conventional, irregular, and cyber warfare. India's defence policy has adapted to address these multifaceted challenges by enhancing its cyber capabilities, intelligence, surveillance, and reconnaissance (ISR) assets, and strategies to counter non-conventional threats [Chari, 2016].

3. Regional and Global Role: India's evolving defence policy aligns with its aspirations for a more prominent regional and global role. In the wake of the Russia-Ukraine war, India is positioning itself as a reliable partner in conflict resolution, peacekeeping, and humanitarian assistance. It's diplomatic and defence engagement reflects its commitment to enhancing regional and global stability [Pandey, 2021].

In summary, the Russia-Ukraine war has compelled India to reassess its defence and strategic alliances, diversify its defence procurement, and adapt its defence policy to the changing security environment.

These developments aim to reinforce India's national security while enhancing its role as a responsible global actor in the ever-evolving world order.

Economic Implications

Investigating Consequences for India in Energy and Trade Dynamics
The Russia-Ukraine war unfolds as a pivotal factor shaping India's economic landscape, exerting notable consequences in both energy and trade dynamics. This section delves into an in-depth exploration of these economic implications and their far-reaching effects on India.

Energy Dynamics
Dependency on Russian energy resources: India's energy security is intricately tied to its reliance on Russian energy resources, particularly oil and gas. The conflict introduces a layer of vulnerability in this dependence, impacting the stability of India's energy supply chain.

Oil and Gas Imports
Russia has been a significant supplier of oil and gas to India. Any disruptions in these imports due to the conflict can lead to increased energy prices and supply uncertainties, affecting various sectors of India's economy [Kudaisya, 2022].

Diversification Strategies: To mitigate these risks, India is actively exploring alternative energy sources and supply routes. Diversification efforts include increasing investments in renewable energy, expanding domestic production, and seeking partnerships with other energy-rich nations [*Money Control*, 2022].

Trade Dynamics: Impact on Bilateral Trade and Global Markets: The economic implications of the Russia-Ukraine war extend to India's trade dynamics, influencing both bilateral and global markets

Sanctions and Trade Routes: As Western nations impose sanctions on Russia, India faces challenges in navigating its trade relationships. Sanctions may impact bilateral trade agreements, and disruptions in traditional trade routes can necessitate recalibrations in India's global trade strategies [*The Economic Times*, 2022].

Trade Balance: The conflict indirectly affects India's trade balance. Economic penalties against Russia, a significant trading partner, can have ramifications for Indian exports and imports. This dynamic necessitates a careful balancing act to ensure economic stability amid shifting global trade dynamics [CNBC-TV18, 2022].

Global Economic Ripples:

Impact on Global Commodity Prices and Inflation: The war's economic consequences extend beyond India's borders, influencing global commodity prices and inflation rates.

Commodity Price Volatility: The conflict contributes to volatility in global commodity prices, impacting essential commodities that India imports. This volatility can lead to inflationary pressures, affecting the cost of living and overall economic stability [Observer Research Foundation, 2022].

Supply Chain Disruptions: Disruptions in global supply chains, especially in critical sectors like energy and commodities, can reverberate through India's economy. These disruptions may necessitate adjustments in trade policies and resource allocation to manage potential shortages [*ECB Economic Bulletin*, 2021].

Research Findings:

Addressing Key Questions: This section presents the key findings of the study, providing insights into the impact of the Russia-Ukraine war on India's security, diplomatic efforts, defence policies, and economic landscape, as outlined by the research questions.

1. **Impact on India's National Security and Strategic Interests**

   Finding: The Russia-Ukraine war poses direct threats to India's national security, particularly concerning regional stability in Eurasia. Instabilities in neighbouring regions, influenced by the conflict, have the potential to impact India's security environment significantly.

2. **Evolving Role of India in Diplomatic Efforts**

   Finding: India's diplomatic role in mediating the Russia-Ukraine war is characterized by active engagement in forums such as the

United Nations Security Council and bilateral dialogues. While the effectiveness of India's mediation efforts is influenced by complex regional dynamics, its commitment to diplomatic dialogue is evident.

3. **Adaptation of Defence Strategies and Alliances**

   Finding: India's defence policy has undergone a strategic shift in response to the conflict. Diversification of defence suppliers, modernization efforts, and a focus on technological advancements are integral aspects of India's adaptation to the changing security environment. The study identifies a deliberate move towards reducing dependence on Russian arms exports.

4. **Economic Implications for India**

   Finding: The economic implications of the Russia-Ukraine war for India are substantial. Energy dynamics are affected by the vulnerability of Russia's energy supplies, prompting India to diversify its energy sources. Trade dynamics witness challenges due to sanctions and disruptions, leading to a recalibration of India's global trade strategies.

5. **Broader Implications for India's Global Positioning**

   Finding: The study identifies the broader implications of the conflict for India's global positioning. India's nuanced foreign policy, emphasizing non-alignment and active participation in international forums, contributes to its role in shaping the evolving global order. The conflict provides India with opportunities to redefine its geostrategic position on the world stage.

In summary, the research findings illuminate the multifaceted impact of the Russia-Ukraine war on India. From direct threats to national security and the evolving role in diplomatic efforts to the adaptation of defence strategies, economic consequences, and broader global implications, the study provides a comprehensive understanding of how this conflict shapes India's responses and positioning in the international arena.

Conclusion

In summary, this article has extensively explored the multifaceted impact of the Russia-Ukraine war on India, analyzing its implications across various domains. The key findings shed light on crucial aspects that shape India's security, foreign policy, and global positioning.

1. **Security Challenges and Strategic Adaptation**: The Russia-Ukraine war introduces direct threats to India's national security, emphasizing the need for strategic adaptation. Instabilities in Eurasia and uncertainties in defence procurement necessitate a nuanced approach. India's move towards diversifying defence suppliers and modernizing its armed forces reflects a deliberate effort to navigate these challenges.

2. **Diplomatic Engagement and Global Influence**: India's diplomatic role in mediating the war showcases active engagement on the international stage. While the effectiveness of these efforts is influenced by complex geopolitical dynamics, India's commitment to diplomatic dialogue and peacekeeping aligns with its non-alignment principles. The war provides India with an opportunity to strengthen its global influence.

3. **Economic Realities and Policy Adjustments:** Economically, the war significantly impacts India. Energy dynamics are vulnerable due to dependence on Russian resources, prompting a shift toward diversification. Trade dynamics face challenges from sanctions and disruptions, necessitating recalibrations in India's global trade strategies. This study underscores the importance of adapting economic policies to navigate through global economic uncertainties.

4. **Broader Geopolitical Implications:** The broader geopolitical implications highlight India's dynamic role in shaping the evolving global order. Emphasizing a nuanced foreign policy, India seeks to balance relationships with key players. The war provides India with opportunities to redefine its geostrategic positioning and contribute to regional and global stability.

Implications for India's Security and Foreign Policy: The research findings underscore the complexity of India's position in the face of the Russia-Ukraine war. Adaptations in defence strategies and alliances are crucial for safeguarding national security. Diplomatic engagement, characterized by a commitment to peacekeeping and non-alignment, positions India as a significant player in global conflict resolution. Economically, diversification strategies and policy adjustments are imperative for mitigating vulnerabilities.

Final Thoughts: As India navigates through the intricate web of challenges posed by the Russia-Ukraine war, it finds itself at a critical juncture. The nation's ability to balance security, diplomatic finesse, economic resilience, and global influence will determine its trajectory in an ever-changing international landscape. This study serves as a comprehensive guide, offering insights into the complexities and opportunities that define India's responses to the challenges of the contemporary geopolitical scenario.

Policy Recommendations: Navigating the Geopolitical Landscape Building upon the research findings, the following policy recommendations are proposed for India to effectively navigate the complexities arising from the Russia-Ukraine war:

1. **Strengthen Diversification Strategies**: Diversify Defence Suppliers: Continue the strategic shift in defence procurement by diversifying suppliers, reducing dependence on Russian arms exports, and fostering partnerships with key global players.

   Advance Indigenous Defence Capabilities: Invest in indigenous defence technologies and capabilities to enhance self-reliance and resilience in the face of global uncertainties.

2. **Enhance Diplomatic Agility**: Active Participation in International Forums: Maintain active participation in international forums, especially the United Nations Security Council, to advocate peaceful resolutions and contribute to global stability.

   Bilateral and Multilateral Engagements: Continue engaging in bilateral dialogues with conflicting parties and participating in multilateral efforts to mediate and resolve the conflict.

3. **Energy Security and Economic Resilience**: Accelerate Clean Energy Transition: Fast-track investments in renewable energy sources to reduce dependence on Russian oil and gas, ensuring energy security and aligning with global sustainability goals.

Diversify trade Partnerships: Actively diversify trade partnerships to mitigate the impact of sanctions and disruptions, focusing on maintaining a balanced trade portfolio.

4. **Technological Advancements and Hybrid Warfare Preparedness**: Focus on Technological Modernization: Prioritize technological advancements in defence capabilities, intelligence, and cyber security to counter evolving threats in the realm of hybrid warfare.

   Strategic Cyber-Security Investments: Enhance cyber security infrastructure to safeguard critical systems and data against potential cyber threats and disruptions.

5. **Geopolitical Positioning and Global Leadership**: Balanced Diplomacy: Navigate geopolitical tensions with a balanced approach, maintaining diplomatic ties with key players while upholding non-alignment principles.

   Active Role in Conflict Resolution: Continue actively participating in conflict resolution efforts globally, showcasing India's commitment to fostering peace and stability.

6. **Economic Adaptability and Resilience**: Agile Economic Policies: Develop adaptive economic policies that respond to global market dynamics, ensuring resilience in the face of trade disruptions and commodity price fluctuations.

   Invest in Domestic Industries: Stimulate domestic industries, especially in defence and energy sectors, to reduce vulnerabilities and contribute to self-sufficiency.

7. **Public Diplomacy and Information Campaigns**: Transparent Communication: Engage in transparent communication with the public to ensure awareness of the challenges and the government's strategies to address them.

   Promote Soft Power: Leverage cultural diplomacy and soft power initiatives to enhance India's global image and strengthen international partnerships. These recommendations aim to guide India in navigating the multifaceted challenges posed by the Russia-Ukraine war, promoting national security, diplomatic effectiveness, economic resilience, and global influence. The implementation of these strategies will contribute to positioning India as a proactive and adaptive player on the global stage.

REFERENCES

1. Tellis, Ashley J. 'What is in Our Interest': India and the Ukraine War, Carnegie Endowment for International Peace, 25 April 2022.
2. https://carnegieendowment.org/2022/04/25/what-is-in-our-interest-india-and-ukraine-war-pub-86961
3. Ganguly, R. (2019). Understanding Russia's Involvement in Ukraine and Implications for India. Observer Research Foundation.
4. Balachandran, V. (2022). 'US Sanctions on Russian Arms Exports Can Impact India's Defence Procurement', *The Economic Times*.
5. Kudaisya, M.B. (2022). 'India's Energy Security amid Ukraine Crisis: A Closer Look.' *The Diplomat*.
6. Joshi, S. (2020). The Quadrilateral Security Dialogue and the India-US Strategic Partnership, Observer Research Foundation.
7. Menon, R. (2021). India's Defence Dilemma, *The Indian Express*.
8. Chari, P.R. (2016). Hybrid Warfare: Future Conflicts in the Digital Age. Institute for Defence Studies and Analyses.
9. *The Economic Times*. (2022). India Urges Peaceful Resolution of Ukraine Crisis, Highlights Impact on Trade.
10. Observer Research Foundation. (2022). Rising Commodity Prices: Impact on India's Economy.
11. *Money Control*. (2022). India's Shift Towards Clean Energy Amid Ukraine Crisis.
12. CNBC-TV18. (2022). How the Russia-Ukraine Conflict Could Impact India's Trade.
13. Shukla, A. (2022). 'India's Diplomatic Balancing Act over Ukraine,' *Business Standard*.
14. Pandit, R. (2022). 'India Diversifies Defence Exports to Ensure Uninterrupted Supplies.' The Times of India.
15. Mearsheimer, J.J. (2014). 'Why the Ukraine Crisis Is the West's Fault: The Liberal Delusions That Provoked Putin, 'Foreign Affairs.'
16. Singh, S. (2018). The Role of India's Non-Alignment and Its Diplomatic Challenges. Observer Research Foundation.
17. Pandey, G. (2022). 'India and Peacekeeping: A Potential Catalyst in Conflict Resolution,' *The Diplomat*.
18. *The Economic Times*. (2021). India Takes Over UNSC Presidency for August.
19. Peri, D. (2022).' India Cautious Amid Rising US-Russia Tensions.' *The Hindu*.
20. Debroy, N. (2022). 'Why Ukraine Crisis Is a Rare Geopolitical Opportunity for India.' *The Indian Express*.
21. Rajagopalan, R.P. (2015). India's Role in the Ukraine Crisis. Carnegie India.
22. Bloomberg. (2022). Russia-Ukraine War: Impact on Global Supply Chains.
23. *ECB Economic Bulletin*, (2021), Supply chain disruptions and the effects on the global economy.

4

Russia-Ukraine War: Key Takeaways for India's National Security

Neeraj Singh Manhas

Introduction

The Ukraine War, sparked by Russia's 'special military operation' in February 2022, has profoundly impacted global geopolitics and continues to shape the international order as it extends into its third year in 2024. While the conflict may have begun as a localised military operation, it has morphed into a multifaceted struggle with far-reaching consequences.[1] It is rooted in years of simmering tensions in the aftermath of the Cold War, when the West retained NATO despite the dismantling of the Soviet Union. As NATO membership expanded, its military alliance nearly doubled in size, making Russia feel increasingly insecure, and the 2014 Maidan revolution, the conflict has disrupted energy, food, and fertilizer supplies, widened the East-West divide, and hampered global economic recovery.[2] This insecurity ultimately led to the current conflict. While India has advocated for a ceasefire, dialogue, and respect for territorial integrity, the war's long-term implications for global security and the potential for wider conflict remain a source of grave concern.[3] As the world navigates this complex crisis, India's voice advocating peace and international norms is more crucial than ever. The Ukraine war is being closely studied by India, China, and other nations as they seek to learn contemporary lessons that could be applied to their own conflict scenarios.[4] The impact of the war is ubiquitous, and has dire economic and political consequences for nations already struggling to recover from the pandemic.[5] In the case of India that is already facing a threat of a two-front war from China and Pakistan, it becomes significant to draw some lessons from the Russia-Ukraine war. It serves as a stark reminder of our interconnected world's vulnerability, and underscores the need for diplomacy, international cooperation, and a renewed commitment to the rule-based order.[6] As the world grapples with this complex and evolving crisis, India's voice advocating for peace and respect for international norms remains crucial.[7] India, advocating for ceasefire, dialogue, and respect for territorial integrity, views the war's long-term implications for global security and potential for wider conflict with grave concern. The war is being closely studied by India, China, and other nations for contemporary lessons applicable to their conflict scenarios. The war's impact has dire economic and political consequences for nations already struggling to recover from the pandemic. The conflict underscores the need for diplomacy, international cooperation, and a renewed commitment to a rule-based order. This paper will look into India's immediate concerns and long-term strategic implications and provides a roadmap for India to strengthen its national security posture in the wake of the conflict.

Historical Context

It was a hallmark case of instability that spread throughout the former Soviet Union, and it was the conflict that occurred between Russia and Ukraine in 2014.[8] Putin was able to take advantage of the Maidan protests in Ukraine to apply external provocation in order to intensify the instability that was already present in the country.[9] The Western world was taken aback by Putin's annexation of Crimea as well as his push into the eastern and south-eastern provinces of Ukraine. In the end, the Western world responded by issuing a diplomatic denunciation, imposing economic sanctions, providing non-lethal military aid, and strengthening military forces along the eastern flank of NATO.[10] The sanctions imposed by the West, which were exacerbated by a dramatic decline in the prices of oil and gas around the world, had a significant impact on the Russian economy, but they were not successful in changing Putin's strategy.[11] The pro-European and pro-reform factions in the Ukrainian parliament were strengthened as a result of the elections that took place in October 2014. The democratically chosen reformers, who included civic activists from the Maidan, had a foundation upon which to build their efforts[12] In the beginning of 2014, more than two hundred professionals, civil society organisers, and human rights campaigners collaborated to develop the Reanimation Package of Reforms.[13] This package of reforms included specific steps to combat corruption, increase transparency in procurement, and overhaul taxes and the judicial system. They are supported by the increased knowledge of the Ukrainians in monitoring responsibilities for which they are responsible and the repercussions that would result from failure.[14]

Geopolitical Implications

Significant geopolitical developments have been triggered as a result of the conflict in Ukraine, which has hastened the development of a multi-polar world and posed a challenge to the core structures that underpin the liberal international order.[15] A realignment of alliances is taking place, regional instability is on the rise, and the economy of the entire world is experiencing turbulence.[16] The war's effects are far-reaching and complex, ranging from the availability of food to the security of energy supplies. In order for India to successfully navigate this ever-changing terrain, it is necessary for the country to employ a strategic approach that includes developing alliances, modernising its military, diversifying its energy sources, and playing a leading role in international organizations.[17] It is only through the implementation of such preventative measures that India will be able to secure its future as a powerful and influential power once the conflict is over.[18]

Military and Strategic Implications

The Russia-Ukraine war has exposed significant vulnerabilities in the modern military landscape and sparked a reassessment of strategic doctrines worldwide. This analysis delves into the diverse military and strategic implications of the war:

(a) Modern Warfare Tactics and Weaponry

The importance of combined arms has highlighted the crucial role of combined arms operations, seamlessly integrating infantry, armoured forces, artillery, and airpower for maximum effectiveness.[19] The widespread use of drones, missiles, and other precision weapons has demonstrated their ability to inflict significant damage with minimal collateral damage. This trend will likely accelerate, prompting investments in advanced weaponry and counter-measures.[20] The war has shown the increasing importance of cyber warfare as a tool for disrupting critical infrastructure, communications, and command and control systems. This necessitates robust cyber defences and offensive capabilities. The intense fighting in urban environments like Kyiv has showcased the complexities and challenges of such conflicts requiring specific tactics and training. It has underscored the significance of information dominance in shaping public opinion, influencing political decisions, and disrupting enemy operations.[21]

(b) Implications for India's Military Modernisation

Indigenous defence development has emphasised the need for India to reduce its reliance on imported weapons and develop its indigenous defence capabilities. This includes investing in research and development, encouraging private sector participation, and fostering collaboration with strategic partners. It also emphasis air defence and missile defence as the need for robust air defence and missile defence systems to counter aerial threats, particularly from unmanned aerial vehicles.[22] The war has demonstrated the continued importance of armoured forces and artillery in modern warfare. India needs to modernize its existing inventory and acquire advanced platforms like next-generation tanks and long-range artillery systems.[23] The need is for robust cyber defences to protect critical infrastructure and networks, coupled with offensive cyber capabilities to deter and respond to cyber attacks. It has shown the effectiveness of special forces in conducting unconventional warfare and intelligence gathering. India needs to enhance its special forces capabilities and invest in modern intelligence collection platforms and technologies.[24]

(c) Strategic Planning and Partnerships

A reassessment of India's military doctrines is needed to incorporate the evolving nature of warfare and adapt to emerging threats. This includes developing strategies for dealing with hybrid warfare, cyber warfare, and potential nuclear escalation.[25] It has underlined the importance of strong regional alliances and partnerships for deterring aggression and maintaining peace and stability. India needs to actively engage with its neighbours and other strategic partners to build robust security architecture in the Indo-Pacific region.[26] It has exposed the risks of relying on a single supplier for critical military equipment. India needs to diversify its defence equipment sources to ensure its strategic autonomy and mitigate potential supply chain disruptions.[27] It is important to emphasise on collaborating with international partners on developing and deploying emerging technologies like artificial intelligence, hypersonic weapons, and quantum computing. The Russia-Ukraine war has served as a stark reminder of the ever-changing nature of warfare and the need for constant adaptation and innovation.[28] India's military modernization and strategic planning must take into account the lessons learned from this conflict to ensure its national security in the face of evolving threats and challenges. By focusing on indigenous development, investing in advanced capabilities, strengthening regional alliances, and diversifying its defence partnerships, India can emerge as a strong and capable military power in the post-war world.[29]

Lessons for India's National Security

The whole responsibility lies with the conflict and the military operations, while diplomatic support can only provide a limited reduction in the suffering. It is imperative that India relies on its own military capabilities.[30] It is imperative that India construct a credible deterrence in order to safeguard its interests. Both raising defence budgets and engaging in strategic posturing are required to accomplish this. It is absolutely necessary to have a robust economy in order to keep a robust military.[31] The growth of the economy and the advancement of technology should be India's primary concerns. A significant component of contemporary conflict is the use of information warfare. It is important for India to make investments in story development and to ensure that negative narratives about Russian military equipment are managed effectively.[32] It is essential to diversify both the purchase and trading of military equipment. Free trade agreements in the defence sector should be investigated by India, and the country should diversify its commerce with additional countries. India is concerned about the possibility of enhanced relations between

Russia and China in the aftermath of the crisis in Ukraine. It is imperative that India takes into consideration the repercussions of Russia's increasing trust in China.[33] This is a very worrying possibility of using nuclear weapons. Developing solutions to address this problem and learning from South Asia's experiences in preventing nuclear conflicts are both important things for India to concentrate on.[34]

(a) Role of Air Power in the Ukraine Conflict

The failure of Russia to gain air supremacy can be attributed to the country's emphasis on ground attack strategies and its failure to adequately assess the danger posed by man-portable air defence systems (MANPADS). It has been employed successfully by the Ukrainian Air Force to target Russian aircraft, despite the fact that they have only flown a limited number of flights. On multiple occasions, Russia has proved that it is capable of using air-launched cruise missiles to strike targets in Ukraine.[35] The fact that they do not have the capability to airlift, however, restricts their efficacy. According to the current state of affairs in the realm of modern warfare, air power has become an essential component of the military strategy of any nation. The conflict that is currently taking place between Russia and Ukraine teaches a number of valuable lessons that have enormous repercussions for the national security of India.[36]

(b) Control of Airspace

The significance of controlling the skies in conventional combat has been highlighted by the crisis in Ukraine and brought new attention to the matter. The capability of Russia to prevent Ukraine from achieving effective air superiority has been an essential component of Russia's strategy. When it comes to India, this underscores the importance of giving air defence a higher priority and ensuring that the army and air force effectively coordinate their efforts.[37]

(c) Vulnerability of Helicopters

One of the most important things that we have learned from this fight is the importance of employing man-portable air defence systems (MANPADS) against helicopters. It is imperative that India recognises this vulnerability and incorporates it into its military strategy, particularly when it comes to the planning of airborne attacks in heavily contested airspace.[38]

(d) Role of Air Force in High-Value Targeting

The war has a clear message that the air force plays an extremely important role in achieving wider strategic goals. Both the integration of India's air force into its overall military policy and the maintenance of a robust interdiction capacity are among the most important things that India must do.[39]

(e) Importance of ISR

The conflict highlights the significance of an organisation's skills in the areas of intelligence, surveillance, and reconnaissance (ISR). ISR capabilities that are persistent, such as space-based systems, are something that India has to invest in so that it can keep its situational awareness and take informed decisions.[40]

(f) Integrated Air Defence System

The conflict and the importance of having a strong integrated air defence system have been brought to light. As threats continue to evolve, India must to take into consideration the possibility of offensively projecting its air defence capabilities.[41]

(g) Terrain Challenges

It has been established through the battle that geography can make surface movement extremely vulnerable. When it comes to its military activities, India needs to take into consideration the potential influence that seasonal weather could have.

(h) Multi-domain Approach

The air domain, along with the maritime domain and the continental domain, needs to be incorporated into India's narratives regarding national security initiatives. In order for India to effectively manage complex security concerns, it is essential for the country to adopt a multi-domain, multi-service approach.[42]

(i) Technology Adoption

When it comes to embracing new technology, India needs to exercise caution because of the costs associated with their creation and obsolescence. It is more important to concentrate on the broad military capability that is in line with the military strategy than it is to pay attention to specific objectives or goals of individual services.[43]

(j) Role of Force in National Strategy

The battle has brought to light the necessity of revaluating the function of force in national strategy, particularly in the context of limited wars that are fought quickly and fighting that takes place in grey zones. It is imperative that India modify its military doctrines in order to accommodate these ever-changing circumstances.[44]

(k) Air Power's Strategic Capabilities

When it comes to matters of national security and interests, India must acknowledge and make use of the strategic capabilities of air power, regardless of whether the situation is peaceful or armed conflict. Among these measures is the promotion of a democratic international order that is founded on norms and that guarantees equitable access to common areas both on land and in the air, respectively.[45]

The battle that is taking place between Russia and Ukraine offers India significant insights on the role that air power plays in modern warfare and the implications that this role has for the nation's security. In order to position itself better to face the growing difficulties in its defence policy, India can benefit from these experiences and put itself in a better position.

Conclusion

There is no denying that the conflict between Russia and Ukraine has served as a wake-up call for India, prompting the country to conduct a complete appraisal of its national security landscape. The war highlights the need for accelerated development of domestic military industrial capabilities and self-sufficiency in defence equipment production. According to the information presented in this paper, the conflict has shone light on a variety of difficulties and opportunities, which calls for the Indian authorities to respond in a nuanced manner.[46] The most important thing that India should take away from the war is the necessity of accelerating the development of its domestic military industrial capabilities. As a result of the excessive reliance on imported weapons, particularly those originating from Russia, vulnerabilities have been revealed, and the necessity for self-sufficiency in the fabrication of defence equipment has never been more clear.[47] Having this awareness should serve as a spur for the establishment of robust policy initiatives that are geared at supporting innovation, research, and development within the domestic defence sector.

The importance of well-coordinated joint theatre operations has been emphasised, with particular focus on the critical role that seamless integration between air defence and information gathering plays. Through the course of the war, the effectiveness of such collaborative techniques in deciding the success of operations has been brought to light.[48] The Indian government needs to make use of this information in order to improve its capabilities in joint warfare and ensure that it takes a comprehensive and unified strategy for national defence. There has been a paradigm shift in modern warfare, as seen by the prevalence of developing technologies in the conflict in Ukraine.[49] These technologies include drones, artificial intelligence, and cyber warfare technology. Not only does India need to adjust to new technologies, it also needs to make significant investments in research and development in order to maintain its lead in this technical competition.

In this paper, the researcher calls for a forward-looking approach and urges India to make technology innovation a priority as a cornerstone of its national security strategy. Additionally, the war has brought to light the precarious nature of global supply lines, particularly with regard to essential militaristic weapons.[50] Diversifying India's sources of supply and decreasing its reliance on any one nation for essential military weapons are both necessary steps. In order to guarantee the robustness of its defence supply chain, this entails establishing strategic relationships and working together with a wide variety of countries. As a result of the struggle, India is forced to rethink and adjust its doctrines and force formations according to the new circumstances. There is a critical need for adaptability, agility, and preparedness to adopt shifting paradigms in strategic thinking. In order to better align India's military capabilities with contemporary concerns, this paper suggests that India should begin a complete assessment of its force architecture. This study should incorporate lessons acquired during the Russia-Ukraine war. India can not only negotiate the current challenges that have arisen as a result of the conflict, but it can also position itself strategically for long-term security in a global context that is constantly changing. This is because India has absorbed four crucial points.

Instead of pursuing confrontation as a means of securing their place as superpowers, Russia and the USA might have avoided becoming involved in the crisis in Ukraine by employing diplomacy to find a solution to the dispute on the internal level. They have caused imbalances in the international order as a result of their concentration on power, which ultimately led to the conflict.[51] Should this imbalanced relationship be disregarded, it is possible that similar occurrences may take place in the future, which might eventually result in another cold war or perhaps World War III. In order to have a better understanding of the severity of the war's repercussions and the potential risk of a world war, additional research should be conducted to investigate the conflict's effects not just on the states that were formerly part of the Soviet Union but also on the rest of Europe and the world.[52] By learning from the Russia-Ukraine war, India can strategically position itself for long-term security in a constantly changing global context.

REFERENCES

1. Alam, M.K., Tabash, M.I., Billah, M., Kumar, S. & Anagreh, S. (2022). 'The impacts of the Russia–Ukraine invasion on global markets and commodities: a dynamic connectedness among G7 and BRIC markets.' *Journal of Risk and Financial Management*, 15(8), 352.
2. Bossman, A., Gubareva, M. & Teplova, T. (2023). Asymmetric effects of geopolitical risk on major currencies: Russia-Ukraine tensions. Finance Research Letters, 51, 103440.
3. Cosgrove, J. (2020). The Russian invasion of the Crimean peninsula, 2014- 2015: A post-cold war nuclear crisis case study. Applied Physics Lab, Johns Hopkins University, Laurel MD.
4. Delanoë, I. (2020). 'After the Crimean crisis: towards a greater Russian maritime power in the Black Sea.' *Southeast European and Black Sea Studies*, 14 (3), 367-382.
5. Douhan, A.F. (2022). 'International organizations and settlement of the conflict in Ukraine.' *Heidelberg Journal of International Law*, 75(1), 195-214.
6. Espinas, G.D. (2010). 'Ukraine's Defence Engagement with the United States.'" *Journal of International Affairs*, 63 (2), 53-63.

7. Glaveanu, V.P., Hanchett Hanson, M., Baer, J., Barbot, B., Clapp, E.P., Corazza, G.E. & Sternberg, R.J. (2020). 'Advancing theory and research: A socio cultural manifesto.' *The Journal of Creative Behaviour*, 54(3), 741-745.
8. Guchua, A., Zedelashvili, T. & Giorgadze, G. (2022). 'Geopolitics of the Russia-Ukraine War and Russian Cyber Attacks on Ukraine-Georgia and Expected Threats.' *Ukrainian Policymaker*, 10(1), 26-36.
9. Holdar, S. (1995). 'Torn between East and West: the regional factor in Ukrainian politics.' *Post-Soviet Geography*, 36(2), 112-132.
10. Hunter, R. (2022). 'The Ukraine crisis: Why and what now?' *Survival*, 64(1), 7-28.
11. Karagiannis, E. (2014). 'The Russian interventions in South Ossetia and Crimea compared: Military performance, legitimacy, and goals.' *Contemporary Security Policy*, 35(3), 400-420.
12. Khodunov, A. (2022). 'The orange revolution in Ukraine.' In *Handbook of revolutions in the 21st century: The new waves of revolutions, and the causes and effects of disruptive political change* (pp. 501-515). Cham: Springer International Publishing.
13. Konoplyov, S. (2022). 'Continuities and Ruptures: Tracking the US Interests in the Black Sea Area in the Context of the 'Pivot to Asia'.' *Journal of Balkan and Near Eastern Studies*, 16 (3), 356-369.
14. Legvold, R. (2014). 'Managing the New Cold War—What Moscow and Washington Can Learn From the Last One.' *Foreign Affairs*, 93(5), 32-43.
15. Mahilaj, S. (2023). 'EU and Cooperation in the Russia-Ukraine Conflict: Impacts and Limitations.' *ESI Preprints*, 15, 49-49.
16. Mearsheimer, J.J. & Alterman, G. (2001). *The tragedy of great power politics*. WW Norton & Company.
17. Okoro, I.O., Ndubuisi, J.O. & Ogwu, P.C.A. (2020). *The Russia-Ukraine Conflict and its Impact on Contemporary Global Security*, 11(2), 1-17.
18. Rywkin, M. (2014). 'Ukraine: between Russia and the West.' *American Foreign Policy Interests*, 36(2), 119-126.
19. Simons, G. (2022). Will the war in Ukraine push the country to join NATO? LSE European Politics and Policy (EUROPP) blog.
20. Sinambela, S.I. & Arsyad, R. (2023). 'The OSCE and the Ukraine Crisis: Cooperation over Conflict.' *Journal PIR: Power in International Relations*, 7(2), 174-185.
21. Snyder, G.H. (2002). 'Mearsheimer's World-Offensive Realism and the Struggle for Security: A Review Essay.' *International Security*, 27(1), 149-173.
22. Svensson, D. & Teorell, O. (2007). 'Bracing for Cold Peace. US-Russia Relations after Ukraine.' *The International Spectator: Italian Journal of International Affairs*, vol. 49, issue 4, pp. 76-96.
23. Taliaferro, J.W. (1999). Security Under Anarchy: Defensive Realism Reconsidered. In International Studies Association, 40th Annual Convention, Washington DC.
24. Taliaferro, J.W. (2000). 'Security seeking under anarchy: Defensive realism revisited.' *International Security*, 25(3), 128-161.
25. Taylor, D. Brian. (2021). 'Crisis in Ukraine-Putin's Own Goal: The Invasion of Crimea and Putin's Political Future.' *Foreign Affairs*, 100(2), 75-89.
26. Toal, G. (2017). *Near abroad: Putin, the West and the contest over Ukraine and the Caucasus*. Oxford University Press.
27. Tytarchuk, O. & Khylko, M. (2022). 'NATO involvement in the Handling of the Russia-Ukraine Conflict: Competitive Synergy or 'Freezing' Crisis management. *International Crisis Management: NATO, EU, OSCE and Civil Society*, 87-100.

28. Yousaf, I., Patel, R. & Yarovaya, L. (2022). 'The reaction of G20+ stock markets to the Russia–Ukraine conflict "black-swan" event: Evidence from event study approach.' *Journal of Behavioural and Experimental Finance*, 35, 100723.
29. Zambakari, C. (2022). War Foretold: Ukraine's Crisis, 30 Years in the Making. Available at SSRN.
30. Bryjka F., Rosyjskawojnazastêpcza w Donbasie, Ante Portas–Studia nadBezpieczeñstwem, 1(6), 2016.
31. Thompson, W.R. 'Principal Rivalries,' *Journal of Conflict Resolution*, 2(39), 1995. doi: 10.1177/0022002795039002001.
32. W³odkowska-Bagan A. Rywalizacjamocarstwnaobszarzeporadzieckim, Warsaw, 2013.
33. Zapa³owski A., Bezpieczeñstwo Polski w geopolitycznejgrzeZachodu z Rosj¹, Warsaw, 2015.
34. Antczak-Barzant A., Œliwa Z., Zaniewski R., Wojna XXI wieku. Pocz¹tkiwojny "trzeciejfali", Warsaw, 2016.
35. Bryc A., Cele politykizagranicznejFederacjiRosyjskiej, Toruñ, 2005.
36. Diehl, P.F. & Goertz G. 'War and Peace in International Rivalry,' Michigan, 2000. doi:10.3998/mpub.16693.
37. Domaga³a, M. & Potocki, R. (eds.), FormatowanieUkrainy, II, Warsaw, 2013.
38. Eberhardt, P. KoncepcjaHeartlanduHalfordaMackindera, Przegl¹dGeograficzny, 2(83), 2011. doi: 10.7163/PrzG.2011.2.5.
39. Charles Maynes, 'Russians are feeling the impact of sanctions, but the worst is still yet to come,' *National Public Radio*, 20 April 2022.
40. Mason Bissada. '500 Or 10,000 Deaths? Russian Media Finally Seems to Report Dire Troop Casualty Numbers—And Then Deletes Them.' *Forbes*, 21 March 2022
41. United Nations. 'General Assembly resolution demands end to Russian offensive in Ukraine.' 2 March 2022.
42. Steven Lee Myers. 'Ukraine Invasion Tests the Ties That Bind Putin and Xi,' *New York Times*, 27 February 2022.
43. Joseph Nye. 'The Kindlebeger Trap,' Project Syndicate, 9 January 2017.
44. Belfer Centre for Science and International Affairs. 'Thucydides' Trap', https://www.belfercenter.org/
45. thucydides-trap/overview-thucydides-trap.
46. Biden, Joe. 'President Biden: What America Will and Will Not Do in Ukraine,' *New York Times*, 31 May 2022.
47. Demirjian, Karoun. 'Milley Tries to Clarify His Case for a Negotiated End to Ukraine War,' *Washington Post*, 16 November 2022.
48. Blattman, Christopher. 'The Hard Truth About Long Wars: Why the Conflict in Ukraine Won't End Anytime Soon.' *Foreign Affairs*, 9 November 2022.
49. Cameron, James J. 'Here's What 'High Combat Alert' for Russia's Nuclear Forces Means,' *Washington Post*, 28 February 2022.
50. Fazal, Tanisha M. 'The Return of Conquest? Why the Future of Global Order Hinges on Ukraine,' *Foreign Affairs*, May/June, 2022.
51. Joshi, Shashank. 'Three Scenarios for How War in Ukraine Could Play Out,' *The Economist*, 14 November 2022.
52. Cochran, Shawn. 'Will Putin's War in Ukraine Continue Without Him?' *War on the Rocks*,10 October 2022.

5

The Hybrid Nature of the Russia-Ukraine War and its Lessons for India

Dhruv Ashok

Introduction

Hybrid Warfare is emerging as an important dimension of warfare in the 21st century. It has several kinetic and non-Kinetic components. Though hybrid warfare has gained currency only after Russia's annexation of Crimea in 2014, it has existed since ancient times. Its strategies have been deployed by both state and non-state actors. In the 21st century, the availability of a diverse set of technological tools has increased the hybrid threats faced by nation-states as these technological tools and their widespread diffusion has enabled both state and non-state actors to resort to hybrid warfare to achieve their goals with plausible deniability making it hard for targeted nation-states to respond to hybrid threats in cyberspace.

The hybrid nature of the current Russia-Ukraine conflict has serious security implications for India which has border disputes with China and Pakistan. Both China and Pakistan have deployed hybrid warfare strategies against India ranging from proxies, nuclear weapons, and information/cyber operations. Hence, it is vital for both the Indian armed forces and policymakers to draw vital lessons on hybrid warfare strategies from the current Russia-Ukraine war.

Concept of Hybrid Warfare

Hybrid warfare is defined as "different modes of warfare including conventional capabilities, irregular tactics and formations, terrorist acts including indiscriminate violence and coercion, and criminal disorder, conducted by both sides and a variety of state and non-state actors," according to Frank Hoffman's 2007 paper titled *'Conflict in the 21st century: The Rise of Hybrid wars'*.

After researching Israel's conflict with the Hezbollah in Lebanon in 2006, Hoffman came up with the term 'Hybrid Warfare'. The Hezbollah, which is primarily seen as Iran's proxy army, was successful in bringing the technologically superior Israeli defence forces to a stop through media manipulation, the use of underground tunnels, guerrilla tactics, and the deployment of Iranian-built missiles. The successful use of these tactics by a non-state actor like the Hezbollah against a strong state actor like Israel, according to Hoffman, makes state mastery of hybrid warfare essential in the twenty-first century (Hoffman, 2007).

Following the Second World War and during the Cold War, the proliferation of nuclear weapons re-energized nation-states' employment of proxy armies and hybrid warfare tactics. Due to the USA and the Soviet Union's possession of nuclear weapons and the latter's inability to win a direct conflict, they engaged in an indirect conflict through client-states and insurgent organisations (Celso, 2019). The two superpowers backed insurgencies meant to damage their rivals throughout the Cold War. Regional nations including Pakistan, Saudi Arabia, and Iran also embraced this policy.

Hybrid warfare, however, can also refer to situations in which a nation-state uses hybrid warfare tactics as part of a larger military strategy in a conventional military conflict against an enemy nation or as part of a proxy strategy to avoid the political and economic costs of a conventional military conflict with a neighbouring state, in contrast to Hoffman's narrow application of the term to situations of armed conflict between state and non-state actors. Examples of nation-states using hybrid warfare tactics to assert their territorial claims against their neighbours without engaging in traditional armed conflict include Russia's 2014 annexation of Crimea, Pakistan's use of hybrid warfare tactics against India and Afghanistan, and China's use of hybrid warfare tactics in the South China Sea and along the India-China border. An example of hybrid warfare tactics used in conventional military conflicts is Russia's 2008 war against Georgia, which included cyber attacks, and information operations along with conventional land, sea, and air forces.

Although hybrid warfare has existed since antiquity, it has become a more significant aspect of conflict in the twenty-first century. The availability of a wide range of technological tools in the twenty-first century has increased the hybrid threats that nation-states must deal with because these tools, along with their wide diffusion, have made it possible for both state and non-state actors to use hybrid warfare to further their objectives while maintaining plausible denial, making it challenging for targeted nation-states to counter hybrid threats in cyberspace. Kinetic and non-kinetic hybrid warfare components are the two categories into which hybrid warfare can be divided.

Space weapons, land, sea, and air power, nuclear, chemical, and biological weapons, insurgents, terrorists, special forces, black operators who carry out assassinations and sabotage, violent agitations, etc., are all kinetic components of hybrid warfare (Deshpande and Mehta, 2018).

Diplomacy, information operations, dissension, subversion, economic warfare, resource battles, weather wars, non-violent agitations, etc., are non-kinetic components of hybrid warfare (Deshpande and Mehta, 2018).

Hybrid Nature of the Russia-Ukraine Conflict

The phrase 'hybrid warfare' is controversial when applied by Western experts to Russia's approach to Ukraine because Russia also utilized conventional military forces to intervene in the country. Russian experts recognize the benefits of hybrid warfare from a Western standpoint, even though they do not use the term themselves (Cisco, 2023). Although the term is used controversially, Russian strategy against Ukraine has contained elements of hybrid warfare since 2014.

Together with Russia's concerns over NATO's eastward expansion, these factors contributed to the start of the current Russia-Ukraine war in 2022. As a result, while employing hybrid warfare techniques to invade Crimea, Russia was unable to achieve its main geopolitical objective of maintaining control over Ukraine. Rather, the Crimean crisis of 2014 spurred the Ukrainian government to request NATO's help in preparing its armed forces to confront the Russian-backed separatist movement in the Donetsk and Luhansk regions. The military assistance that Ukraine is receiving from the USA and NATO in the ongoing Russia-Ukraine war is another indication of Ukraine's tight links with NATO. Despite being a traditional military confrontation, both Russia and Ukraine have used hybrid warfare methods in the present conflict. In the present conflict, information and cyber operations, mercenaries and foreign volunteers, and economic sanctions have been the key facets of hybrid warfare.

Information/Cyber Operations

An example of cyber operations in the ongoing conflict between Russia and Ukraine is the hacking of Viasat, a US commercial communications satellite that provided high-speed satellite broadband to military and commercial customers in Ukraine and other European countries during the early stages of the conflict. In May 2022, the UK's National Cyber Security Centre accused Russia of hacking Viasat (Joshi, 2022). Despite Russia's hacking of Ukraine's military command and control systems, cyber experts have observed that they largely spared the country's civilian infrastructure (Copp, 2022). Cyber experts speculate that because they expected a quick military victory, the Russians planned for the Ukrainian network to survive and continue to serve their interests.

Elon Musk's Space X company and its Starlink constellation have been instrumental in helping Ukraine repel Russian intrusions. Since then, Starlink has supported the Ukrainian military by linking drones for targeted attacks and working to restore broadband services across the country (Wadhwa and Salkever, 2022).

In the domain of media operations during the current conflict, Ukraine has also put in place an efficient communication strategy to counter what it perceives to be Russian propaganda, in contrast to the 2014 Crimea crisis, when Russia controlled the narrative around its activities in Crimea. Five primary themes seem to be the focus of Ukraine's media campaigns: the necessity of Ukraine's right to self-defence against Russian aggression; the resilience of Ukrainian resistance; the cruelty of Russian actions; and Russia's poor military planning. Volodymyr Zelenskyy, the president of Ukraine, has emphasised these points in his pleas to the US Congress and the European Parliament. Besides, Ukraine has successfully influenced Western public opinion in its favour through the skilful use of traditional and social media.

Mercenaries/Foreign Volunteers

Both Russia and Ukraine have asserted that numerous mercenaries and foreign volunteers have joined their respective armed units since Russia's invasion of Ukraine in March 2022. Twenty thousand applicants from fifty-two nations submitted applications to join the newly established International Legion of Territorial Defence of Ukraine on 6 March 2022 (Wright, 2022). Americans, Canadians, and people from other European nations are among these foreign volunteers (Wright, 2022).

The deployment of armed mercenaries by Russia in its fight with Ukraine is not new. The Wagner Group, a privately owned Russian paramilitary organisation, is a significant supplier of mercenaries for Russia in its fight with Ukraine (Lawless, 2022). The Wagner Group was established to give Russia plausible deniability in armed combat situations when Russia is not formally at war or when Russian military forces have incurred significant casualties. Russia officially denies the Wagner Group's existence since it is against the law to deploy private military corporations in Russia, according to its constitution.

The friendly regimes in Syria and the Russian Republic of Chechnya are a significant supply of mercenaries for Russia in its confrontation with Ukraine. Additionally, Russia is hiring mercenaries in Syria, where the Russian military supported President Bashar al Assad's government since the start of the Syrian Civil War in 2015. Russia is apparently offering a thousand dollars or more per month to fight in Ukraine; Syria's civil war has spawned informal local militias and some battle-hardened fighters who earn as little as fifteen to thirty-five dollars per month (Hubbard, Saad, and Omar, 2022).

Economic Sanctions

They have played a significant role in the USA and European Union's use of hybrid warfare in the conflict between Russia and Ukraine. The

Central Financial of Russia was among the seven Russian banks that the USA, Canada, and Europe banned from using SWIFT, the international messaging system that facilitates financial transactions, in reaction to the Russian invasion of Ukraine in March 2022. The International Monetary Fund states that the sanctions placed on the Russian financial sector could cause the largest drop in Russia's GDP by 6 per cent since the collapse of the Soviet Union, notwithstanding the various measures the Russian government has taken to attempt to mitigate their effects (Kyobe, 2023). The Western sanctions against Russia's financial sector have hurt the country's economy by causing capital flight, soaring inflation, and possibly even a debt default (Moret, 2023). The primary military impact of the most recent Western sanctions has been to deprive Russia of microchips and drone parts.

In addition to the Russian economy, the sanctions have affected the economies of a number of Western countries, especially those in Europe that rely on the supply of Russian gas. By exploiting Europe's dependence on Russian gas, Russia hopes to weaken EU unity. Russia claimed that the completion of repairs to its gas turbines was delayed as a result of reducing the amount of gas delivered to European nations via the Nord Stream pipeline in response to Western sanctions (Kakar, 2022). European nations would not be able to accumulate the gas needed to meet rising demand during the vital winter months if Russian gas imports decreased. Should the present Russia-Ukraine conflict continue, European nations reliant on the Nord Stream pipeline and heavily on Russian gas for electricity generation are expected to suffer the most from economic consequences. One such country is Germany.

Role of Allies in Russia-Ukraine War

Russia and North Korea agreed to provide mutual military assistance if either faced armed aggression, according to the full text of a pact released by North Korea after a visit by Russian President Vladimir Putin to Pyongyang where he met North Korean leader Kim Jong Un (Park & Kim, 2024). The day after the deal was signed at a Pyongyang summit on 19 June 2024, North Korean state media released the full text of the agreement which vows mutual defence assistance and broader cooperation in military, foreign policy, and trade (*Hindustan Times*, 2024).

During the Cold War era, North Korea signed an alliance treaty with the Soviet Union in 1961 that stipulated immediate military assistance in case of an attack on either of the countries. Following the collapse of the Soviet Union, the 1961 treaty was succeeded in 2000 by a lower-level treaty with Russia.

Putin's visit to North Korea, the first by a Russian leader in twenty-four years, comes as two countries have grown considerably close in the past few years since Russia invaded Ukraine. North Korea is suspected to have provided Russia with millions of artillery shells and other weapons for use in Ukraine, in exchange for food, energy and military technologies (Kuhn, 2024). Hence, this agreement will benefit Russia in its current conflict with Ukraine as a steady supply of North Korean military equipment will enable the Russian military to reinforce its dwindling reserves of military equipment due the prolonged military conflict against Ukraine.

Much of the debate over the recent North Korea-Russia partnership revolves around Article 4 of the agreement that pledges mutual aid. According to the North Korean state media, Article 4 states that if one of the countries is invaded and pushed into a state of war, the other must deploy "all means at its disposal without delay 'to provide' military and other assistance" (Hyung & Heintz, 2024).

The agreement also calls for countries to actively cooperate in efforts to establish a "just and multi-polar new world order," the North Korean Central News Agency said, underscoring how both North Korea and Russia are aligning with each other against their perceived common threat in the international system, namely, the USA (Hyung & Heintz, 2024). North Korea believes the US support to South Korea since the Korean war in the 1950s resulted in the USA preventing the reunification of the Korean peninsula under North Korea's communist government. This along with US-imposed economic sanctions against North Korea for its nuclear weapons program resulted in North Korea having a hostile relationship with the USA and forging close relations with US adversaries like Russia and China.

Another important development was the June 2024 G7 Summit in Italy where the G7 member-nations—the USA, Britain, Germany, France, Germany, Italy, and Japan agreed on continued support for

Ukraine. This included making around $ 50 billion in loans available to help Ukraine in its fight against Russia's invasion (Elliott, 2024). The money will come from the proceeds of Russian assets that have been frozen as a result of the war. This continued supported from Western nations and their allies has enabled Ukraine to continue its military fight back against Russian forces in Ukraine.

Hybrid Conflict Challenges Faced by India

India faces conflicts of a hybrid nature involving both kinetic and non-kinetic components from its two nuclear armed neighbours, China and Pakistan, with whom it has long contested borders.

Pakistan's use of Hybrid Warfare against India

Pakistan's use of proxy terrorist groups

In addition to regular fighters drawn from the military, paramilitary, and intelligence services, Pakistan has depended on irregular fighters and razakars (volunteers) (Fair, 2011). These regular combatants from Pakistan's paramilitary and military forces were either disguising themselves as irregular fighters or wearing mufti, or civilian attire (Fair, 2011). The goal of Pakistan's deployment of irregular forces or regular forces undercover in mufti has been to provide the Pakistani state with a plausible deniability and protect it from international criticism and overt Indian military retaliation. However, in spite of this, Pakistan's strategy has led to three wars between India and Pakistan in 1947, 1965, and 1999 as well as to several crises that have brought India and Pakistan to the brink of conflict.

Pakistan has managed to impose considerable costs on India in the Jammu and Kashmir insurgency, which started in the late 1980s, despite its inability to take Jammu and Kashmir from India through proxies as part of its hybrid warfare strategy. Approximately 6,000 Indian security force personnel in Jammu and Kashmir died as a result of attacks by terrorist proxy groups supported by Pakistan, such as Lashkar-e-Taiba and Jaish-e-Mohammed (Kapur and Ganguly, 2012). During this time, 15,000 Indian civilians also lost their lives in Jammu and Kashmir (Kapur and Ganguly, 2012).

Nuclear Weapons

These weapons are emerging as an important component of hybrid warfare particularly in cases when the threat of nuclear escalation is used by a state as part of its hybrid warfare strategy to deter an adversary from escalating a limited or localized military conflict into a full-fledged conventional military conflict. An example in this regard is the Kargil conflict of 1999. In 1998, both India and Pakistan conducted nuclear tests which resulted in condemnation by the USA and its allies and the imposition of economic sanctions on both countries as both India and Pakistan had consistently refused to sign the Nuclear Non-Proliferation Treaty (NPT) which sought the limit the spread of nuclear weapons among existing non-nuclear weapon states. Much of the international concern over the nuclear tests was relieved by the signing of the Lahore Declaration on 21 February1999 (Krolikowski, 2016). The Lahore Declaration of 1999 was the first major bilateral document signed between India and Pakistan since the end of the last armed conflict in 1971 (Krolikowski, 2016).

The Lahore Declaration committed both parties to reach a peaceful solution regarding the problem of Kashmir and to implement confidence-building measures with regard to nuclear and conventional arms. However, the Lahore Declaration was soon overshadowed by the Kargil conflict of 1999. It ended on 26 July 1999 by which time India had recaptured the heights in the Kargil sector which had been previously seized by Pakistani forces. In the aftermath of the Kargil conflict, Pakistan was criticised by other countries such as the USA for instigating the conflict by sending military and paramilitary forces to seize territory on the Indian side of the LOC. In response, the Pakistani government applied the strategy of 'plausible deniability', arguing that the military action in Kargil was carried out by 'Kashmiri freedom fighters" which had ultimately failed (Krolikowski, 2016).

Also, Pakistan's attempts to draw analogies between its military operation in Kargil and India's capture of the Siachen glacier in 1984 found less credibility in the international community in the current nuclearized environment in South Asia post the 1998 nuclear tests (Lavoy, 2009). Pakistan's initiation of the Kargil conflict in spite of the Lahore peace process enabled India to secure the widespread support of the international community as it responded with heavy military force to the Pakistani incursions in Kargil.

Pakistani military planners assumed that the risk of escalation to a general war was minimal because the presence of nuclear weapons might deter India and would also ensure the involvement of the international community to pressure India against turning a limited high-altitude adjustment of the LOC into a full-fledged war and that India would accept the Pakistani fait accompli in the Kargil sector just as Pakistan was forced to accept India's 1984 military seizure of the Siachen glacier (Lavoy, 2009). However, where Pakistani military planners miscalculated was in their assumption that India would restrict the combat in the Kargil sector to the infantry units of the Indian army and did not expect the heavy deployment of artillery and air power in support of the Indian military.

Information/Psychological Warfare

In Jammu and Kashmir, information warfare dates back to the late 1980s and early 1990s when anti-India and pro-Pakistan elements communicated with Kashmiri society through local newspapers, leaflets, mosque announcements on loudspeakers, elimination of pro-India and moderate voices, sloganeering and shutting down of cinema halls by dubbing them as un-Islamic (Bhatt, 2018). While such tactics by pro-Pakistan groups have continued even today, digital media platforms for radicalisation by pro-Pakistan terrorist groups are an emerging threat. Social media platforms such as Facebook, Telegram and Instagram have been weaponized by pro–Pakistan terrorist groups to wage a psychological war against the Indian state in Jammu and Kashmir by radicalizing sections of the youth in Jammu and Kashmir.

The use of modern information technology by pro-Pakistan terrorist groups reflects an important departure from past strategies in physical space to radicalise local Kashmiri youth as they exploit the internet for recruitment, propaganda and support, as well as for strengthening their cross border linkages (Kaura, 2017). A shift in the information/psychological warfare strategies of pro-Pakistan terrorist groups from the physical to the virtual domain became visible during the 2010 protests in the Kashmir Valley. In 2010, angry and misguided Kashmiri youth displayed their resentment against the Indian state and Indian security forces by engaging in heavy stone pelting and massive protests using social media tools, particularly text messaging via mobile phones (Snedden, 2015). The number of people in Jammu and Kashmir with access to social media has increased significantly from twenty-five per cent in 2010 to about seventy per cent by the end of 2015.

The violent protests in 2016 in Jammu and Kashmir after the killing of Hizbul Mujahedeen (HuM) commander Burhan Wani surprised the Indian security forces, which rendered them incapable of responding appropriately. In the last five years before his death Burhan Wani had emerged as the face of the HuM as he threatened Indian security forces with attacks and attracted more Kashmiri youth to insurgency. Known as a top jihadist recruiter in the Kashmir Valley, Burhan Wani was part of the breed of the educated youth, who joined the insurgency after the 2010 protests (Kaura, 2017).

Before Burhan Wani, most of the local Kashmiri terrorists belonging to Pakistan-sponsored terrorist groups in the 1990s and early 2000s operated clandestinely covering their faces when in public spaces. They were not commonly known among the people, except when their names were released by the Indian security forces after being killed. However, Burhan Wani was the first local Kashmir terrorist commander who posted his photographs and posts on social media. In August 2015, Burhan Wani uploaded a video on Facebook, carrying messages released by other jihadist leaders that called for setting up an Islamic caliphate in the region. Wani also urged Kashmiri youth to join him in his campaign of terrorism and insurgency against the Indian state and Indian security forces and asked the police to abandon their fight against the separatist insurgency supported by Pakistan. The video which was made with Wani and two others in combat fatigues, with a Kalashnikov and a holy Quran at his side, was widely circulated on WhatsApp in Kashmir (Rashid, 2015). In another video in early 2016, this time uploaded on both Youtube and Facebook, Wani threatened to launch attacks against the proposals to set up separate sainik colonies and townships for Kashmiri pundits.

Zakir Rashid Bhatt, the HuM's new commander who succeeded Burhan Wani, released a new video message in August 2016, which was widely circulated through WhatsApp in which he called upon Kashmiri youth to support protests against Wani's killing by Indian security forces (Hussain, 2016). Through the use of relatively cheap and accessible social media, he called upon HuM local Kashmiri youth to join the pro-Pakibehrestan separatist insurgency in Jammu and Kashmir. Wani's expanding base of supporters has translated into a sudden upsurge in the numbers of local militants. In 2015, the Jammu and Kashmir police examined the cases of 111 youngsters who had joined militancy and terrorism; 58 of them eventually returned home (Unnithan, 2015). At least 88 of them were between the ages of 15 and 30, and more than half of them were radicalized through the internet (Unnithan, 2015). According to Intelligence Bureau sources, more than 100 Kashmiri youth joined the pro-Pakistan separatist insurgency in Jammu and Kashmir after Wani's death (Agarwal, 2016).

Following the example of the Islamic state terrorist group in Iraq and Syria, Pakistan-based terrorist groups like Lashkar-e-Taiba (LeT) and Jaish-e-Mohammad (JeM), along with the HuM have entered cyberspace. It was reported that the Jamaat-ud-Dawah (JUD), LeT's charity arm, launched its cyber initiative during a conference on social media that it organized in Lahore in December 2015 (Sharma, 2016). Emphasising the growing importance of social media in disseminating propaganda, the JUD chief, Hafiz Saeed, called upon his followers to use this medium to strengthen the separatist insurgency in Jammu and Kashmir against the Indian state (Sharma, 2016).

On numerous occasions Pakistan has accused Prime Minister Narendra Modi's government of fascism, promoting Hindu supremacy, and being anti-Muslim (Ahuja and Diwan, par. 1). The Pakistan army's Inter Services Public Relations Agency (ISPR) uses various social media handles and think tank reports to spread propaganda against India (Ahuja and Diwan, 2018). The Pakistani media, too, has compared Indian Prime Minister Narendra Modi with the Nazi leader Adolf Hitler and claimed that the condition of Indian Muslims was similar to the persecution of Jews in Germany and Nazi-occupied Europe in the 1940s. To advance this narrative, Pakistan has leveraged various events in India. For instance, the Delhi riots in late February 2020 saw massive tweet traffic from accounts linked to Pakistan, with hashtags like

#Hinduterrorism and #RSSKillingMuslims (*Business Standard*, 2020). In addition, there was an active sharing of fabricated and edited media reports on various social media platforms belonging to different countries and timelines, claiming to be from India (Anand, 2020).

China's use of Hybrid Warfare against India

The three warfare strategies of China's conceptual framework classify various data pertaining to non-kinetic operations for changing the behaviour of the enemy into three categories:

Psychological Warfare

The purpose of psychological warfare is to scare and demoralise the enemy in order to undermine their resolve to fight. In addition to individuals and society, PSYOPS also aim to affect the enemy's governing bodies and command structures (Behrendt, 2022). In order to intimidate opponents and encourage compliance with the PRC's desired outcomes, the People's Republic of China (PRC) employs psychological warfare. This includes the deployment of Chinese military and paramilitary forces prior to a conflict as well as the application of other national power instruments (diplomatic, economic, cultural) (Livermore, 2018). This strategy has been deployed by China in its various border clashes with India including the 2017 Doklam standoff and the 2020 Galwan Valley clashes.

Media Warfare

The manipulation of public opinion is the aim of the PRC's media warfare. It involves the use of materials delivered to public audiences through established news services, informal internet sites, and other social media to influence domestic and international perspectives on issues involving the PRC's interests (Livermore, 2018). An example of such media warfare was seen during the 2020 clash between Chinese and Indian soldiers in Ladakh's Galwan region. China was eager to draw attention to the nearly twenty Indian soldiers who died in the conflict in 2020 in Galwan, something India had already acknowledged in public. Chinese official media also released images of purportedly captured Indian soldiers (Behrendt, 2022). At the same time, the Chinese media was reluctant to emphasise the full extent of Chinese military casualties. It wasn't until several months later that Chinese state media acknowledged that China had also experienced military casualties and formally acknowledged the deaths of only four Chinese soldiers in the Galwan clash because acknowledging other numbers would have undermined the official Chinese state narrative of Chinese military superiority relative to its Asian neighbours. (Behrendt, 2022).

Cyber Operations

Two Indian vaccine manufacturers, Bharat Biotech and the Serum Institute of India (SII), had their IT systems breached by Chinese state-backed hackers, according to a March 2021 report from Singapore-based CyFirma (NDTV, 2021). The most important component of India's national immunization program and vaccine diplomacy has been the vaccines provided by these companies. Chinese hackers targeting of SII is significant when examining the reach of its vaccine, Oxford-AstraZenica/Covishield which is being used in 183 countries, as against almost half the reach of China's flagship Sinopharm vaccine (used in 90 countries) (Patil and Mahajan, 2022). Therefore, it can be expected that China will broaden the scope of its Indian targets for commercial cyber espionage reasons to include sectors like services where India has barred Chinese investments.

In October 2020, in one of the worst power outages, large parts of Mumbai witnessed a widespread blackout which affected suburban train services and hospitals. Months later, Recorded Future noted that a China-linked hacker group, 'Red Echo' had breached the Indian power sector, which may have caused Mumbai's power outage—a charge refuted by a Maharashtra government's technical audit committee examining the incident (Scroll, 2021). Recorded Future also added that besides the power sector, Chinese hackers had also targeted two Indian ports and some parts of the railway infrastructure. Coming in the wake of the violent June 2020 Galwan Valley clash between the Indian and Chinese armies, this targeting of India's critical infrastructure suggested a combination of intimidation and retribution which forms part of Chinese strategy of deploying psychological warfare against an adversary.

The extent of Chinese hackers targeting India is shown by the

Advanced Persistent Threat 30 (APT30) vector (Scroll, 2021). This threat actor's espionage operation ran for a decade before its discovery in 2015. It harvested information from Indian computer networks on geopolitical issues relevant to the Chinese Communist Party, such as the India-China border dispute, Indian naval activity in the South China Sea, and India's relations with its South Asia neighbours. (Scroll, 2021).

Hybrid Warfare Lessons for India from the Russia-Ukraine Conflict

Information/Cyber Warfare

Enhancing its information/psychological warfare capabilities using the latest information communications technologies and deploying such capabilities to achieve strategic national aims is an important lesson that India s military and political decision-makers can take away from the current Russia-Ukraine conflict especially Ukraine's effective use of information communication technologies to ensure support for its narrative of self-defence against Russian aggression among the public and decision makers in Europe and the USA. India needs to be able to effectively propagate its narrative on Jammu and Kashmir as well as on border disputes with China to a larger international audience. To achieve this, India needs to have a whole-of-government approach with regard to both cyber and information warfare for both offensive and defensive purposes.

Offensive cyber and information warfare could be aimed at an adversary's critical infrastructure as well as trying to subvert the loyalties of restive sections of the adversary's population. Defensive cyber and information warfare is aimed at protecting one's own critical digital infrastructure from an adversary's cyber attacks as well as limiting the adverse impact of an adversary's propaganda on vulnerable sections of one's own domestic population such as the online propaganda directed by Pakistan-based terrorist groups aimed at indoctrinating and radicalizing the minds of Kashmiri youth to continue the terrorist insurgency in Jammu and Kashmir and propagating the false narrative of Muslims being second class citizens in India.

In 2020, the Indian Army established the post of Director-General Information Warfare (DGIW) to counter propaganda from China and

Pakistan. However, the DGIW adopts a mainly defensive approach to counter anti-India narratives which will be effective only in the short term. Hence, the Indian government must develop a grand strategy involving all ministries to combat information warfare by hostile state and non-state actors that targets the Indian psyche, especially the youth, to generate discontent against the Indian government and sow communal discord.

The Indian Army and Indian intelligence agencies must allocate funds and develop capabilities to conduct psychological operations, electronic and cyber warfare and utilize new technologies like artificial intelligence for disseminating pro-India narratives. In the cyber domain, India needs to develop a solid manufacturing base as part of the government's *Atmanirbhar Bharat* scheme to create indigenously manufactured technologies for its security needs and digital infrastructure which is essential as imported technology, especially from China, is vulnerable to being hacked.

Mercenaries/Proxies

Another important lesson for India from the Russia-Ukraine war is the effective use of mercenaries as proxies as a means to undermine an adversary's conventional fighting capabilities. In the current Russia-Ukraine war, we see that both Russia and Ukraine are deploying foreign mercenaries and volunteer fighters to bolster the fighting capabilities of their conventional armed forces. Though the Indian context is different, Indian decision makers should consider exploiting the ethnic fault lines of India's adversaries such as the Baloch separatist insurgency in Pakistan and the Tibetan and Uighur separatist problems in China by extending all possible material, financial and diplomatic support to these separatist elements there. Extending such support to these separatist elements will force the Chinese and Pakistani states to devote considerable resources to managing their own domestic separatist problems and will considerably affect the support provided by Pakistan and China to separatist movements in India in regions such as Jammu and Kashmir and India's North-East states.

Ancient Indian Strategic Thought

Finally, India must draw inspiration from its own ancient strategic thought when it comes to formulating its own hybrid warfare strategies. In his treatise, the *Arthashastra*, the ancient Indian thinker Kautilya refers to four types of war:

- ***Mantrayuddha* or War by Counsel:** This is the exercise of diplomacy to win wars. It is to be utilized when the king is in a weaker position and engaging in a battle is not wise or beneficial (Deshpande, 2018).
- ***Prakasayuddha* or Open Warfare:** This is a form of conventional warfare that follows all the rules laid down of fighting a battle (Deshpande, 2018).
- ***Kutayuddha* or Concealed Warfare:** This form of warfare includes irregular methods, ambushes, and treachery in the enemy camp (Deshpande, 2018).
- ***Guda Yuddha* or Clandestine War:** Kautilya argues this type of war is waged by covert means to achieve the objective without actually waging battle, usually by assassinating the enemy. Regarding *Guda Yuddha*, Kautilya argues that the king should use agents, double agents, allies, vassals, tribal chiefs and suborned friends and supporters of the enemy (Deshpande, 2018).

Despite being an ancient treatise, Kautilya's *Arthashastra* is relevant in examining the modern concept of hybrid warfare as it identifies several components of what today constitutes hybrid warfare which are diplomacy, information operations, conventional warfare and unconventional warfare including subversion, sabotage, covert operations, assassinations, etc.

Conclusion

The Russia-Ukraine war, despite being a traditional military confrontation, has several hybrid warfare dimensions such as information/cyber operations, mercenaries/foreign volunteers, economic sanctions and role of allies in sustaining the hybrid Russia-Ukraine conflict. India faces hybrid warfare threats from its neighbours—China and Pakistan—with whom it has territorial disputes. The hybrid warfare strategies deployed by Pakistan against India include proxy terrorist groups, nuclear weapons and information/psychological warfare. The hybrid warfare strategies deployed by China against India include psychological warfare, media warfare and cyber operations. There are hybrid warfare lessons that India can learn from the Russia-Ukraine war. Enhancing its information/psychological warfare capabilities using the latest information communications technologies and deploying such capabilities to achieve strategic national aims is an important lesson that India's military and political decision makers can take away from the current Russia-Ukraine conflict, especially Ukraine's effective use of information communication technologies to ensure support for its narrative of self-defence against Russian aggression among the public and decision makers in Europe and the USA.

The Indian Army and Indian intelligence agencies must allocate funds and develop capabilities to conduct psychological operations and electronic and cyber warfare and utilize new technologies like artificial intelligence for disseminating pro-India narratives. In the cyber domain, India needs to develop a solid manufacturing base as part of the government's *Atmanirbhar Bharat* scheme to create indigenously manufactured technologies for its security needs and digital infrastructure which is as essential as imported technology, especially as those from China are vulnerable to being hacked.

Another important lesson for India from the Russia-Ukraine war is the effective use of mercenaries as proxies as a means to undermine an adversary's conventional fighting capabilities. In the current Russia-Ukraine war, it is observed that both Russia and Ukraine are deploying foreign mercenaries and volunteer fighters to bolster the fighting capabilities of their conventional armed forces.

Finally, India must draw inspiration from its own ancient strategic thought when it comes to formulating its own hybrid warfare strategies such as Kautilya's *Arthashastra*. Kautilya refers to four types of war which are *Mantrayuddha* or war by counsel, *Prakasayuddha* or open warfare, *Kutayuddha* or concealed warfare, and *Guda Yuddha* or clandestine war.

REFERENCES

1. 'Mumbai power outage: Supply restored in most parts, Uddhav Thackeray orders investigation,', Scroll,12 October 2020, https://scroll.in/latest/975566/power-outage-in-mumbai-due-to-supply-failure-suburban-trains-get-delayed. Accessed 16 November 2023.
2. 'Chinese hackers target India's Serum Institute, Bharat Biotech: Report,' NDTV, 1 March 2021, https://www.ndtv.com/india-news/chinese-hackers-target-india-s-serum-institute-bharat-biotech-report-2381309. Accessed 14 November 2023.
3. 'What are the Delhi riots 2020,' *Business Standard*, 5 September 2023, https://www.business-standard.com/about/what-is-delhi-riots-2020. Accessed 15 November 2023.
4. Ahuja, Sarthak and Diwan, Samridhi. 'India's two- front information war,' Observer Research Foundation, 10 May 2023, https://www.orfonline.org/expert-speak/indias-two-front-information-war/
5. Anand, Arun. 'Imran Khan party wing showed Delhi riots as anti-Muslim, spread fake news: Delhi police,' The Print, 6 March 2020, https://theprint.in/india/imran-khan-party-student-wing-showed-delhi-riots-as-anti-muslim-spread-fake-news-report/376224/. Accessed 14 November 2023.
6. Ashiq Hussain. 'Ex-engineering student emerges as Wani's successor in Hizbul video,' *The Hindustan Times*, 17 August 2016, http://www.hindustantimes.com/india-news/former-engineering-student-emerges-as-burhan-wani-s-successor-in-new-hizbul-video/story-qiH7PAEO0cmr1X9w9SvDTM.html. Accessed 13 November 2023.
7. Behrendt, Pawel. 'San Zhong Zhanfa or Three Warfares. Chinese Hybrid Warfare,' Boym Institute, 19 April 2022, https://instytutboyma.org/en/san-zhong-zhanfa-or-three-warfares-chinese-hybrid-warfare/
8. Bhatt, Paranjanya. 'Building effective counterterror narratives in Kashmir,' Observer Research Foundation, 18 September 2018, https://www.orfonline.org/expert-speak/44307-building-effective-counterterror-narratives-in-kashmir/
9. Celso, Anthony. 'Superpower Hybrid Warfare in Syria.' *The Marine Corps Gazette*, vol. 9, 2019, pp. 94-99. http://dx.doi.org/10.21140/mcuj.2018090206. Accessed 10 November 2023.
10. Copp, Tara. 'Why is Ukraine's Internet Still Up? Perhaps Because the Invaders Need It,' *Defence One*, 7 March 2022, https://www.defenseone.com/threats/2022/03/why-ukraines-internet-still-perhaps-because-invaders-need-it/362854/
11. Deshpande, Vikrant. *Hybrid Warfare: The Changing Character of Conflict*. 1st edn., Pentagon Press, 2018.
12. Fair, C. Christine. 'The Militant Challenge in Pakistan,' *Asia Policy*, no. 11, 2011, pp. 105–38. JSTOR, http://www.jstor.org/stable/24905028. Accessed 19 November 2023.
13. Hoffman, Frank G. 'Conflict in the 21st century: The rise of hybrid wars,' Arlington, VA: Potomac Institute for Policy Studies, 2007.
14. Hubbard, Ben et al. 'Syrian Mercenaries Deploy to Russia en Route to Ukrainian Battlefields,' *New York Times*, 31 March 2022, https://www.nytimes.com/2022/03/31/world/middleeast/syrian-mercenaries-ukraine-russia.html. Accessed 9 November 2023.

15. Joshi, Manoj. 'The Russia-Ukraine War: Ukraine's resistance in the face of hybrid warfare,' Observer Research Foundation, 6 June 2022, https://www.orfonline.org/expert-speak/ukraines-resistance-in-the-face-of-hybrid-warfare/
16. Kakar, Harsha. 'Sanctions as a Tool of War: Time for West to Look for Alternatives,' News 18, 11 August 2022, https://www.news18.com/news/opinion/sanctions-as-a-tool-of-war-time-for-west-to-look-for-alternatives-5729083.html
17. Kapur, S. Paul, and Sumit Ganguly. 'The Jihad Paradox: Pakistan and Islamist Militancy in South Asia,' *International Security*, vol. 37, no. 1, 2012, pp. 111-41. JSTOR, http://www.jstor.org/stable/23280406. Accessed 19 November 2023.
18. Kaura, Vinay. 'Countering insurgency in Kashmir: The cyber dimension,' Observer Research Foundation, 10 January, 2017, https://www.orfonline.org/research/countering-insurgency-kashmir-cyber-dimension/
19. Królikowski, Hubert. 'Indo-Pakistani 'hybrid war ' for Kargil,' *Politeja*, no. 40, 2016, pp. 395–414, JSTOR, http://www.jstor.org/stable/24920214. Accessed 20 November 2023.
20. Kyobe, Annette. 'International Monetary Fund Report.' Accessed 10 November 2023.
21. Lavoy, Peter. *Asymmetric Warfare in South Asia: The Causes and Consequences of the Kargil Conflict.* 1st edn., Cambridge University Press, 2009.
22. Lawless, Robert. 2022. 'Are Mercenaries in Ukraine,' Lieber Institute, West Point, 21 March 2022, https://lieber.westpoint.edu/are-mercenaries-in-ukraine/
23. Livermore, Doug. 'China's Three Warfares in Theory and Practice in the South China Sea,' *Georgetown Security Studies Review*, 25 March 2018, https://georgetownsecuritystudiesreview.org/2018/03/25/chinas-three-warfares-in-theory-and-practice-in-the-south-china-sea/
24. Moret, Erica. 'Sanctions and the Costs of Russia's War in Ukraine,' *Global Observatory*, 12 May 2023, https://theglobalobservatory.org/2022/05/sanctions-and-the-costs-of-russias-war-in-ukraine/
25. Munish Sharma. 'Lashkar-e-Cyber of Hafiz Saeed,' Institute for Defence Studies and Analyses, 21 March 2016, http://www.idsa.in/idsacomments/lashkar-e-cyber-of-hafiz-saeed_msharma_310316
26. Patil, Sameer and Mahajan, Kishika. 'Expanding Chinese cyber-espionage threat against India,' Observer Research Foundation, 18 April 2022, https://www.orfonline.org/expert-speak/expanding-chinese-cyber-espionage-threat-against-india/
27. Poonam Agarwal, 'Terrorists or Rebels? Here's What Kashmiri Militants' Families Say,' The Quint, 17 December 2016, https://www.thequint.com/kashmir-after-burhan-wani/2016/12/17/terrorists-or-rebels-the-quint-meets-bereaved-kashmiri-families-hizbul-mujahideen-jammu-and-kashmir-burhan-wani. Accessed 11 November 2023.
28. Rashid, Toufiq. 'In new video J-K militant Burhan Wani asks youth to join him,' *The Hindustan Times*, 26 August 2015, https://www.hindustantimes.com/india/in-new-video-j-k-militant-burhan-wani-asks-youth-to-join-him/story-q83k8ndWm2Wf6TUWI5TtmN.html. Accessed 14 November 2023.
29. Sandeep Unnithan. 'Kashmir's new militant tide,' *India Today*, 30 July 2015, http://indiatoday.intoday.in/story/kashmirs-new-militant-tide/1/455226.html.

Accessed 14 November 2023.

30. Snedden, Christopher. *Understanding Kashmir and Kashmiris.* 1st edn., Hurst Publishers, 2015.
31. Wadhwa, Vivek and Salkever, Alex. 'How Elon Musk's Starlink got battle tested in Ukraine,' *Foreign Policy*, 4 May 2022, https://foreignpolicy.com/2022/05/04/starlink-ukraine-elon-musk-satellite-internet-broadband-drones/
32. Wright, Robin. 'Will Mercenaries and Foreign Fighters Change the Course of Ukraine's War?' *The New Yorker*, 5 April 2022, https://www.newyorker.com/news/daily-comment/will-mercenaries-and-foreign-fighters-change-the-course-of-ukraines-war
33. Jack, K. and Park, J. (2024). 'New North Korea-Russia pact calls for immediate military aid if needed.' Retrieved from ttps://www.reuters.com/world/north-korea-russia-pact-give-all-available-military-help-if-other-is-invaded-2024-06-20/#:~:text=SEOUL%2C%20June%2020%20%28Reuters%29%20-%20North%20 Korea %20and,the%20North%27s%20KCNA%20news%20agency%20reported%20on%20Thursday
34. Gong, S. (2024). 'Russia and North Korea vow stronger partnership against the West with new treaty. Retrieved from https://origin-www.mprnews.org/story/2024/06/19/npr-russia-north-korea-treaty-mutual-defense
35. 'North Korea, Russia sign mutual defence pact; immediately to help if either is attacked, '*The Hindustan Times*, Retrieved from https://www.hindustantimes.com/world-news/north-korea-russia-sign-mutual-defence-pact-immediately-to-help-if-either-one-attacked-101718864433105.html
36. Kuhn, A. (2024). 'What North Korea's shift toward Russia means for its global strategy.' Retrieved from https://www.npr.org/2023/12/07/1214799117/north-korea-russia-china-us-foreign-policy
37. Hyung, K.and Heintz, J. (2024). 'What's known and not known, about the partnership agreement signed by Russia and North Korea.' Retrieved from ttps://www.latimes.com/world-nation/story/2024-06-20/whats-known-and-not-known-about-the-partnership-agreement-signed-by-russia-and-north-korea
38. Elliott, D. (2024). 'G7 Summit talking points: From Ukraine and Gaza to the impact of AI.' Retrieved from https://www.weforum.org/agenda/2024/06/g7-italy-summit-key-talking-points/

6

The Russo-Ukrainian War: India's Diplomatic Stance and Strategic Engagement

Abhigya Langeh

Introduction

Amidst historical, cultural, and political complexities, a long-lasting and intricate geopolitical conflict arose: the Russo-Ukrainian conflict. Its origins may be seen in Ukraine's 1991 declaration of independence and the disintegration of the Soviet Union. In the years that followed, Ukraine struggled to define its own identity and geopolitical direction, which had a big impact on how it interacted with Russia. After Russia annexed Crimea in 2014 and ousted Viktor Yanukovych, the pro-Russian president of Ukraine, tensions increased on both regional and global levels. The annexation, which was strongly denounced by the international world, was a watershed moment that set off a sequence of events that eventually developed into a major war. The eastern parts of Ukraine, especially Donetsk and Luhansk, which have substantial populations of Russian speakers, turned into focal points of contention. Following the declaration of independence by pro-Russian separatist forces in these areas, the Ukrainian government retaliated militarily.

The conflict also underscored the struggle between Russia's desire to maintain influence in its periphery and Ukraine's aspirations for autonomy and alignment with Western institutions. Ukraine's pursuit of closer ties with the European Union through the signing of an Association Agreement in 2014 exacerbated tensions with Moscow, which perceived such a move as a direct challenge to its historical sphere of influence. The annexation of Crimea, coupled with Russia's support for separatist movements in Eastern Ukraine, marked a strategic attempt to prevent Ukraine from drifting towards the West (Hahn, 2017).

The struggle was made more complex by ethnic and cultural factors. There is a rift in the way that society views loyalty and identity as a result of Ukraine's varied population, which includes a sizable minority that speaks Russian. Some people tried to embrace their own Ukrainian identity, while others were more strongly aligned with their historical and cultural links with Russia. This internal division made it easier for outside players like Russia to take advantage of existing fault lines to further their geopolitical goals (D'Anieri, 2023).

A complicated mix of military battles, economic pressures, and diplomatic manoeuvres has defined the war. The goal of the 2014–2015 Minsk Accords was to create a foundation for a political settlement and truce in the war. However, the way these accords have been put into practice has been uneven, with recurring breaches and rekindled hostilities, underscoring the persistent difficulties in coming up with a long-term, all-encompassing solution (Plokhy, 2023).

In addition to straining ties between Russia and Ukraine, the Russo-Ukrainian war has had an impact on world affairs. In response, Western nations—most notably the USA and the EU—imposed sanctions on Russia and denounced its activities in Eastern Ukraine and Crimea. NATO's position in the area has also been re-evaluated as a result of the war, with a greater emphasis now being placed on strengthening the defence capacities of Ukraine and other Eastern European nations (Mpoke Bigg, 2022).

The impact of the ongoing fighting goes beyond the actual battlefield. A complex situation has been brought about by population relocation, humanitarian concerns, and the economic costs to both Russia and Ukraine. To sway public opinion around the world, each side has presented its version of events, fuelling a war of narratives (Johny, 2023).

The Russia-Ukraine war continues in 2024, with significant developments on both sides. Ukrainian President Volodymyr Zelenskyy has recently emphasized Ukraine's determination to end the war on its own terms (Welle, 2024). Ukraine has made strategic advances, including striking a Russian S-300/400 air defence battery in Belgorod Oblast using HIMARS. Germany has strengthened its diplomatic ties with Ukraine, opening a repair centre for armoured vehicles in Ukraine and pledging billions in aid for defence and reconstruction efforts. Meanwhile, Russian forces continue their offensive in eastern Ukraine, making advances near Kharkiv and other regions. Russia is also seeking to increase its military, political, and economic cooperation with several African states, while engaging in information operations to undermine international support for Ukraine. These developments indicate a prolonged and complex conflict with significant military, economic, and diplomatic dimensions, as both Ukraine and its allies intensify their efforts to counter Russian aggression and prepare for post-war reconstruction (Russian Offensive Campaign Assessment, 2024).

In essence, opposing national interests, historical legacies, and larger geopolitical challenges are what have led to the Russo-Ukrainian war. It serves as a reminder of the difficulties in striking a balance between the region's geopolitical realities and the quest for national identity and autonomy, as well as the complexity inherent in the post-Soviet environment. Given that the war is still ongoing, it is critical to develop diplomatic solutions that take into account the justifiable worries of all sides and open the door to a safe and stable future for both Ukraine and the wider region (Tripathi, 2023).

India's Historical Relationship with Russia and Ukraine

India's historical relationship with Russia and Ukraine is a tale woven through the intricate fabric of geopolitics, diplomacy, and shared experiences. India and Russia have a long association dating back to the Soviet Union when they first established a strategic alliance that has withstood political upheaval and the test of time. During the Cold War, India and the Soviet Union developed a close relationship based on their common commitment to non-alignment, mistrust of superpower supremacy, and pursuit of independent global identities (MEA, 2017).

The Indo-Soviet Treaty of Friendship and Cooperation, signed in 1971, was a watershed moment that solidified the strategic relationship between the two nations. This treaty not only strengthened diplomatic and economic ties but also laid the groundwork for defence collaboration, with the Soviet Union emerging as a crucial ally for India during times of regional instability. The Soviet support during the Indo-Pakistani war of 1971, which led to the creation of Bangladesh, further cemented the bond between Moscow and New Delhi (Budhwar, 2007).

Russia emerged as the successor state after the Soviet Union's breakup in 1991, causing a profound upheaval in the geopolitical environment. The Indo-Russian partnership survived the shift and moved smoothly into a new period. The 2000 signing of the Declaration on Strategic Alliance, which reflected the common commitment to expanding cooperation in a variety of domains like commerce, energy, defence, and culture, served to reinforce the strategic alliance.

The historical course of India's connection with Ukraine, however, is distinct. When India and Ukraine established diplomatic ties in 1992, it signalled the start of a bilateral relationship characterised by respect for one another and shared goals for development. With the fall of the Soviet Union came the emergence of sovereign states, and Ukraine, with its deep cultural legacy and strategic location, emerged as a unique player in India's diplomatic sphere (MEA, 2020).

India and Ukraine's relationship has matured over the years, encompassing various spheres such as trade, technology, education, and cultural exchange. The Joint Declaration on Strategic Partnership, signed in 2011, laid the groundwork for deepening collaboration in areas like space exploration, science, and technology. This strategic partnership reflects a shared commitment to fostering economic development and leveraging each other's strengths for mutual benefit (MEA, 2020).

Significant advancements have occurred in India's defence ties with both Russia and Ukraine. Russia has long been one of India's main suppliers of defence hardware, with Russian-made weapons accounting for a sizable share of the Indian military's inventory. Strong defence cooperation involves combined research, development, and manufacturing of cutting-edge military gear and goes beyond simple transactions. The depth and tenacity of the defence relations between

India and Russia are demonstrated by their continued cooperation on projects like the BrahMos missile system (Mankoff, 2022).

Ukraine has also had an impact on India's defence environment. The bilateral cooperation in the defence industry is shown in the purchase of Ukrainian engines for India's defence aircraft as well as the cooperation on modernising and updating military hardware. Furthermore, to improve military-to-military cooperation and exchange knowledge, both countries have participated in discussions and exchanges.

Economic ties form another pillar of the triangular relationship between India, Russia, and Ukraine. India's economic engagements with Russia span diverse sectors, including energy, pharmaceuticals, information technology, and agriculture. The annual bilateral summits and mechanisms like the Inter-Governmental Commission on Trade, Economic, Scientific, Technological, and Cultural Cooperation provide platforms for enhancing economic collaboration and addressing challenges.

India and Russia have a long association dating back to the Soviet Union when they first established a strategic alliance that has withstood political upheaval and the test of time. During the Cold War, India and the Soviet Union developed a close relationship based on their common commitment to non-alignment, mistrust of superpower supremacy, and pursuit of independent global identities (MEA, 2017).

Cultural exchanges and people-to-people ties have served as an intangible yet vital dimension of India's historical relationship with Russia and Ukraine. The shared appreciation for literature, art, music, and cinema has fostered a sense of cultural affinity. Educational exchanges and scholarships have facilitated the exchange of knowledge and ideas, contributing to a deeper understanding between the peoples of these nations.

India's connections with Russia and Ukraine are complex and historical, yet the geopolitical environment is ever-changing and offers both possibilities and problems. India is in a difficult position because of the Russo-Ukrainian war in particular, considering its historical links with Russia and the necessity to strike a balance between several diplomatic issues. India's strategic approach aims to strike a careful balance by acknowledging its worries about the conflict and highlighting the significance of diplomatic communication and a peaceful conclusion (Mahapatra, 2021).

India's past diplomatic ties with Russia and Ukraine demonstrate the intricacy of such interactions in a world order that is undergoing fast change. An important component of India's foreign policy remains the long-standing alliance with Russia, which is based on common historical experiences and strategic goals. Concurrently, the developing relationship with Ukraine highlights India's dedication to interacting with new partners in a way that is consistent with its development objectives and aspirations for the world. India addresses this complex web of ties with diplomatic skill and strategic savvy, striking a delicate balance between historical allegiances and the demands of modern geopolitics (Tripathi, 2023).

India's Neutrality and Non-Interventionist Approach

India's foreign policy, deeply rooted in the principles of non-alignment, neutrality, and non-interventionism, reflects a unique approach to navigating the complex currents of global geopolitics. These principles were crystallized during the Cold War, as India, under the leadership of Prime Minister Jawaharlal Nehru, sought to chart an independent course amidst the ideological confrontations between the USA and the Soviet Union. Non-alignment, as articulated in the Bandung Conference of 1955, aimed at maintaining equidistance from power blocs, advocating for sovereign decision-making, and promoting peaceful coexistence (Raghavan, 2017).

As India transitioned from a colonial past to a newly independent nation, the architects of its foreign policy recognized the imperative of safeguarding national interests without aligning with any particular alliance. The non-interventionist stance was not merely a strategic choice but a reflection of India's commitment to ethical and moral considerations in international affairs. This commitment found expression in India's response to various global conflicts, emphasizing diplomatic resolutions and adherence to the principles of the United Nations Charter.

In the contemporary context, India's commitment to neutrality and non-interventionism faces new challenges, notably in the Russo-Ukrainian War. As tensions between Russia and Ukraine escalate, India finds itself navigating a delicate balance between historical ties with Russia and the imperative of responding to unfolding global events. India's diplomatic finesse becomes particularly evident as it refrains from taking sides and advocates a peaceful resolution through dialogue and negotiation (Ransome, 2023).

The non-interventionist strategy is a proactive dedication to using diplomatic channels to resolve conflicts rather than a passive withdrawal. This dedication is demonstrated by India's participation in international organisations, such as the UN. India has continuously supported diplomatic efforts and constructive conversations as ways to resolve disputes, such as the Russo-Ukrainian war, in the UN Security Council. This strategy is consistent with India's view that states should be respected for their sovereignty and given the freedom to choose their paths free from outside interference (Raghavan, 2020).

The focus India places on establishing and maintaining bilateral and multilateral partnerships based on respect and common interests is one of the main features of its non-interventionist strategy. India has established a reputation as a responsible global actor by abstaining from military alliances and meddling in the domestic affairs of other countries. India's capacity to interact with a wide range of nations and build ties across political and economic systems has been facilitated by this approach (Bjørn, 2017).

The Russo-Ukrainian war, however, poses a nuanced challenge to India's traditional stance. Given that Russia is both an important military, energy, and technological partner and a historical ally, India must balance upholding its neutrality with voicing worries about the conflict's potential effects on international stability. India's measured response demonstrates its dedication to diplomacy as it calls on all sides to pursue a negotiated resolution that upholds Ukraine's sovereignty and takes Russia's valid concerns into account (Ransome, 2023).

India is dedicated to using conversation and negotiation as a means of resolving conflicts, which serves as the foundation for its non-interventionist policy. This commitment also includes South Asia, where

India has encountered several difficulties such as border conflicts with bordering nations. India has persistently promoted nonviolent resolutions to regional disputes, taking part in diplomatic endeavours and steps to boost confidence to promote stability. India's approach to conflict has been centred on non-coercive diplomacy and dedication to dialogue, which is consistent with its vision of a world order marked by mutual respect and collaboration (*The Hindu*, 2023).

India's non-interventionist policy is heavily influenced by economic factors as well. India, a growing country with aggressive growth goals, aims to capitalise on its economic alliances while maintaining its strategic independence. India has reduced its reliance on any one country or bloc by diversifying its economic connections with other partners across the world. This economic pragmatism guarantees that political or strategic decisions are not influenced by economic factors, in line with the larger non-interventionist ideology.

Critics argue that in the face of global challenges, strict adherence to non-interventionism might limit India's ability to play a more assertive role in addressing pressing issues such as human rights violations or authoritarianism in certain regions. However, proponents of India's approach contend that non-interventionism allows for a more measured and principled engagement avoiding the pitfalls of unilateral interventions that often lead to unintended consequences and protracted conflicts.

India has its share of difficulties and problems with its non-interventionist policy. Challenges are ever-present due to the dynamic character of global conflicts, the emergence of new geopolitical processes, and the interdependence of national interests. Nonetheless, India's foreign policy continues to be based on its dedication to peaceful resolutions, respect for national sovereignty, and avoiding armed confrontations. India's approach to the developments in the Russo-Ukrainian war will remain a delicate dance between historical allegiances, pragmatic concerns, and the need to respect the ideals of non-interventionism and peacekeeping in the international sphere. In doing so, India hopes to contribute to the development of a global order founded on communication, collaboration, and understanding in addition to navigating the complexity of the current world (*The Hindu*, 2023).

India's Stance on the Russo-Ukrainian War

India's position on the Russo-Ukrainian war is a careful balancing act that takes into account its historical links with Russia, neutrality, and the need to address global issues. India found itself at the nexus of geopolitics and diplomacy as tensions between Russia and Ukraine increased, necessitating a sophisticated strategy to manage the situation's intricacies. India's foreign policy has always been based on the concepts of non-interventionism and non-alignment, which are at the heart of its position. India has a formidable diplomatic obstacle in the form of the Russo-Ukrainian war as it tries to preserve strategic ties, especially with Russia, while also voicing worries about the conflict's effect on regional and international security (Raghavan, 2020).

From the days of the Soviet Union, India and Russia have had a strong and diverse historical relationship. An important turning point in the strategic alliance of two countries was the 1971 signing of the Indo-Soviet Treaty of Friendship and Cooperation. This collaboration has covered several industries throughout the years, including space exploration, energy, military, and technology. Russia has been India's main supplier of defensive equipment, and the two nations have collaborated and entered into joint ventures, demonstrating a level of cooperation that goes beyond simple business dealings.

India's historical connections to Russia provide a particular problem in the context of the Russo-Ukrainian war. Sanctions and diplomatic tensions have resulted from the conflict's impact on ties between Russia and Western nations. India, which cherishes its independence and non-alignment, has to tread carefully in these geopolitical waters. India has adopted a measured and cautious stance in its reaction to the war. India has voiced worries about the changing circumstances but has not publicly denounced Russia, preferring to place more emphasis on communication, diplomatic solutions, and respect for international law.

The geopolitical landscape surrounding the Russo-Ukrainian war has further complicated India's stance. The conflict has sparked debates about the nature of alliances and the shifting dynamics of global power.

India's position is intricately linked to its commitment to multi-polarity and the belief that the world benefits from a diversity of voices and perspectives. In a multi-polar world, India contends, no single nation or bloc should dictate the course of global affairs. This philosophy aligns with India's historical resistance to aligning with major power blocs during the Cold War and reinforces its commitment to non-alignment in the present context (Shubhrajeet, 2023).

India's stance on the Russo-Ukrainian war has been articulated through diplomatic channels, international forums, and official statements. At the United Nations Security Council, India has consistently emphasized the need for a peaceful resolution, dialogue, and respect for the sovereignty of nations. The call for diplomacy and negotiation is a reflection of India's broader commitment to the principles enshrined in the UN Charter. It underscores India's belief that disputes should be resolved through dialogue and that military interventions often exacerbate conflicts, leading to human suffering and prolonged instability.

Economic considerations also play a role in shaping India's stance. Russia is an important economic partner, particularly in the energy sector. India has a strategic interest in securing energy resources to fuel its growing economy, and Russia has been a reliable supplier of oil and natural gas. The economic ties between India and Russia add a layer of complexity to India's response to the conflict, as disruptions in these ties could have implications for India's energy security and economic stability.

Simultaneously, India recognizes the humanitarian aspects of the conflict. The displacement of civilians, the impact on regional stability, and the potential for broader geopolitical ramifications are all factors that weigh on India's approach. Humanitarian concerns align with India's commitment to the principles of justice, equity, and compassion in international affairs. While balancing its economic and strategic interests, India also acknowledges the importance of addressing the human toll of the conflict.

India is using conservative diplomacy in response to the Russo-Ukrainian war. The subtleties of its position include actively participating in diplomatic attempts targeted at de-escalation and conflict settlement in addition to vocalising concerns about the war. India has always demanded that all sides show restraint, put an end to hostilities, and have meaningful conversations. India's diplomatic activities are a reflection of its commitment to actively contribute to international efforts towards conflict resolution as well as its conviction in the effectiveness of peaceful discussions.

The evolving nature of the conflict poses a challenge for India in terms of navigating the changing dynamics and adapting its stance to emerging developments. The careful calibration of India's response reflects a diplomatic acumen that seeks to balance competing interests and uphold principles of justice and fairness. India's stance is not static; it is responsive to the fluid nature of global affairs, and it remains grounded in the principles that have defined its foreign policy for decades.

Critics of India's position on the Russo-Ukrainian war come in several forms. Many contend that India's circumspect stance demonstrates its dedication to sovereignty, non-alignment, and ethical diplomacy. Some, on the other hand, argue that India ought to be more proactive in addressing the humanitarian aspects of the war and pushing for a more forceful conclusion. Finding the ideal balance is a difficult undertaking that calls for a rigorous evaluation of India's economic interests, historical links, and dedication to international security (Mahapatra, 2021).

In March 2024, Prime Minister Narendra Modi held special separate phone conversations with Ukrainian President Volodymyr Zelenskyy and Russian President Vladimir Putin. During these calls, PM Modi emphasized that the path to ending the war lay in dialogue and diplomacy. He assured both leaders that India would continue to support efforts aimed at achieving a peaceful resolution to the conflict.

As India reinforces its principles of non-alignment, it is increasingly seen by other countries as a pivotal player in uniting nations from the Global South. This positioning allows India to potentially spearhead a diplomatic initiative proposed by Ukraine to resolve the war. Such an initiative would likely make other nations feel more secure and comfortable, encouraging them to join the peace efforts alongside India (Krishnan, 2024).

India reserves the right to shape its policies based on pragmatic realism and its core national interests. It believes that maintaining a neutral stance anchored in strategic autonomy best serves its interests. India's cautious neutrality, such as condemning civilian killings and abstaining from UN votes, is reflected in its strong response to Russia's invasion of Ukraine. The West recognizes India's strategic market importance and democratic influence needed to counterbalance China. To address Chinese expansionism, border conflicts, and the void left by the US military's departure from Afghanistan, India requires cooperation from both the USA and Russia. Achieving self-reliance in arms is crucial for India to assert its position confidently on the global stage.

Furthermore, India's position on the Russo-Ukrainian war captures the nuances and difficulties that come with modern geopolitics. India, a country that cherishes its independence and non-aligned status, needs to move deftly through the complex web of international ties. In the light of shifting global dynamics, the Russo-Ukrainian war puts India's historical connections with Russia to the test. India's unwavering dedication to diplomacy, non-interventionism, and observance of international law serve as a framework for its contributions to attempts towards a peaceful resolution of the conflict. India's foreign policy has to be dynamic and adaptable, reflecting the country's commitment to an international order that is characterised by collaboration, discussion, and the pursuit of common interests. The current events in the area will continue to impact India's attitude (Abraham, 2008).

Conclusion

In recapitulating India's diplomatic stance and strategic engagement amidst the Russo-Ukrainian war, a nuanced and pragmatic approach emerges as the hallmark of the nation's foreign policy. India's commitment to neutrality and non-interventionism, deeply rooted in its historical principles of non-alignment, has shaped its response to the crisis. The delicate balance between its historical ties with Russia and the imperative of addressing global concerns highlights India's diplomatic finesse. Throughout the conflict, India has consistently advocated a peaceful resolution, emphasizing the importance of dialogue and adherence to international law (Raghavan, 2020).

India plays a crucial role in maintaining regional peace through its dedication to diplomatic solutions and participation in international fora. India promotes discussion, moderation, and respect for national sovereignty to establish itself as a stabilising influence in the area. India's multidimensional approach to promoting peace is exemplified by the careful calibration of its reaction, which acknowledges the humanitarian aspects of the conflict while also addressing its economic and geopolitical implications.

The prospects and long-term effects of India's involvement in the Russo-Ukrainian war continue to remain floating in the air. Given the dynamic character of the situation, India must possess the strategic flexibility to modify its position in response to new information. India is in a unique position to influence the course of regional and global events because of its dedication to multi-polarity, non-alignment, and the pursuit of international cooperation.

While economic considerations and historical ties with Russia present challenges, India's principled stance on diplomacy and conflict resolution provides a foundation for constructive engagement. The potential long-term implications may extend beyond the immediate conflict, influencing India's broader foreign policy outlook and its standing on the global stage.

India is a perfect example of how to skilfully navigate geopolitical complexity, as seen by its diplomatic posture and strategic participation in the Russo-Ukrainian war. The country is unwavering in its commitment to principled diplomacy even as it works to promote stability in the area. The future depends on India's capacity to use its economic connections, diplomatic skills, and historical links to constructively contribute to the conflict's resolution and the creation of a cooperative, stable, and peaceful global order. The current events highlight the significance of India's place in the world and the demand for a flexible, nuanced foreign policy that responds to the demands of the dynamic geopolitical environment and is consistent with India's basic values.

REFERENCES

1. Abraham, I. (2008). *From Bandung to NAM: Non-alignment and Indian Foreign Policy, 1947–65. Commonwealth & Comparative Politics*; Taylor & Francis. https://www.tandfonline.com/action/showCitFormats?doi=10.1080%2F14662040801990280
2. Bjorn Moller. (2017). 'India and the responsibility to protect.' *Third World Quarterly*, 38:8, pp. 1921-1934.
3. Budhwar, P. K. (2007). 'India-Russia Relations: Past, Present, and the Future. '*India Quarterly*, 63(3), 51–83. http://www.jstor.org/stable/45073205
4. D'Anieri, P. (2023). *Ukraine and Russia*. Cambridge University Press.
5. Hahn, G. M. (2017). *Ukraine Over the Edge*. McFarland.
6. Johny, S. (23 February 2023). 'The past and present of Russia's war in Ukraine.' *The Hindu*. https://www.thehindu.com/opinion/op-ed/explained-the-past-and-present-of-russias-war-in-ukraine/article66544858.ece
7. Mahapatra, C. (2021). 'India's Approach to the War in Ukraine.' *Indian Foreign Affairs Journal*, 16(2), 95–108. https://www.jstor.org/stable/48720483
8. Mankoff, J. (2022). 'Russia's War in Ukraine: Identity, History, and Conflict.' CSIS Centre for Strategic and International Studies. https://www.csis.org/analysis/russias-war-ukraine-identity-history-and-conflict
9. MEA. (2017). India-Russia Relations. Ministry of External Affairs. https://www.mea.gov.in/Portal/ForeignRelation/India_Russia_May.pdf
10. MEA. (2020). India- Ukraine Relations. MEA; MEA. https://www.mea.gov.in/Portal/ForeignRelation/India_Ukraine_July_2020.pdf
11. Mpoke Bigg, M. (26 March 2022). 'A history of the tensions between Ukraine and Russia.' *The New York Times*; The New York Times. https://www.nytimes.com/2022/03/26/world/europe/ukraine-russia-tensions-timeline.html
12. PIB. (4 September 2019). India-Russia Joint Statement during visit of Prime Minister to Vladivostok. Press Information Bureau; PIB. https://pib.gov.in/Pressreleaseshare.aspx?PRID=1584171
13. Plokhy, S. (2023). *The Russo-Ukrainian War: The Return of History*. W. W. Norton & Company.
14. Raghavan, P. S. (2017). 'The Making of India's Foreign Policy: From Non-Alignment to Multi-Alignment.' *Indian Foreign Affairs Journal*, 12(4), 326–341. http://www.jstor.org/stable/45342011
15. Raghavan. (8 September 2020). 'What is in a NAM and India's alignment' *The Hindu*. The Hindu. https://www.thehindu.com/opinion/op-ed/what-is-in-a-nam-and-indias-alignment/article32555378.ece
16. Ransome, D. (28 March 2023). India's neutrality in the Russia-Ukraine war. The Round Table. https://www.commonwealthroundtable.co.uk/commonwealth/eurasia/india/research-article-indias-quest-for-security-and-its-neutrality-in-the-russia-ukraine-war/
17. Shubhrajeet Konwer. (2023) 'The Ukraine crisis and India: quandaries and implications.' *Canadian Foreign Policy Journal*, 29:3, pp. 317-331.
18. *The Hindu*. (13 April 2023). 'Neutral, not passive' Editorial on India's stand on the Russia-Ukraine conflict, The Hindu. https://www.thehindu.com/opinion/editorial/neutral-not-passive-the-hindu-editorial-on-indias-stand-on-the-russia-

ukraine-conflict/article66733363.ece

19. Tripathi, S. (27 June 2023). 'India's delicate balancing act: Relations with Russia and the United States during the war in Ukraine.' *Times of India* Blog. https://timesofindia.indiatimes.com/blogs/abhiram/indias-delicate-balancing-act-relations-with-russia-and-the-united-states-during-the-war-in-ukraine/
20. Welle, D. (11 June 2024). *Ukraine: Zelenskyy says Kyiv will end war on "own terms" – DW – 06/12/2024*. Dw.Com; Deutsche Welle. https://www.dw.com/en/ukraine-zelenskyy-says-kyiv-will-end-war-on-own-terms/live-69326832
21. *Russian Offensive Campaign Assessment, 3 June 2024 | Institute for the Study of War*. (n.d.). Institute for the Study of War. Retrieved 20 June 2024, from https://www.understandingwar.org/backgrounder/russian-offensive-campaign-assessment-june-3-2024
22. Krishnan, M. (29 March 2024). *Ukraine seeks India's help in ending war with Russia – DW – 03/29/2024*. Dw.Com; Deutsche Welle. https://www.dw.com/en/ukraine-seeks-indias-help-in-ending-war-with-russia/a-68699328

SECTION II

GLOBAL IMPACT AND GEOPOLITICAL IMPLICATIONS OF THE RUSSIA-UKRAINE WAR

7

The Impact of the Russia-Ukraine War on Global Diplomacy and Geopolitics

Bharti Das

Introduction

In the initial days of the Russia-Ukraine war, no one thought that Russia's aggression would escalate to extent that it would leave 9,083 civilians dead and 15,779 people injured (the Office of the United Nations High Commissioner for Human Rights verified the number as on 18 June 2023) and persist the war for over 480 days now. Where Moscow seems determined to invade and attack the Ukrainian lands and restricting it from joining the NATO and the EU, Kyiv continues to launch counteroffensives against the enemy's forces with all the diplomatic and military support from the NATO, the USA, the UK, and the EU. Considering the latest developments, the war continues with no end in sight. It is hard to say if peace and agreement will be settled between the two countries soon.

Current Scenario

President Volodymyr Zelenskyy recently claimed that Ukrainian forces are annihilating Russian troops in the two main battle areas in the east and south of the nation. On 20 June 2023, Russia began a large air campaign against Kyiv and other cities in a west to east direction. Twenty-eight of the 30 Iranian-made Shahed drones that Russia launched were shot down by Ukraine's air defence systems. Russia's defence minister, Sergei Shoigu, promised to retaliate if Ukraine attempted to assault Crimea using long-range HIMARS artillery and Storm Shadow missiles.

Russia annexed Ukraine's Crimean peninsula in 2014. Ruslan Strilets, Ukraine's environment minister, estimated that the Nova Kakhovka hydroelectric dam collapse cost the country 1.2 billion Euros ($ 1.3 billion) in damages and warned that mines uncovered by flooding would wash up on the coastlines of neighbouring European nations. Russia blocked UN aid for the victims of this collapse. According to the Ukrainian Ministry of Defence, the EU's Military Assistance Mission for Ukraine (EUMAM) will train 30,000 soldiers this year.

Ukraine has shifted its strategy from a counteroffensive to an 'Active Defence,'[1] focusing on deeper trenches and anti-tank measures to protect its territory, while also conducting drone attacks on Russian infrastructure. Concurrently, Russia continues its military operations in southern and eastern Ukraine. Switzerland will host a Peace Summit in June 2024, initially excluding Russia but aiming to involve it in future negotiations. The summit seeks to engage the Global South, including India, to foster dialogue. The USA has accused Russia of using chemical weapons in Ukraine and criticized China and Iran for supporting Russia. Sanctions have been imposed on nearly 300 Chinese entities in response to their involvement, highlighting the broader implications for USA-China relations and global arms trade concerns, including Russia-North-Korea exchanges.[2]

Recently, Russian President Vladimir Putin visited North Korea on 19 June 2024. Putin and Kim Jong Un signed an agreement reinstating a mutual defence pact reminiscent of their Cold War-era alliance, which had been dissolved in 1990. The agreement, part of a broader 'comprehensive strategic partnership,' commits both countries to provide immediate military assistance in the event of armed aggression against either party, invoking Article 51 of the UN Charter and respective national laws.[3] This move is viewed as a significant geopolitical manoeuvre by Moscow in Asia, signalling deepening ties with Pyongyang amid their respective international isolations. The pact underscores their shared opposition to Western influence, particularly in the light of US support for Ukraine, and includes provisions prohibiting either side from signing treaties with third parties that undermine the other's interests. Additionally, the agreement outlines joint efforts to enhance defence capabilities aimed at regional and global peace and security, while raising concerns among US allies like South Korea and Japan over potential implications for regional stability and arms control.

The Ukraine conflict, now in its third year, has had significant regional and global impacts, disrupting supply chains and straining the European security architecture. Western fatigue and emerging crises in the Middle East have divided attention, while the roles of China, Iran, and North Korea in supporting Russia have drawn scrutiny. The upcoming elections in the USA and Europe may shift focus inward, but there is a growing, albeit, quiet, push for a peace accord. The planned peace conference in Switzerland is strategically important, aiming to involve all stakeholders eventually. India's invitation to the summit reflects its recognized role in promoting dialogue and diplomacy, alongside its substantial humanitarian aid to Ukraine and consistent calls for an end to hostilities.

Diplomacy

German Chancellor Olaf Scholz asked Beijing to use its clout with Moscow in relation to the conflict in Ukraine and to refrain from arming Russia while speaking at a high-level meeting in Berlin. Next week, EU leaders intend to request China's assistance in putting an end to the conflict in Ukraine, a senior EU official told Reuters. On 29-30 June, EU leaders will gather in Brussels for a summit. For the next four years, the EU will provide Ukraine with a credit and grant package of 50 billion Euros ($ 55 billion). Given the potentially extensive effects of any nuclear catastrophe, Norway's foreign ministry announced it will put aside 250 million kroner ($ 23 million) for nuclear safety and security in Ukraine. Russia's invasion of Ukraine, according to the US envoy to the UN, Linda Thomas-Greenfield, was 'primarily responsible' for the rise in the number of refugees in 2022. A new $ 21.9 billion ($ 3.2 billion) aid package for Ukraine was revealed by the Danish defence ministry. It would include firearms, other military hardware, first aid supplies, and training.[4]

The Possible Ways to End the War

As the war seems to have no end, there still are numerous ways to bring both the parties to equal terms. To begin with, working out an end to a long-term war. The use of military aggression until or unless one side claims its victory can be a prolonged process. This will carry high risks as it can turn out to become a full-fledged nuclear war. Neither Kyiv nor Moscow seems to accept the defeat and drop their weapons in front of their rival at the present height of dispute. This will leave a high number of casualties at both ends, with a more count of civilians in Ukraine.

In addition to this, one of the sides surrendering is another way. If Russia retreats its troops from the region and surrenders, Ukraine will be autonomous to plan upon joining the NATO and the EU. The USA will get an upper hand in eastern Europe and will use Ukraine as a military base to spy on Russia. A long-term peace settlement cannot be assured, keeping in account the security and military concerns of Russia. However, the chances of this happening seem bleak. If Ukraine surrenders, it will risk its democracy and sovereignty. It will lose its chance to be an autonomous nation in Europe. Moreover, Russia's invasion and hegemony in the region will magnify.

Furthermore, diplomatic talks between both the countries can be effective in establishing peace deals. The challenge here is to bring them to talk without any external mediation. Coming to a mutual conclusion is also very debatable due to the differing approaches of the parties towards negotiations. Considering the latest developments, neither of the sides seems keen to choose a diplomatic path. Then, a 'mutually agreed' (by Russia and Ukraine) mediation of a third party. This point has been discussed in detail later in this article. Lastly, strong intervention of forces like the UN and the NATO and establishing ceasefire in Ukraine. It will not be an end, but will bring active warfare to rest, temporarily. Putting sanctions on Russia and mutual agreements between both the parties will be necessary to ensure a long-term dispute settlement, although, NATO's interference will be less likely to interest Russia to have any round of talks with either the West or Ukraine.[5]

Third Party Mediation

The Broader Picture

There is a territorial conflict involving four other regions in the area: South Ossetia, Transdniester, Abkhazia, and Nagorniy-Karabakh. They are all territorial disputes taking place on former Soviet Union territory. The current conflict focuses on eastern Ukraine which has shown weak fidelity to the centre and is more Russophile. Then Crimea, since 1921, has been a part of Russia, but according to international law, is a part of the Ukrainian state. The mediator should be able to maintain a balance between all the arenas of the dispute and take action accordingly.

According to the Ukrainian Ministry of Defence, the EU's Military Assistance Mission for Ukraine (EUMAM) will train 30,000 soldiers this year. Mediation is a stepping-stone to a shared future and strong bond. But in this case, Germany and France have co-managed two cease-fire agreements in Ukraine, with Ukraine, Russia, Donetsk, and Luhansk as signatories; Russia observes the pact rather than act as a guarantor. Given that Russia's involvement is not mentioned expressly in any of the provisions, it could be argued that allowing one of the main actors to withdraw from or be exempt from the agreement at any point gives this actor an advantage over others.

Can Mediation Help Resolve the Conflict?

There have been arguments that, according to some, Ukraine is the victim; thus, the decision of 'if and when' to have diplomatic talks or mediation should lie with the Ukrainian government. There is a fear of losing, lack of trust and reluctance of either party to negotiate.

None the less, mediation is the most effective way of bringing both the parties on equal terms if the needed criteria of equal participation, inclusiveness, maintenance of decorum of international law, etc., is met. A 'mutually decided' mediator (by Russia and Ukraine) who is neutral enough to provide a space to both the parties to put forward their arguments and reflect their best interests can serve as a crucial asset. Anything less will just continue magnifying the 'frozen' situation.[6]

Can China or India Mediate in the Russia-Ukraine War?

China has been coming forward to act as a mediator in the Russia-Ukraine war. China has not yet sent any weapons to Russia, but the proposal to mediate between the two rivals seems unlikely to fructify, considering China's stance on the war. Beijing has not only constantly blamed the NATO for the conflict and has taken a pro-Russian position but has also maintained strong ties with Moscow throughout history.

China's neutrality can be its strategy to stabilize its tense relations with the USA and the EU, but the chances of achieving this is little. If China imposes sanctions, it will alienate itself from the only great power partner and bring hurdles in its bond with Russia. If it doesn't, its relations with the West would become even more strained. It's possible that future improvements in relations with the West will be partially contingent on Beijing penalising Moscow. Both solutions would cost China politically and economically. In another case, the only gain for China in a failed mediation would be that it would slightly improve its political image in the eyes of the West. Thus, mediating in the war is a risky factor for China.

India's stance has been neutral since the beginning of the war. It has shown its concern towards the loss of lives and livelihood in Ukraine but has never openly commented in favour of or against any side, believing that it would not help ending the conflict. India believes that staying on its ground is advantageous for its foreign policy of maintaining strong relations with the West and Russia. India has constantly emphasised the need for diplomatic talks as the only effective means to end the crisis between the rivals.

The question whether India can act as a mediator is quite complicated considering differing views of Ukraine and Russia on India's stance. Ukraine is sceptical about India's intentions as India continues to purchase oil from Russia which, they believe, is contributing funds to Russia to go against them. India, to its defence, said that it will not restrict itself from procuring the best oil available in the market for its people, on account of the ongoing crisis. On the other hand, the bilateral relations between Russia and India have strengthened ever since the war started. In India, for example, Russia now accounts for 225 per cent of all crude oil imports, outpacing both Iraq and Saudi

Arabia as the country's leading oil suppliers. Russia has always referred to India as a 'steady and time-tested partner.' Russia's foreign minister had earlier noted, in reference to India's function as a mediator, "India is an important country. India can support such a process if it perceives itself as playing a role that offers a solution to the issue, if it is taking the position of a just and reasonable approach to international issues (India Can Act as a Mediator Between Moscow and Kyiv).

India's history of its 'non-alignment' approach and a friend, of both the West and Russia, can be seen as a key mediator. On 24 February 2022, as hostilities started, New Delhi moved quickly to assist Ukraine's humanitarian needs. The government of Prime Minister Narendra Modi claims that India's foreign and defence policies are consistent with its decision to refrain from criticising Moscow's activities at the UN. In response to Modi's recent concerns over the conflict, Russian President Vladimir Putin recognised them and told him at their meeting in Uzbekistan that Moscow would make every effort to put a halt to the fighting "as soon as possible."[7]

Conclusion

The ongoing Russia-Ukraine war shows no signs of imminent resolution, underscoring the urgent need for diplomatic engagement. Both nations must recognize that a sustainable settlement can only be achieved through diplomatic talks facilitated by a mutually agreed third-party mediator who can fairly represent the interests of both sides. This mediator's role is crucial in conveying the message that political gains cannot justify the loss of lives and livelihoods, and that continued military aggression risks escalating into a nuclear conflict.

Meanwhile, the geopolitical landscape is further complicated by Russia's renewed alliance with North Korea. During President Vladimir Putin's visit to Pyongyang, he and Kim Jong Un signed a comprehensive strategic partnership reviving their Cold War-era mutual defence pact. This agreement, which pledges immediate military assistance in the event of armed aggression, highlights Russia and North Korea's shared opposition to Western influence and US support for Ukraine. The pact's stipulations, including prohibitions on treaties with third parties that could harm the other's interests, and commitments to enhance defence capabilities, have raised alarms among US allies. As these developments unfold, it is clear that the path to peace and stability requires not just regional cooperation but also a broader, more nuanced approach to international diplomacy.

REFERENCES

1. War in Ukraine, Global Conflict Tracker, CFR, 24 April 24, 2024, https://www.cfr.org/global-conflict-tracker/conflict/conflict-ukraine. Accessed online on 2 May 2024.
2. Australia-Republic of Korea 2+2 Foreign And Defence Ministers' Meeting. AUKUS Pillar Two. Hanwha bid for Austal; foreign interference; Korean peninsula security.
3. 'North Korea, Russia sign pact to give all available military help if other is attacked,' story by SEOUL (Reuters). Reported by Jack Kim, Kim Coghill and Gerry Doyle. North Korea, Russia sign pact to give all available military help if other is attacked (msn.com)
4. Russia-Ukraine war: List of key events, day 483: https://www.aljazeera.com/news/2023/6/21/russia-ukraine-war-list-of-key-events-day-483; Putin's War Against Ukraine: The End of The Beginning, https://carnegieendowment.org/2023/02/17/putin-s-war-against-ukraine-end-of-beginning-pub-89071
5. How to End the War in Ukraine: https://www.bostonreview.net/forum/how-to-end-the-war-in-ukraine/; How will the Russia-Ukraine war end? https://www.hindustantimes.com/world-news/explained-three-situations-that-could-end-russia-ukraine-war-101677308923799.html
6. Is Peace Mediation in Ukraine Possible, and How?: https://www.c-r.org/news-and-insight/peace-mediation-ukraine-possible-and-how
7. Mediating the Russia–Ukraine war a risky role for China: https://www.voanews.com/a/china-offers-to-act-as-mediator-in-russian-war-with-ukraine-/7068167.html ;

8

Impact of the Russia-Ukraine War on Global Economy

Dhirendra Dwivedi and Mayank Saraswat

Introduction

The Russians renewed invasion of Ukraine on 24 February 2022 and the endless international sanctions on Russia have led to economic, security and humanitarian crises in the region that is causing wide-ranging spill over effects globally and likely to trammel the economic recovery of nations from the COVID-19 pandemic. The COVID-19 pandemic created an unprecedented global crisis and impacted almost all aspects of the global, regional, national and local elements of the economy, trade and social life.[1]

The Russia invasion in Ukraine has completed more than two years and the world is facing trade disruptions, inflationary pressures and security concerns to weigh on consumer and investor sentiment, reducing real incomes and depressing global demand. If the war is not ended soon, it may lead to a more widespread regional and potentially global economic recession and increase the risk of social unrest in both developed and developing economies. The war has increased the risk to global growth. Financial markets have been disturbed and lead to global economic crisis that compound pre-existing ones created by the pandemic. Human capital has also been affected in the region and in neighbouring countries by food insecurity, energy insecurity, production and consumption, inflation and trade barriers.

In 2021, there was a surge in demand for physical goods that resulted from economic stimulus programs and a sharp shift in spending from services to consumer durables, while supply remained restricted by pandemic-induced constraints on production and transportation. This condition worsened after the Russian invasion in Ukraine.[2] Several sanctions were imposed on Russia that placed an additional strain on the supply chain. These developments resulted in supply-demand imbalances in the global economy.

Recently, Russian President Vladimir V. Putin stated that Russia would order a cease-fire and enter into negotiations if Ukraine withdrew its troops from the four regions Russia claims and abandons its NATO aspirations. Ukraine's foreign ministry rejected this, accusing Putin of trying to mislead the international community and undermine diplomatic efforts for peace. Putin's conditions include Ukraine surrendering significant territory, a stance Kyiv opposes, demanding Russian withdrawal from all recognized Ukrainian territory. Putin's announcement, preceding a peace conference in Switzerland, aims to influence global opinion and pressure Ukraine. Despite incremental battlefield gains, Russia faces Ukrainian resistance and Western support delays. By presenting himself as open to negotiations with unrealistic demands, Putin may be seeking to sway Western opinion and reduce support for Ukraine. Analysts believe Putin's objectives remain unchanged, aiming for broader territorial claims beyond the specified regions.[3]

According to UN Secretary-General Antonio Guterres, "The war in Ukraine in all its dimensions is setting in motion a crisis that is devastating global energy markets, disrupting financial systems and exacerbating extreme vulnerabilities for the developing world."[4] In addition to the tragic loss of thousands of human lives and the exposure of humanitarian crisis, the war has affected not only the Russian and Ukrainian economies and security but also the global economy and security.

Global Supply Chain

The military operation commenced by Russia against Ukraine has completed more than two years. This invasion has affected many sectors including the global supply chain. The embargo on Russian exports and retaliation against foreign imports by Russia, including refusal to allow foreign shipments through its airspace and waterways during the military operation disrupted the global supply chain that led to scarcity and rise in the prices of imported goods.

Prior to the war, Ukraine was the top exporter of agricultural products (46%) followed by manufactures (42%).[5] Ukraine's primary export destinations were the European Union (39%), China (12.1%), Turkey (6.1%) and Russia (5.1%).[6] Russia's main export commodities were fuels and energy products (63%), metals (10%), machinery and equipment (7.4%), and chemical products (7.4%). It is notable that Russia produces 25 per cent of the world's nitrogen fertilizer and exports most of its energy to the European Union. Russia and Ukraine together accounted for 28 per cent of the global wheat exports. The immediate effect of the war on the supply chain was the hike in the prices of commodities like petrol, diesel and other resources which had been hit hard. This situation forced the companies to find alternative sources of material and labour to keep up the demand. First the COVID-19 pandemic and then the Russia-Ukraine war fuelled an increasing interest in creating an alternative strategy.

The war has created obstacles in trade including global transport routes and added strain to the existing supply interruption. Air space was closed by European countries and in retaliation, Russia too closed its airspace. Due to supply chain-related constraints, the world is facing high inflation, food shortages, decreased growth, high oil and energy prices, etc. Supply and demand are imbalanced. As Ukraine is big exporter of grain, and supply of grain was not possible at that time, it increased the problem of supply shortage and higher prices. Due to various trade barriers and sanctions, supply was not possible through the Black Sea.

There are some key impacts on the global supply chain:

(i) Organizations are looking for alternative supplies with cheapness and surety.

(ii) Cost of labour increased in Europe.

(iii) Risk management is no longer optional.

(iv) Production, growth rate and import disruption.

Thus the war escalated supply chain interruption where the current climate is unpredictable. Business needs to be proactive and consider how the situation may develop after the end of the war and what scenario might arise.

Oil and Natural Gas

Russia's invasion in Ukraine is first and foremost an energy tragedy. Energy is the most important resource in production and shipping. Before the invasion, the condition of the oil market was already stiff. Due to COVID-19, demand was low and the price of crude oil slipped to 10 dollars per barrel. This placed companies in significant deficits. Due to the lockdown in almost every country, demand was low. But it increased after relaxation of COVID cases. But before COVID ended, Russia invaded Ukraine; this worsened the situation. Prices of oil and natural gas reached an all-time high. The high prices led to a deep effect on global energy markets. Price fluctuation, supply shortages, security issues and economic uncertainty have contributed to what the IEA called "the first truly global energy crisis that will be perceived for years to come." The increased price of both oil and natural gas resulted in an economic burden for countries. Most of the countries imported oil and gas. Due to high energy cost, the share of oil and natural gas prices to GDP increased. Since Russia is the world's second largest oil producer it exported most of its crude oil and gas to European countries through the Nord Stream pipeline. After the invasion, various sanctions were imposed on Russia preventing it from export its oil and natural gas. Russia used her resources as a weapon and cut the supply to European countries. A serious energy crisis emerged in these countries; sanctions were also imposed on purchasing Russian crude oil. This situation hit the world hard. But some countries, including India, regularly purchased oil from Russia at low prices.

Russia's invasion has disrupted lives and livelihoods. The energy sector like all other industries is now operating in an uncertain environment. Oil prices rose to 140 dollars per barrel even prior to the full escalation of war. The price of crude oil was already high even before the war due to high demand by the recovery of global economies from COVID-19 and low investment in the oil and gas industry. A global disruption in oil and gas supply affected not only the prices of these commodities but also every economic activity reliant on these resources. Countries that were dependent on Russian imports have explored alternative sources for their needs and re-examined their energy security policies. Now, two years and three months into the invasion, oil prices are down to 80-90 dollars per barrel from 130-140.

Food

The Russian invasion in Ukraine has caused extensive damage and loss of life in the major cities of Ukraine, spread across rural areas and sparked massive displacement of the population. It is quite clear that war has resulted in a severe food crisis across the world and disrupted livelihoods during the agriculture growing season in Ukraine, which ultimately affected global food security. Before the war, the international food commodity had reached an all-time high. This was mainly due to market conditions, but the high prices of energy, fertilizers and other agricultural services worsened the condition. In March 2022, the FAO Food Price Index reached a new high in its history recording 12.6 per cent in February and 33.6 per cent from its earlier level of 15.8 per cent, which was higher than the peak reached in February 2011.[7]

Russia and Ukraine were prominent players in the global trade of food and agricultural products in 2021. They accounted for 30 per cent of the global market in exports of food and agricultural products. So, the invasion in Ukraine has multiple implications for the global economy and food supplies, representing a challenge for food security for many countries, and especially for the low-income food import dependent countries and vulnerable population groups.

The war has created constraints on physical access to inputs and damage to home, productive assets, agricultural and forest land and environment too. Due to the war, several ports were closed; oilseed crushing operations were suspended. Some crops and food products were also banned. As a result, this war shocked the global market, when food markets are already struggling with high prices and the challenges that the world has been facing as a result of COVID-19.

After the beginning of the war, exports of goods collapsed as the Russian war efforts were entirely focused on the Black Sea of the Azove coast. Some of Ukrainian port cities such as Mariupol and Kherson were under Russian control that enforced a naval blockade in the waters of the Black Sea. The sanctions imposed by Western countries on Russian exports crippled the situation. About 50 countries, including most of the African countries, faced a serious food crisis. Prices reached an all-time high. The world faced global inflationary pressure. People of less developed or developing countries were vulnerable to the food shortage and hunger issues. Countries that relied on imports of food grains and oil seeds in their consumption basket were especially at risk.

The Black Sea Grain Initiative, brokered by Turkey to allow Ukraine to export grain amidst its conflict with Russia, initially provided global relief by reducing food commodity prices. However, Russia's decision not to extend this agreement has heightened concerns about grain and fertilizer prices, exacerbating the global food crisis. This issue is particularly pressing for China, the world's largest food importer, as it faces numerous challenges, including pandemic-related disruptions, systemic competition with the USA, and climate-related shocks.

Inflation

COVID-19 crippled the global supply chain, the war in Ukraine knocked it to its knees. The world was facing inflationary pressure already when the war rapidly increased global inflation, with a sharp increase in uncertainty and risk of severe adverse outcomes. The economies of Russia and Ukraine are shrinking sharply as a direct result of the war and the sanctions imposed on Russia by the Western countries. Since the beginning of the conflict, commodity markets have been in turmoil and financial markets have been highly volatile. According to IMF data, the world inflation rate for 2021 was 3.50 per cent, that is, 1.57 per cent increase from 2020. The world inflation rate for 2020 was 1.92 per cent, that is, 0.27 per cent decline from 2019. The world inflation rate for 2019 was 2.19 per cent, that is, 0.25 per cent decline from 2018.[8] The global inflation rate is expected to peak at 9 per cent in the fourth quarter of 2022.[9] The global inflation rate is expected to fall to 6.6 per cent in 2023 and 4.3 per cent in 2024, which is still above the pre-pandemic levels.

Due to higher inflation, household consumption will be less and the expected fall in business investment and exports will lower GDP growth. Not only Europe, other countries of the world felt the economic shockwaves in the form of inflated prices of food items and energy. Due to sanctions on Russian exports and seizure of ports, grains were highly inflated worldwide. Most of the African, Latin American and Asian countries faced severe food crises. The prices of oil and natural gas were at an all-time high. The ratio of imports of oil and natural gas to the GDP increased due to the price rise. It is quite clear that the economies of various countries were hit hard by the war, of course at different intensities; where some were able to balance their budgets, others failed. Due to inflation, not only economic pressure, but political pressure also increased. Governments were changed due to inflation in some countries.

Stock Market

Following the collapse in March 2020 due to the COVID-19 pandemic, stock markets grew due to tech and pharma companies benefiting from the pandemic. This trend finally ended on 24h February 2022 after the Russian invasion of Ukraine. Due to uncertainty, investors fled to safety. Stock prices were the lowest on the day of the invasion. Due to the ongoing conflict, financial markets across the world experienced a strong dynamic regarding supply chain and commodity prices. After the financial crisis of 2008, this affect was considered as the biggest change in the stock market. The prices of commodities are strongly connected with the stock market. Due to supply chain disruption, high rise in prices of oil and natural gas, sanctions imposed on Russia and uncertain environment, the stock market collapsed. This unexpected attack on Ukraine signalled the beginning of a humanitarian crisis. This attack also affected investor decisions. The relationship between the war and the stock market is a negative one. Now, the war has completed more than two years, but the growth rate and inflation in the world is perhaps leading to recession.

Banking Sector

After the Russian invasion of Ukraine, many governments responded with a series of financial sanctions on Russia including freezing assets and banning Russian banks from Worldwide Interbank Financial Telecommunication (SWIFT), which is a messaging service used to facilitate cross-border payments. Sanctions imposed on Russia are the largest package of sanctions ever adopted in history.

First, there are so many payment firms like Visa, MasterCard, American Express, PayPal, etc., that are both domestic and international, that reacted to the war by announcing bans and withdrawing from Russia and Belarus. SWIFT measures were designed to put economic and political pressure on Russia, which affected the Russian economy and payment market. Imports and exports were disrupted by payment measures, and that finally affected the global supply chain.

The direct impact of the Russia-Ukraine war on the global banking system is minimal. Foreign banks that were operating in Russia were severely impacted by the invasion. They were impacted after many countries imposed financial sanctions on Russian banks and Russian individuals.[10]

Exchange Rate, Debt and Growth Rate

After being invaded by Russia, the Ukraine Hryvnia fell to a record low against the US dollar with a likely reaction on Ukrainian agriculture, including a boost to its export competitiveness and imposing a limit on its ability to import. The economic sanctions imposed on Russia led to a significant decrement in the ruble. The USD to ruble value lost significant ground reaching a low of 135 rubles in March 2022.[11] Lastly, ruble decrement negatively affected investment and productivity growth prospects in the region.

Economic forecasts from various economic organizations were downgraded following the outbreak of war in Ukraine. Before the start of the war, the International Monetary Fund (IMF) estimated that the world GDP would grow at 4.4 per cent in 2022 and the volume of goods trade would increase to 6 per cent.[12] After calculating the impact, the WTO estimated that the war would reduce the world GDP growth to between 0.7 and 1.3 percentage points.[13] The most recent IMF world economic outlook of October 2022 forecast was 3.4 per cent in January 2023. The GDP forecast for 2023 was revised at the same time, from 2.7 to 2.9 per cent.[14]

Indian Economy

After COVID-19, the Indian economy was recovering gradually but the Russian invasion of Ukraine restrained it again. The spill over effect was seen in India as well. In line with global nods, the stock market shuffled, and inflation reached a record high; the rupee tumbled again the US dollar. The common reaction to the war was a fall in investor sentiments globally due to the uncertain environment that led to one of the worst falls in the Indian stock market after 2008. However, the impact of the war was not felt so much in India as in other major economies. Disruption of major trade routes, and subsequent sanctions imposed on Russia by Western countries made a huge impact on global supply chains. As a result, prices of oil and natural gas surged to a record high which, in turn, pushed inflation. However, the Indian economy showed extreme resilience to such factors and expanded by 13.5 per cent in the first quarter of the financial year 2022-23.[15] India's growth is projected to slow down in the coming financial year but is still the fastest growing among the major economies of world. One of the biggest impacts of the war is high inflation. India's retail inflation jumped to a an eight year high of 7.79 per cent and remained above the Reserve Bank of India's tolerance band of 2-6 per cent.[16] The main reason behind it was the massive surge in global crude oil prices.

Global Security

After the Second World War, it is for the first time that Russia challenged the security order established by Western democracies. The expansion of NATO towards the east created a security dilemma for Russia. The Russian invasion of Ukraine galvanized the Western alliance; endless economic sanctions were imposed on the Russian economy and it was isolated by various UN bodies. The Russian aggression also prompted Finland and Sweden to request entry to NATO; both were neutral throughout the Cold War. NATO members admitted Finland as their 31st member recently. All the countries within NATO have notably increased their military expenditure. The arms race has started again at a rapid pace.

According to a SIPRI report, imports of major arms by European states increased by 47 per cent between 201317 and 2018-22. The US share of global arms exports increased from 33 to 40 per cent, while

Russia's fell from 22 to 16 Per cent.[17] Due to the invasion of Ukraine and tensions between Russia and other European countries, there is a sharp rise in arms transfers in Europe while arms transfers have declined globally. US and French arms exports increased as Russian exports declined. Ukraine became the third-largest importer of weapons in 2022 due to the ongoing war. There was a big setback to the disarmament process. There is a sharp incline in military expenditure. According to the SIPRI report, 86 nuclear weapons were added last year of which 60 were by China alone.[18] International security is in an uncertain environment due to different geopolitical tensions in various regions of the world. India-China military stands-off at the LAC, China-Taiwan issue, West Asian crisis, unstable African countries, and the power game in Indo-Pacific are heating up the security environment. In this scenario, efforts of disarmament and arms control slowed down.

Defence Modernization of India

The Russia-Ukraine war once again highlighted the strategic dilemma of foreign dependency on military preparedness. The ongoing strategic and diplomatic enigma faced by India best illustrates the scenario. On many occasions, India abstained from UN votes against Russia. There are short-term and long-term implications for India's defence modernization. India's core security priorities are focused on its land border disputes with China and Pakistan and maritime competition with China in the Indo-Pacific. These priorities will continue to influence India's defence capabilities and preparedness. The war has created pressing concerns for India about Russia's ability to deliver its defence requirements. As the war is going on, Russia is paying attention towards its own requirements first. This will surely delay the timely delivery of the four remaining units of advanced surface-to-air defence system S-400 missiles, Talwar class frigates, upgrades for AN-32, R-27 air-to-air missile and a propulsion system for frigates. There is also a delay in the Akula class nuclear submarines, and T-90 main battle tanks which involves technology transfer, the jointly manufactured Brahmos missile system and Ak-203 rifles. In 2014, India convinced Ukraine to provide the propulsion system for the construction of two frigates, but Russian strikes on defence industries are hampering Ukraine's export capacity. So, there is a huge impact on India's defence modernization. In this situation, India will have to make efforts for rapid indigenization of defence industries.

Lessons Learnt by India

The ongoing Russia-Ukraine war highlights the changing nature of modern-day warfare. The war has thrown up multiple lessons for militaries across the world. Indian strategists paid attention to the war and assimilated some lessons that are as follow:

(i) India must be self-reliant in defence production. The defence industrial ecosystem will maintain supply of weapons and other requirements of war.

(ii) Another big take-away from the war for the Indian military is the possibility of a long war. Before the war, strategists largely thought about a future war being short and swift.

(iii) Conventional firepower still matters and will play a big role in future wars.

(iv) Well-trained infantry will play a significant role in war. Maybe there will not be trench warfare but India needs trained soldiers to push into and occupy enemy territory.

(v) The effectiveness of drones is questionable in a heavily challenged air space.

(vi) The relevance of hard power still exists with land continuing to be the decisive domain of warfare and the notion of victory by occupying enemy territory.

(vii) The country must have a big store of petroleum products; in case of supply chain disruption we can fulfil our requirements.

Conclusion

This article examines the effect of the Russian invasion of Ukraine on global economy and global security in the 21st century. This is the era of globalisation. Economic growth and security cannot be dealt with separately. Geopolitical conflicts tend to have economic effects all over the world. The Russia-Ukraine war, like the COVID-19 pandemic, has accelerated existing problems in the global supply chain and emphasized the interconnected nature of the global economy. This war highlighted the importance of domestic and global supply chains and emphasized on limiting trade dependencies on other countries. Due to the war, prices of oil and natural gas, food and other commodities increased and that led to global inflation ultimately affecting global growth. Many sanctions were imposed on Russia by Western countries but their impact was global. Russia and Ukraine were the largest exporters of grain, but the war hampered supply. The financial sector collapsed due to the uncertainty created by the war. Moreover, the uncertain security environment lead to an arms race. There was a sudden increase in arms expenditure in Europe.

As of June 2024, the Indian economy continues to experience stress due to the ongoing Russia-Ukraine war. Prices of oil and gas increased significantly due to disrupted crude oil supplies, causing inflation to reach an all-time high. However, Russia's offer to sell oil at lower prices has helped India reduce inflation, minimizing the overall economic impact. Despite this relief, the modernization of India's armed forces has been adversely affected by the war. Consequently, strategists are increasingly advocating the rapid indigenization of the defence industry to reduce dependency on imports.

The Russia-Ukraine war has surpassed the two-year mark, but there is some relaxation in supply chains leading to lower food prices; oil and natural gas prices have also decreased. The war has impacted every sector of the global economy, with the repercussions felt far beyond Russia and Ukraine. Indian Prime Minister Narendra Modi emphasized, "This is not an era of war," urging for a swift end to the conflict. He stressed that ending the war would allow the world to breathe a sigh of relief and gradually reduce the war's impact on the global economy.

REFERENCES

1. *Journal of Applied Economics and Business Research*, p. 58, (2022).
2. Congressional Research Service. Russia's 2022 war Against Ukraine: Global Economic Effects, 12 May 2022.
3. Putin Makes Cease-Fire Offer With Sweeping Demands on Ukraine's Territory, *The New York Times* (nytimes.com) Accessed on 18 June 2024.
4. http://www.un.org/en/desa/fragile-economic-recovery-covid19-pandemic-upended-war-Ukraine.
5. News.uft.edu/2023/02.
6. 'Impact of the Ukraine-Russia conflict on global food security,' Food and

Agricultural Organisation of the UN, 117th session, 13-17 June 2022.

7. Ibid.
8. http://www.macrotrends.net/countries/wLD/world/Inflation-rate-cpi.
9. Balba, M. 'The impact of the Russian-Ukrainian war on the Global Economy,' Researchgate, April 2022.
10. http://www.statista.com
11. 'War in Ukraine, assessing the impact on global trade development,' WTO, oneyukr-e.pdf 2023
12. Ibid.
13. Ibid.
14. Ibid.
15. Ibid.
16. https://www.sipri.org/
17. Ibid.
18. 'Russia-Ukraine War: Military modernization and operational challenges for India,' *South Asian Voice*, 17 May 2022.

9

The Russia-Ukraine War: A Historical Survey

Raghvendra Pratap Singh

Introduction

The Russia-Ukraine war is the most intricate geopolitical conflict of the present time. It includes their history, contemporary politics, and uncertain action. It has captured global attention and sparked debates on sovereignty, territorial integrity, and the balance of power in a post-Cold War world. Here, it is important to understand the intricacies of this ongoing crisis. The historical and strategic background of this conflict goes back to the common heritage of Russia and Ukraine. In fact, it originated from the Kievan Rus. Centuries of combined history, armed struggle, and cooperation set the stage for contemporary tensions. The crisis took a dramatic turn in 2014 when Russia annexed Crimea. It shattered the status quo. This bold move resulted in a chain reaction of events that affected the world. The international community condemned and put sanctions in place. It became the stage for a protracted struggle.

As of today, the war in eastern Ukraine, particularly in the Donetsk and Luhansk regions, persists. Despite multiple attempts at ceasefires and peace negotiations, sporadic violence endures. The involvement of external actors, both overt and covert, has further complicated the geopolitics of the region. Looking to the future, the resolution of the Russia-Ukraine conflict still remains distant. The positions of the involved parties are deeply involved, and global powers have large interests. Beyond the immediate conflict, and its broader implications on global politics, the expansion of organisations like NATO and the European Union, and the balance of power between East and West are of significant concern.

Conflict in the Strait of Kerch

The armed struggle in the Strait of Kerch is a regional maritime dispute between Russia and Ukraine. The Kerch Strait became the focal point. It connects the Black Sea to the Sea of Azov. This area has seen tensions and incidents related to control over navigation and territorial claims.

The conflict escalated after Russia annexed Crimea in 2014. It transformed the strategic dynamics of the region because Crimea's control gave Russia control over the northern access points to the Black Sea, including the Kerch Strait. Russia has tried to show its supremacy over the waters around Crimea, including the Kerch Strait. This had led to disputes over territorial waters and maritime boundaries, and Russia claimed the strait as its territorial waters. Ukraine, on the other hand, asserted its claim to openly navigate the Kerch Strait as an international waterway because it was governed by international maritime law. This became a bone of contention as both countries asserted conflicting claims to the area. Several naval incidents in the area followed, including confrontations between Russian and Ukrainian naval vessels. The most notable incident occurred in November 2018, when Russian forces seized three Ukrainian naval vessels near the Kerch Strait. It led to tensions and international condemnation by the worldwide community.

The conflict has deep economic implications, particularly for Ukraine's ports in the Sea of Azov. Russia's control over the Kerch Strait has permitted it to exert influence over Ukrainian maritime traffic to these ports. The international community, including Western countries and international organisations, has expressed deep concern over the situation in the Strait of Kerch and has called for a peaceful resolution of the conflict. In response to the annexation of Crimea and related actions, Western nations imposed sanctions on Russia, which have far-reaching consequences. The conflict in the Strait of Kerch is part of the broader Russia-Ukraine crisis and is characterised by disputes over maritime boundaries and territorial control. It has had implications for regional security, navigation, and economic activities in the area, as well as contributing to ongoing tensions between Russia and Ukraine.

The Crimean Conflict and the Minsk Declaration

The Russia-Ukraine war has deep historical roots, current complexities, and a challenging path forward. As one navigates this intricate landscape, it becomes evident that this conflict transcends borders, encompassing a multitude of factors that will shape the geopolitical order for years to come. The ongoing crisis between Russia and Ukraine, particularly in the eastern regions of Donetsk and Luhansk, closely links the Crimean conflict and the Minsk Agreements. Here's an overview of how the Crimean conflict and the Minsk Declaration are connected.

The Crimean conflict started in 2014 when Russia seized Crimea. It was a region that was previously an important part of Ukraine. This annexation was widely condemned by the international community, as it violated Ukraine's sovereignty and territorial integrity. The annexation led to a sharp deterioration in Russia-Ukraine relations. It sparked a confrontation that extended beyond Crimea into eastern Ukraine. Following the annexation of Crimea, pro-Russian separatist movements erupted in the Donetsk and Luhansk regions of Eastern Europe. These separatist forces, often with alleged support from Russia, clashed with Ukrainian government troops. This escalation resulted in a protracted conflict. It was characterised by sporadic violence, civilian casualties, and displacement.

The Minsk Agreements are a set of ceasefire and peace agreements brokered through diplomatic efforts involving the Organisation for Security and Cooperation in Europe (OSCE), Russia, Ukraine, and the separatist groups in eastern Ukraine. There are two main Minsk agreements: Minsk I (September 2014) and Minsk II (February 2015). Negotiators negotiated the Minsk Agreements to tackle the ongoing conflict in eastern Ukraine, further intensified by the events in Crimea. These agreements aimed to establish a ceasefire, withdraw heavy weaponry, facilitate humanitarian access, and outline a political process for resolving the crisis. The agreements have been a focal point of international efforts to de-escalate the situation and find a peaceful resolution.

However, the implementation of the Minsk Agreements has faced significant challenges, with ceasefires repeatedly violated and political and security provisions remaining unfulfilled. The conflict in eastern Ukraine has not ended, and the Minsk Agreements failed to provide a comprehensive and lasting resolution. Negotiators negotiated the Minsk Agreements in response to the Crimean conflict, which served as a catalyst for the broader crisis in eastern Ukraine, with the aim of seeking a peaceful resolution. While the Minsk Agreements represent a diplomatic framework, their full implementation has proven difficult, and the conflict continues to impact the region.

Russia and the G7

The Group of Seven (G7) is an intergovernmental organization comprising the world's largest advanced economies: Canada, France, Germany, Italy, Japan, the United Kingdom, and the USA, with participation from the European Union. Originally established as the G6 in the 1970s, Canada's inclusion expanded it to the G7. In the 1990s, the group briefly expanded to include Russia as the G8, but after international criticism and sanctions stemming from Russia's annexation of Crimea, the other G7 members suspended Russia in 2014, effectively reverting to the G7. In 2017, Russia announced its permanent withdrawal from the group. Despite complex relations marked by disagreements and mistrust, dialogue persists on global issues such as climate change, terrorism, and health crises.

During the G7 2024 summit in Italy, leaders met Ukrainian President Volodymyr Zelenskyy, reaffirming staunch support for Ukraine amid its steadfast resistance to Russia's illegal two-year invasion. Commending Ukraine's bravery, the G7 condemned Russia's breaches of international law and pledged unwavering assistance towards achieving a just and enduring peace. The leaders also paid tribute to Alexei Navalny's anti-corruption efforts and urged Russia to release unlawfully detained individuals. Emphasizing defence, security, and economic stability support for Ukraine, they highlighted the imperative of reforms and Euro-Atlantic integration. Condemning Russia's war crimes and efforts to weaponize food supplies, the G7 committed to impose further sanctions and ensure accountability for damages caused by the conflict, while promising reconstruction aid until Ukraine's sovereignty was fully restored.

Vladimir Putin and Russia's Imperial Identity

Many strategic experts felt that Vladimir Putin's leadership in Russia was closely associated with a reassertion of Russian imperial identity and influence on the global stage. This connection between Putin and Russia's imperial identity could be understood in various important aspects. Russia believes in a long history of empire-building. It included the Russian Empire, the Soviet Union, and the Russian Federation. Putin, then a KGB officer, has often portrayed himself as a protector of Russia's historical legacy and a leader who tries to balance the nation's prestige and power. His tenure has witnessed certain nostalgia for the Soviet era because some Russians looked back at the superpower status and worldwide influence that the Soviet Union once held. Putin himself has often praised the great achievements of the Soviet age and emphasised Russia's role as a global player.

Putin has promoted the idea of Eurasianism. He has emphasised Russia's role as a bridge between Europe and Asia. This concept is crucial to Russia's efforts to maintain influence in its neighbouring countries, particularly in the former Soviet Union. Russia took military action in Georgia in 2008 and Ukraine in 2014. The aim was to protect what it perceives as the interests of Russian-speaking populations and to maintain influence in its periphery. People perceived these actions as an attempt to assert Russian supremacy in the region.

Putin's leadership has been marked by symbolic actions that reinforce Russia's imperial identity, such as the annexation of Crimea in 2014, which was seen as reclamation of historically Russian territory. Russia has put forward a more assertive foreign policy by challenging Western dominance. It also seeks to partner with countries that have similar worldviews, often thinking of Russia as an alternative world power centre.

Cultural and Political Control: Domestically, the Russian government has enough control over the media and cultural narratives. This has fostered a sense of national pride and unity that aligns with the imperial identity.

It's important to note that Putin's leadership and Russia's imperial identity vary widely, both within Russia and internationally. Some view Putin as a pragmatic leader who defends Russian interests in a changing world, while others see his actions as destabilising and expansionist. Overall, Vladimir Putin's leadership has been intertwined with a vision of Russia as a world power with an imperial legacy. This has significant implications for Russia's domestic and foreign policies.

Western European and American Concerns

Western European countries and the USA have expressed significant concerns about various aspects of the Russia-Ukraine war. These concerns encompass a range of political, security, and humanitarian issues. Western European countries and the USA strongly support the principle of Ukraine's territorial integrity and sovereignty. They have condemned Russia's annexation of Crimea and its support for separatist movements in eastern Ukraine as violations of international law. The ongoing conflict in eastern Ukraine is a cause for concern. Western nations fear that further escalation of the conflict could lead to a wider regional crisis and increased instability in Eastern Europe.

The humanitarian toll of the conflict, including civilian casualties, displacement, and suffering, is a source of deep concern. Western nations have provided humanitarian aid to affected areas and called for the protection of civilians. All these compelled Western countries to impose economic sanctions on Russia because of its actions in Ukraine. It included the annexation of Crimea and ongoing support for separatist groups. Sanctions include potential economic effectiveness and the need to maintain a united front among Western nations.

The conflict has raised serious concerns about European security among the members of NATO. Its members, particularly those in Eastern Europe, are worried about Russia's offensive actions in the region and their impact on the security landscape. Western European countries, along with the USA, are actively involved in diplomatic efforts to find a suitable peaceful resolution to the conflict. They support the Minsk Agreements and have called for all parties to adhere to the agreed-upon ceasefire and political provisions. Western European countries are concerned about energy security. They are too dependent on Russian natural gas supplies. The conflict has pointed out vulnerabilities related to energy dependence and the necessity to diversify energy sources. There are concerns about cyber attacks and disinformation campaigns. It originated in Russia. It has targeted Western nations and institutions. These raise cyber security threats, and the integrity of democratic processes became important to having a viable and peaceful atmosphere in the region.

The conflict has led to wider geopolitical implications. It has had an impact on the current balance of power in Eastern Europe and affected relations between Western nations and Russia. Further questions, like the future of NATO and the European Union's eastern expansion, have been highlighted by these governments. Western European countries and the USA have raised serious concerns about various dimensions of the Russia-Ukraine war. It has ranged from violations of international law to humanitarian suffering, security challenges, and broader geopolitical consequences. They have been actively engaged in efforts to address these concerns through diplomatic means and sanctions while reaffirming their support for Ukraine's sovereignty and territorial integrity.

Western Economic and Military Aid to Ukraine

Western countries, particularly the USA and European nations, have provided significant economic and military aid to Ukraine, especially in response to the ongoing conflict in eastern Ukraine and Russia's annexation of Crimea. This assistance included supporting Ukraine's defence capabilities, strengthening its economy, and promoting stability in the region.

Non-Lethal Assistance: Western countries, including the USA, have provided non-lethal military aid to Ukraine. It included items such as medical supplies, non-lethal equipment, and humanitarian assistance to support Ukrainian forces. Some Western countries have also given lethal military aid to Ukraine. This includes weapons and ammunition to increase Ukraine's defence capabilities. The USA, in particular, has supplied anti-tank missiles. Western nations have offered military training and advisers to the Ukrainian armed forces. This assistance was intended to promote the professionalism and effectiveness of Ukrainian troops.

Financial Aid: Western countries have given economic assistance to Ukraine to normalise its economy and address fiscal challenges. This has come in the form of loans, grants, or financial guarantees. Western nations have encouraged and supported economic reforms in Ukraine, particularly in areas such as governance, anti-corruption measures, and economic restructuring. These reforms are essential for long-term economic stability.

Humanitarian Aid: Western countries have provided humanitarian assistance. This includes food, medical supplies, and shelter. It was also provided to help alleviate the suffering of civilians affected by the conflict in eastern Ukraine. Western countries have imposed economic sanctions on Russia in response to its actions in Ukraine. The purpose of these sanctions is to apply economic and diplomatic pressure on Russia, and promote a peaceful resolution to the conflict. Besides economic sanctions, Western countries have been engaged in diplomatic efforts to find a viable and peaceful resolution to the conflict. They have supported initiatives like the Minsk Agreements and even called for a ceasefire and political dialogue. Beyond direct aid, Western countries have cooperated with Ukraine on security matters, including intelligence sharing and cyber security support, to counter threats in the region.

Western aid to Ukraine is a clear reflection of the international community's commitment to Ukraine's territorial integrity, sovereignty, and stability. It has fully supported Ukraine's efforts to address the security challenges posed by the ongoing conflict. It has even implemented reforms and developed a more stable and bright future. The nature and extent of this aid will depend on the changing circumstances in the region.

Road to War and Beyond

The Russia-Ukraine war was marked by Russia's annexation of Crimea in 2014 and the ongoing conflict in the Donbas region. It has followed a complex path with significant consequences. The historical relationship between Russia and Ukraine is characterised by shared histories, territorial disputes, and complex dynamics. Ukraine became an independent country in 1991 after the demise of the Soviet Union, but historical legacies and regional differences did not alter the relations between the two countries. The conflict's immediate precursor was the Euromaidan protests in Ukraine, which began in late 2013. These protests were the result of then-President Yanukovych's action to abandon an association agreement with the European Union in favour of closer ties with Russia. The protests led to a broader movement and paved the way for political reforms against corruption.

In February 2014, as the protests intensified, Russia interfered militarily in Crimea, leading to its annexation. This move was widely condemned globally. This marked a turning point in the crisis. Russia's argument was that it was safeguarding the rights of ethnic Russians in Crimea. After Crimea's annexation, pro-Russian separatist movements erupted in eastern Ukraine, particularly in the Donetsk and Luhansk regions. These separatist groups declared independence, leading to a conflict between Ukrainian government forces and the separatist forces. Multiple ceasefire agreements, known as the Minsk Agreements, to end the conflict were finalised. However, these agreements did not bring any positive change, as they were seen as having limited success while sporadic fighting continued.

The conflict has had a severe humanitarian impact, with civilian casualties, displacement, and infrastructure damage. Humanitarian organisations have been involved in providing aid and relief. The conflict has had economic repercussions for both Russia and Ukraine. Ukraine's economy has faced challenges, and Russia has experienced sanctions and economic pressure from Western countries. The conflict has strained Russia's economic relations with Western countries. It has resulted in sanctions and diplomatic isolation. It has also raised questions about the future of NATO and the European Union's eastern expansion. Western countries, particularly the USA and the European Union, have imposed sanctions on Russia in response to its actions in Ukraine. These sanctions have targeted individuals, entities, and sectors of the Russian economy. The post-conflict period will also require reconstruction efforts in eastern Ukraine and reconciliation among affected communities. Diplomatic efforts to resolve the conflict continue, with negotiations involving Ukraine, Russia, and the Organisation for Security and Cooperation in Europe (OSCE). However, reaching a lasting resolution remains challenging. Besides, the conflict has raised security concerns in Europe, with NATO member-countries, particularly those in Eastern Europe, worried about Russia's assertiveness in the region. The Russia-Ukraine war remains an ongoing and complex conflict with far-reaching implications. The solution to war remains uncertain, and the impact of the conflict continues to shape the geopolitics of the region and the wider international landscape.

Global Impact

The Russia-Ukraine war, with its past, present, and future developments, has a significant global impact on both economic and political fronts. The USA and the European Union have imposed economic sanctions on Russia in response to its actions in Ukraine. These sanctions have targeted key sectors of the Russian economy such as finance, energy, and defence, leading to economic challenges for Russia. The conflict has raised concerns about energy security in Europe, where some countries depend heavily on Russian natural gas. Efforts to diversify energy sources and reduce reliance on Russian energy have gained importance. The economic sanctions and counter-sanctions imposed by Russia have disrupted trade flows and had repercussions for global supply chains, impacting international trade and commerce. The conflict has created uncertainty in the investment climate, affecting foreign direct investment in the region. Companies and investors have to assess the risks associated with operating in Ukraine and Russia. The economic consequences of the conflict have influenced global commodity prices, particularly oil and natural gas.

The conflict has increased geopolitical tensions between Russia and Western countries. It has affected diplomatic relations and raised questions about Russia's intentions and ambitions. European security has become important as NATO member-countries in Eastern Europe have enhanced their defence capabilities and shown their readiness to respond to security threats from Russia. The annexation of Crimea had challenged the established norms of international law regarding sovereignty and territorial integrity. It also led to deliberations about the sanctity of borders and state sovereignty. International organisations, including the United Nations and the Organisation for Security and Cooperation in Europe (OSCE), are working to mediate in the conflict. It highlighted the importance of multilateral diplomacy in addressing regional crises. The conflict has led to discussions about the world's balance of power. On the other hand, Russia has tried to assert itself as a major player in international affairs, and, on the other hand, Western countries have responded to these ambitions. The international community is actively participating in humanitarian efforts to alleviate the suffering resulting from the conflict. It included aid to affected populations and support for internally displaced persons. The region has accused Russia of engaging in cyber attacks and disinformation campaigns. It raises concerns about cyber security attacks and the integrity of democratic processes in Western nations.

Role of NATO

Founded in 1949, NATO (North Atlantic Treaty Organization) is a military alliance. Its primary aim was to counter the Soviet Union during the Cold War period. Today, it consists of 30 member-countries from North America and Europe. Russia regarded NATO's push towards eastward expansion as a threat. While Ukraine is not a member of NATO, it has sought closer ties with the alliance, especially following the 2014 annexation of Crimea by Russia. This interest intensified in the light of the conflict in Eastern Ukraine. NATO has not directly intervened militarily in the conflict between Russia and Ukraine. Its involvement has been primarily in the form of political support and military aid. It condemned Russia's actions and provided non-lethal aid and capacity-building assistance to Ukraine.

NATO has increased its presence in Eastern Europe. It conducted military exercises and provided training missions to bolster the defence capabilities of its member-states and partners, including Ukraine. Russia views this as provocative. Beyond political support, NATO has provided Ukraine with substantial non-lethal military aid. This includes secure communications, medical equipment, cyber defence expertise, and trust funds to support various defence and security-related projects. In response to the overall security situation in Eastern Europe, NATO has enhanced its defence and deterrence posture, including the establishment of enhanced Forward Presence battle groups in the Baltic states and Poland. NATO has reaffirmed its open-door policy. This means that Ukraine may join the alliance in the future if it meets the required criteria. However, NATO members cannot agree on when or whether Ukraine should receive membership, making this a contentious issue.

NATO has consistently advocated a peaceful resolution to the conflict. It has even supported various diplomatic efforts, including the Minsk Agreements. While NATO has not been militarily involved in the Russia-Ukraine conflict, its role has been important in terms of political support, capacity-building, and shaping the security setup of Eastern Europe. The alliance has also highlighted the delicate balance of supporting a partner country. It avoided direct military competition with a nuclear-armed state like Russia.

Role of the EU (European Union)

The EU's relationship with both Russia and Ukraine has been strategically important. Ukraine's Western tilt to get closer to the EU was one of the significant factors in the 2014 Euromaidan protests. It eventually led to the ousting of President Viktor Yanukovych. The subsequent annexation of Crimea by Russia and the conflict in Eastern Ukraine increased tensions between the EU and Russia.

In response to the annexation of Crimea and Russia's perceived role in the Eastern Ukraine conflict, the EU imposed a series of sanctions on Russia. These sanctions targeted individuals, entities, and sectors of the Russian economy. Since their introduction, the EU has regularly renewed them, contingent on the situation in Ukraine. The EU has provided Ukraine with substantial financial assistance to stabilise its economy, foster reforms, and support its path towards European integration. This aid has come in various forms, including loans, grants, and technical assistance. In 2014, the EU and Ukraine signed an Association Agreement, which was one of the catalysts for the initial unrest in Ukraine. This agreement seeks to strengthen political and economic ties between the EU and Ukraine, offering Ukraine a path to deeper integration with the European market and regulatory standards.

The EU has played a vital role in diplomatic efforts to resolve the conflict. Key EU member-states, especially Germany and France, were instrumental in the Minsk negotiations, which sought to bring about a ceasefire and peaceful resolution to the conflict. They are still playing an active role in bringing peace and stability to the region while pressing for a ceasefire. The conflict has affected the European energy sector, given the significant amount of natural gas that flows from Russia to the EU through Ukraine. The EU has been keen to diversify its energy sources and ensure that energy disputes between Russia and Ukraine will not disrupt supplies to member-states.

Conclusion

The Russia-Ukraine conflict remains one of the most pressing geopolitical challenges in the post-Cold War era. Since its inception in 2014, political shifts, territorial disputes, and the present state of unresolved tensions have not been resolved. The conflict reflects deeper issues of regional influence, national sovereignty, and international alliances. Looking forward, the pathway to resolution is quite difficult and uncertain. It ranges from diplomatic settlements to prolonged hostilities. The situation underscores the importance of international collaboration, mutual respect for sovereignty, and the pursuit of peaceful solutions in an increasingly interconnected global landscape.

The Russia-Ukraine conflict has underscored the complexities of post-Cold War geopolitics in Eastern Europe. NATO's non-combative role has been crucial in shaping the regional security environment and providing support to Ukraine. The alliance's involvement illustrates the challenges of navigating strategic interests, alliance commitments, and the wider perspective of maintaining global peace and stability. As the situation does not remain stable, the delicate interplay between diplomacy, deterrence, and defence becomes ever more critical. The ongoing dynamics between Russia, Ukraine, and NATO focus on the significance of dialogue and diplomacy while addressing international tensions and seeking sustainable solutions.

REFERENCES

1. Alam, M.K.; Tabash, M.I.; Zillah, M.; Kumar, S. & Anagram, S. (2022). 'The impacts of the Russia–Ukraine invasion on global markets and commodities: a dynamic

connectedness among G7 and BRIC markets.' *Journal of Risk and Financial Management*.

2. Bossman, A.; Gubareva, M.; & Teplova, T. (2023). 'Asymmetric effects of geopolitical risk on major currencies: Russia-Ukraine tensions.' *Finance Research Letters*.
3. Guchua, A.; Zedelashvili, T.; & Giorgadze, G. (2022). 'Geopolitics of the Russia-Ukraine War and Russian Cyber Attacks on Ukraine-Georgia and Expected Threats.'
4. Mahilaj, S. (2023). 'EU and Cooperation in the Russia-Ukraine Conflict: Impacts and Limitations.' *ESI Preprints*.
5. Simons, G. (2022). 'Will the war in Ukraine push the country to join NATO?' *LSE European Politics and Policy* (EUROPP).
6. Taylor, D. Brian. (2021). 'Crisis in Ukraine-Putin's Own Goal: The Invasion of Crimea and Putin's Political Future.' *Foreign Affairs*.
7. Yousaf, I.' Patel, R. & Yarovaya, L. (2022). The reaction of G20+ stock markets to the Russia–Ukraine conflict "black-swan" event: Evidence from event study approach.' *Journal of Behavioural and Experimental Finance*.

10

Russia-Ukraine War: Historical Development and Current Scenario

Arvind Kumar Kushwaha

Introduction

The day was 25 December 1991. On that day, Soviet Russia (USSR–Union of Soviet Socialist Republics) disintegrated and 15 new countries were formed. Ukraine and Russia were also among these 15 countries. Before 1991, Soviet Russia used to lead the communist bloc in the bipolar world order system and it had tremendous competition from the USA. At that time, there was such fierce rivalry between Soviet Russia and America that both the countries came on the verge of war several times. This period from 1945 to 1991 is known as Cold War era. But the capitalist USA was victorious in this race and on 25 December 1991, the USSR was divided into 15 countries. With this, the USA became the leader of the whole world in various ways.

The USSR split into several parts in 1991. Many Russians drank this development like a sip of humiliation, because the Russian Republic was the leader of the 15 republics that were included in the USSR and the splitting was very difficult for him. At that time, the condition of Russia was very weak. It had to bear the downfall of its empire even without wanting to. It remained heartbroken. Even after the disintegration of the USSR, America continued to suppress Russia in different ways. In this order, many factors like geography, global military alliance, world hegemony, global trade, and unseen competition between the USA and other power blocs have created a very severe condition in front the entire world, in the form of the Russia-Ukraine war. On 24 February 2022, war erupted between two countries. More than two years have passed, but war has not ended yet. At present, the Russian annexation of Crimea and parts of four southeast Ukrainian oblasts in 2014 and 2022, respectively has resulted in Russian occupation of more than 18 per cent of Ukrainian territory as of June 2024. In the same manner Ukraine has regained many areas from Russia.

Situation after Disintegration of the USSR

Through the military organization NATO (North Atlantic Treaty Organization) America started persuading the countries separated from the USSR to bring them under its influence. In 1991, 15 countries were formed after separating from the USSR. These are the countries: Armenia, Azerbaijan, Belarus, Estonia, Georgia, Kazakhstan, Kyrgyzstan, Latvia, Lithuania, Moldova, Russia, Tajikistan, Turkmenistan, Ukraine, and Uzbekistan.

In 2004, three countries of these 15—Latvia, Lithuania and Estonia—became members of NATO. This meant that America had now reached Russia's borders because these three countries located in the Baltic region were part of the USSR and had contiguous. Here is very important linkage that there is an agreement between NATO (North Atlantic Treaty Organisation) countries that if any one member-country is attacked, all the other members will consider it an attack on them and will respond jointly with combined military power. There are currently 31 countries in NATO. In this way America started the siege of Russia through NATO. The borders of Ukraine and Russia meet. Ukraine also wanted to join NATO to increase its strength. Taking advantage of its geographical position, Ukraine started demanding from America that it should also be made a member of NATO. Putin was extremely irritated by this step of Ukraine's President Zelenskyy. He sent his army to the Ukraine border. This is the immediate reason for Russia's tension with Ukraine.

In 2014, Putin annexed Crimea, which was part of Ukraine. Crimea is a region located along the Black Sea. It is close to both Ukraine and Russia. Most of the population there speaks Russian. Putin first formed a pro-Russian government there and then sent his army and occupied the area.

The Russian occupation of Crimea put America and NATO in tension. America has understood that if Russia is not stopped, then the independent existence of Ukraine will end. That's why efforts started to integrate Ukraine into NATO. But Putin was opposing it. Actually, Russia has a wide influence in the population of Ukraine. One out of every five people there speaks Russian. There is a cultural influence of Russia there.

If we talk about the eastern part of Ukraine, then the people there consider themselves close to Russia while the people of the west consider themselves closer to Europe. There is a fight for supremacy in the country. The eastern part of Ukraine is adjacent to Russia and here people speak Russian while in the west it is just the opposite. Russian elites justify the merger of the eastern part of Ukraine with Russia by citing this cultural influence.

President Putin first recognized two regions of Ukraine, Luhansk, and Donetsk, as independent countries. Both these regions are located in the same eastern region of Ukraine. Russia encourages separatist forces and openly describes this region as part of the historical republic of Russia citing history and geography. Working on this strategy, on 21 February Vladimir Putin recognized two troubled regions of Ukraine as sovereign nations.

Causes

1. The struggle over Central European territoriality in the post-Cold War era and the desire to revive a glorious Russian past are at the core of the Ukraine crisis.
2. Ukraine and Russia share hundreds of years of cultural, linguistic, and family ties.
3. For many people in Russia and in ethnically Russian parts of Ukraine, the shared heritage of the two countries is an emotional issue that has been exploited for electoral and military purposes.
4. As a part of the Soviet Union, Ukraine was the second most powerful Soviet republic after Russia and held a strategic, economic, and culturally important position.
5. The regional balance of power: Ukraine, being an important buffer

zone between Russia and the West, its bid for NATO membership and Russia's interests in the Black Sea region, as well as protests in Ukraine, are the main reasons for the current conflict.

Current Scenario

1. The conflict is the largest attack by one state on another in Europe since World War II. Along with this, it is the first major conflict after the Balkan conflict in the 1990s.
2. With Russia's invasion of Ukraine, agreements such as the Minsk Protocols of 2014 and the Russia-NATO Act of 1997 have become virtually ineffective.
3. The G-7 countries have strongly condemned Russia's invasion of Ukraine. Sanctions have also been imposed on Russia by the USA, the European Union (EU), the UK, Australia, Canada and Japan in response.
4. China has rejected calling Russia's action on Ukraine an 'aggression' and urged all sides to exercise restraint.
5. India did not join the Western powers in condemning Russia's intervention in Crimea and refrained from making any public statement on the issue.
6. In the present case, India chose to abstain from voting on a US-sponsored UN Security Council resolution that "condemned in the strongest terms" Russia's 'aggression' against Ukraine. On this occasion, India emphasized on the words 'Dialogue' and 'Diplomacy' and said that dialogue is the only way to resolve differences and disputes and expressed 'regret' that the way of diplomacy in this matter was ignored.
7. Apart from India, the United Arab Emirates (UAE) and China also abstained from voting.

Russian Side

1. Russia's view is that NATO expansion violates promises made prior to the disintegration of the Soviet Union that Ukraine's entry into NATO would overcome Russia's threat status and that NATO's strategic posture would provide Russia with a continuing security against danger.

2. The expansion of NATO as a politico-military alliance following the dissolution of the Soviet Union and the Warsaw Pact was a US initiative aimed at containing European ambitions for strategic autonomy and countering Russia's resurgence.
3. The Ukraine crisis was justified by the Russian president on grounds of security interests and protecting the rights of Russians in the former Soviet republics.
4. Russia seeks assurances from the West that Ukraine will never be allowed to join NATO. It currently has the status of a 'partner country' which means it will be allowed to join this military alliance in the future.

Indian Side

1. India abstained on a US-sponsored United Nations Security Council (UNSC) resolution that deplores in the strongest terms Russia's aggression against Ukraine.
2. India abstained from a United Nations General Assembly resolution that censured Russia for its military actions in Ukraine.
3. India also abstained from the IAEA (International Atomic Energy Agency) resolution that was related to safety at four nuclear power stations and a number of nuclear waste sites including Chernobyl as the Russians seized control of them.
4. Condemnation of civilian killings.
5. Abstention from UN votes.

Effect on India

1. The Russia-Ukraine crisis will increase cooking gas, petrol and other fuel costs for Indian homes and businesses. Higher oil prices also increase freight/transportation costs.
2. Tensions arising in the event of prolonged high global oil prices may call into question the credibility of the RBI with respect to inflation projections, while also impacting the government's budgetary calculations, particularly the fiscal deficit.
3. A rise in crude oil prices will increase India's oil import bills and with the rupee already under pressure, gold imports may rise again.

4. India's import of petroleum products from Russia is only a fraction of its total oil import bill and thus can be offset.
5. Exports to Russia account for less than 1 per cent of India's total exports, but exports of pharmaceuticals and tea may face some challenges, while shipments to CIS (Commonwealth of Independent States) countries will also face some difficulty. The increase in freight rates may also make overall exports less competitive.

Conclusion

Russia and India share a 'special and privileged' strategic partnership; simultaneously, India's relations with the West are also strengthening day by day. Additionally, it has friendly connections with Ukraine, one of the top countries for Indian students to study abroad, particularly in the medical profession. Due to this dynamic, India has been pushing all sides to decide to address the continuing situation via diplomacy and discussion. India has so far refrained from voting against Russia in both the UN Security Council and the UN General Assembly, but has endorsed the request for 'immediate ceasefire' made by the world community.

A key result of the Russia-Ukraine war is the further development of relations between Russia and China in the latter's rivalry with the USA. Russian economic decline and isolation from the Western economies would drive the country farther towards China, indicating severe repercussions for India. Russia would like China and India to have cordial relationship. But the deep mistrust that divides China and India makes that unlikely. China is more tightly connected to Russia as compared to India, literally by pipelines and railways, but also possesses economic and technological strengths that India lacks. There is little doubt that China and Russia share a common adversary, the USA, making Beijing a more reliable partner.

China's strengthening of ties with Russia may motivate it to aggressively advance its interests in South Asia. Also, that may alter the balance of power between China and India and increase regional tensions. India has attempted to address this threat by fostering closer ties with countries like Australia, Japan, and the USA, among others.

But India's embrace of the West has been relatively sluggish. However, India could wish to quicken the pace given how close the Russian-Ukrainian war has pushed China and Russia nearer to each other.

At present (June 2024), both countries have lost their major resources during this war. Any war brings many problems and opportunities. Here the problem is how will this war end because it creates many difficulties in front of the world in various ways. It has changed the scenario of present threats. It teaches us that physical clashes between two countries are not only two-way affairs but they could be escalated in chain reaction, and the chain reaction may be direct or indirect. In the G-20 summit, India and most the world's countries raised the Russian-Ukraine issue, but due to some inevitable reasons a proper and peaceful solution on this issue could not be worked out. Currently Russia and Ukraine are attacking each other. Its effect is being seen not only on the common man but also on our environment. Along with the G-20, we have to end this war as soon as possible; only after that will there be peace once again in whole world.

REFERENCES

1. Saini, M.; Yadav, M.; Aggarwal, V. & Kumar, M. (2023). 'All weather friends: How did the Russia-Ukraine war impact Indian stock markets.' *International Journal of Diplomacy and Economy*, 9(1), 93. https://doi.org/10.1504/ijdipe.2023.128806
2. Jargin, S. (2023). The Conflict in Ukraine: An Update. SSRN Electronic Journal. https://doi.org/10.2139/ssrn.4344546
3. Flockhart, T. & Korosteleva, E.A. (24 June 2022). 'War in Ukraine: Putin and the multi-order world.' *Contemporary Security Policy*, 43(3), 466–481, https://doi.org/10.1080/13523260.2022.2091591
4. Doyle, M.W. (27 June 2023). 'Cold Peace: Avoiding the New Cold War.'
5. Kuzio, T.; Zhuk, S.I. & D'Anieri, P. (eds.). (28 January 2022). *Ukraine's Outpost: Dnipropetrovsk and the Russian-Ukrainian War.*
6. Kuzio, T. & D'Anieri, P. (28 May 2018). *The Sources of Russia's Great Power Politics: Ukraine and the Challenge to the European Order.*
7. The Russo-Ukrainian War by Serhii Plokhy review—deeply personal study of 'an old-fashioned imperial war.' (30 April 2023), *The Guardian*. https://www.theguardian.com/books/2023/apr/30/the-russo-ukrainian-war-by-serhii-plokhy-review
8. NATO-Russia relations: the facts. (n.d.). Retrieved 23 April 2023, from https://www.nato.int/cps/en/natohq/topics_111767.htm
9. Luthra, G. (n.d.). 'The Russia-Ukraine Conflict and Sanctions: An Assessment of the Economic and Political Impacts', ORF. ORF. https://www.orfonline.org/research/the-russia-ukraine-conflict-and-sanctions/

11

In the Nexus of Power: Analyzing Geopolitical, Geo-Strategic, and Geo-economic Forces in the Russia-Ukraine War

Mohammad Afsar Alam and Md. Abusaad

Introduction

Applying a geo-cultural framework allows one to better understand the nature of the interaction between the two nations. Nevertheless, the degree of mutual mistrust between these two nations plummeted to an alarmingly low point, leading to the current scenario, particularly after 2004. It is undeniable that Russia's military power is far greater than Ukraine's. Even though it has sought membership in the military alliance since 2008, Kiev is still not a part of NATO, which might have offered effective protection. That Russia attacked Ukraine so easily is thus not surprising. Moscow was especially concerned about NATO's further expansion in the wake of Ukraine's 2004 Colour Revolution, although this is now mostly seen as a source of war between the two countries. According to Bharat *Shakti* (31 January 2023), here is where the fighting between the two Slavic brothers began, which in turn led to the current strategic deadlock.

Recall that in the mid-1990s, the Partnership for Peace (PfP) Programme was established by NATO, and that both Russia and Ukraine were members. But starting in 2000, under Vladimir Putin's leadership, Russia's image shifted from one of timidity under Boris Yeltsin to one of assertiveness. Russian President Vladimir Putin's administration made measures to limit NATO's growth because

Moscow saw the alliance's liberal principles—including democracy, human rights, and others—as at odds with its own culture. The core of the war is the Ukrainian leadership's increasing closeness to NATO. The frequent naval manoeuvres, particularly in the Black Sea, and the stationing of NATO soldiers also caused concern among Russian leaders. In a similar vein, Russia has been aggressively pursuing its Greater Eurasian policy goals for some time now, particularly in the post-Soviet region. Russia aspires to become a dominant maritime force by consolidating its influence in the Black Sea and the Mediterranean Sea, according to this policy. The strategically vital maritime route will be pushed under Moscow's authority as a result. So, to make a strong statement to NATO, Russia picked Ukraine as its target (Bharat *Shakti*, 31 January 2023).

The level of Western intervention in the ongoing crisis is another issue that comes to light. Regarding this matter, it should be noted that many sources indicate that France has pledged to provide weapons to Ukraine and that the USA has sent naval vessels to neutralize Russia. According to reports, NATO has also maintained a reserve of soldiers ready to respond to any future events. Russia has already conquered a large portion of Ukrainian territory; thus this military aid will not help them much right now. Any more escalation on either side will have the unfortunate consequence of endangering innocent people. The situation might worsen to the point that World War III breaks out as a result of this (Bharat Shakti, 31 January 2023).

European energy security will also feel the effects of the current crisis to a greater extent. Russia has always sold its electricity to Europe. According to Eurostat, Russia supplies the European Union with almost 25 per cent of its oil and roughly 45 per cent of its gas. There has already been disruption to this energy supply chain as a result of the war. Not only that, the current war has its epicentre in the Black Sea, which means it will have repercussions for the transportation of Caspian gas and oil along this route. The global energy market may be greatly affected by this. Since Russia's economy is heavily dependent on energy exports to Europe, Western sanctions are expected to have a significant negative impact on Moscow's interests. Given this backdrop, the potential imposition of more sanctions by Western nations might render Russia's economy completely inoperable. According to sources, the ruble's value is falling precipitously; if this trend continues, the challenge facing Russia's policymakers will be enormous. Also, Russia will be increasingly exposed as its reliance on China increases. Actually, Moscow may find itself capitulating to Beijing's demands. In contrast, India has both opportunities and challenges in the geopolitical landscape that has emerged as a result of the war between Russia and Ukraine. India would feel the effects of the global increase in petrol and oil prices. Investments made by India in Russia, especially in the energy and mineral industries, would be severely impacted by Western sanctions. Russia may potentially pose difficulties for India's military industry when it comes to acquiring equipment. To sum up, there may be some significant obstacles that India's economic recovery faces (*The Economic Times*, 1 March 2022).

Objectives of this Study

This study has three-fold objectives.

(a) To examine the geopolitical, geostrategic and geo-economic impulsions of the Russia-Ukraine war.

(b) To find out the extent of the spill over effect on neighbouring European countries, and

(c) To analyze the evolving Middle East geopolitical scene.

The Approach to Research

The study is descriptive in nature and uses secondary sources for its data. The majority of the information came from books, both published and unpublished, periodicals, and online sources. Besides, we consulted a number of research papers published in scholarly publications on a national and worldwide scale, as well as newspaper stories written by relevant specialists.

Discussions

Not only has the war between Russia and Ukraine changed global geopolitics and the international system, it has also reshaped political blocs in significant ways. This is due to the fact that the nature of the war is multi-faceted, including not just political violence between Russia and Ukraine but also Russia, the USA, and Europe. The USA is using the crisis between Russia and Ukraine as a means to strengthen and preserve its worldwide hegemony while simultaneously attempting to restructure and reorganize its system of global allies. When asked about the war between Russia and Ukraine, the attitudes of other nations to the USA and Russia have been all over the map. Because they did not follow American leadership or take a stand between Russia and the USA, US friends in the developing world—Central Asia, South Asia, and the Middle East—mostly reflect the relative fall of the West and the USA in global affairs (Zhongmin Liu and Meng Shu, June 2023).

Global Political Consequences

We are staring down the nose of a protracted battle of attrition that might eventually lead to geopolitical turmoil and circumstances beyond the control of even the most powerful nation, the USA. It stands to reason that it and the Western allies in NATO will maintain their full support for Ukraine in all spheres, including but not limited to military, economics, diplomacy, intelligence sharing, information warfare (or global perception management), and psychology. While doing so, they are testing boundaries that may erupt at any moment, raising the risk of escalation in terms of the length of the fight (a nuclear firestorm) and attracting other countries, particularly NATO, to side with either side. Overall, the Middle East has benefited from a more diverse and balanced influence of big powers outside the area and from nations in the region gaining greater autonomy (Liu, 2022a). There has been little disruptive influence on Middle Eastern regional dynamics from the Russia-Ukraine war. The opposite is true: there has almost never been a trend towards greater autonomy in Middle Eastern foreign relations. Regarding the game between the USA and Russia, most Middle Eastern nations have opted to stay neutral (Zhang, 2022; She, 2022; Yang, 2022; Wu, 2022).

To further establish its dominance in Eurasia, Turkey used the crisis as an opportunity to negotiate between all sides, particularly on the transportation of food and the security of the Black Sea waterway. Turkey's diplomatic stance is well-rounded since the country values protecting its own interests and recognizes the multi-faceted historical roots of the crisis between Russia and Ukraine. This is a product of Turkey's diverse and complicated identity, as well as efforts to achieve strategic autonomy and maintain political harmony among the country's many groups (Yang, 2022).

Israel has been quite generous with humanitarian aid to Ukraine, but it has turned down a request for offensive weaponry. Israel has sought to satisfy Ukraine's expectations for political assistance and has shown concern about the situation in Ukraine on several diplomatic occasions (Wu, 2022).

Among the world's most Jewish nations, Ukraine stands out. The majority of Ukraine's Jewish population—anywhere from 200,000 to 400,000—lives in the cities of Kiev, Dnipro, Kharkov, and Odessa (Dashefsky and Shekin, 2022). While mediating the dispute between Russia and Ukraine, the Israeli government has regularly contacted and coordinated with Russia to ensure the safety of Jewish communities in Ukraine, as well as Diaspora Jews. Israel has changed its policy in response to mounting pressure from the West and the USA. For example, it now sanctions Russia with the West and supplies defence weaponry and equipment to Ukraine (Wu, 2022).

Already, the war's effects on the world economy have been severe and negative, particularly in the South of the globe. A stable security environment and the interests of other countries are being sacrificed in order for non-conformist authoritarian and autocratic governments to pursue their own national objectives. Concerns of a new Cold War, an energy catastrophe, right-wing expansionism, a decrease in globalization and multilateralism, and the emergence of the 'My Nation First' strategy are heightened by China's adventurism and the USA's overreaction. Because of this, many countries have decided to remain neutral on strategic or moral grounds so that they are not entangled in the political games played by either side. This is particularly true of smaller and poorer states.

The West's ultimate goal is to weaken Russia's CNP to the point that it cannot exert its influence in Europe and beyond. To get to that point, Russia must suffer a defeat and Putin must be removed from office. So far, the repercussions have been enormous and terrible: as many as six million Ukrainians have fled their homes, over a million have died in the war, Ukraine's vital infrastructure has been destroyed, the country's economy has been in free fall, and a stronger, more united

Europe has banded together to confront Russia, all the while cutting off its energy and product supplies to further escalate the situation.

During his trip to Israel, Palestine, and Saudi Arabia in July 2022, President Biden attended the Security and Development Summit. The summit brought together heads of state from six Gulf Cooperation Council member-states—Saudi Arabia, the United Arab Emirates, Oman, Qatar, Kuwait, and Bahrain—as well as the USA, Egypt, Jordan, and Iraq. The summit's primary objective was to rally support from Middle Eastern nations in favour of US sanctions and war with Russia. But nothing came out of Biden's Middle Eastern tour. He was unsuccessful in his attempts to forge a regional coalition opposed to Russia and Iran, and he was also unsuccessful in winning over Saudi Arabia and other supporters in the battle. To sum up, "the lack of predictable policy direction and credible political commitment" (She, 2022) is more to blame than the USA's dwindling absolute physical strength for its waning influence in the Middle East.

The Information War is Being Won by the West and Ukraine

The Russian government has kept the international community in the dark about its position, the reasons for its disastrous war, and the impact of sanctions on Russia's economy. The majority of the information comes from the Western media and the internet, which have drawn their conclusions based on what should have been the Russian point of view. It isn't easy to find good content coming out of Russia, and this piece focuses on the Russian viewpoint without passing judgement. 'The Mother of All Information and Psychological Wars,' which the world's largest digital and IT companies have joined in promoting, has even them bolstering their narrative. They are now leading in this crucial area of information.

Russia's Red Lines: Life-Challenging Worries

Russia has long seen Ukraine's membership in NATO as 'The Mother of Red Lines,' according to the available information and the opinions of most military and geopolitical specialists. Everyone in Russia, from government officials to regular citizens, sees this as a matter of life and death that threatens Russia's proper position in international affairs. Despite its name change to the Soviet Union, Russia remained a world power with the greatest nuclear arsenal for hundreds of years, until about 20 years ago. It is logical to assume that any Russian leader other than Putin would have attacked Ukraine earlier, before it became a fait accompli and a NATO member.

The Resilience of the Russian People and Their Widespread Support

Despite what you may expect from Western media, Russia's economy, leadership, and army have all managed to stay afloat, and the country is stronger than many had anticipated. For the most part, Putin's confidence and mystique remain intact in his encounters with the media and public addresses. Repetition of losses would demoralize the Russian army, and Russia certainly does not have the widespread and strong backing that Ukraine enjoys from its friends and allies. It has endured, gained wisdom, and strengthened its defensive positions by reducing the length of its front line and logistic tail. Its economy has weathered the storm, albeit it will gradually decline; as of now, it is down 3 per cent, which is much less than what some had anticipated. The country's economy and financial system have shown to be stable and long-term viable. The use of economic sanctions and pressure has historically been ineffective in ending of war. Russia's military apparatus is still well-funded and -equipped, but it faces the same shortcomings as the West and Ukraine, with less access to vital and sensitive equipment and ammunition.

The majority of Russians still back the Russian government and refuse to admit defeat, which the West reluctantly accepts, given the current climate of hyper-nationalism. The average Russian has heard Putin's dire warning that sanctions imposed by the West are an attempt to subdue the Russian people. Many people think it's worth fighting for Crimea and Sevastopol, and Putin is still the one who guarantees Russian stability and sovereignty.

A loss and Putin's ouster is a worst-case scenario that many oligarchs and even the average Russian fear would cause Russia to collapse. For this reason, the fate of Russia hangs in the balance of the war.

Throughout his career, Putin has made statements such as, "We always considered the Ukrainian people as brotherly, and I still think so," and, "What's going on is certainly a tragedy, but it's not a result of our policy." Support for Putin might swiftly shift against him as casualties mount and loss becomes more certain, as is typical of authoritarian governments. Putin knows full well what a loss would mean for Russia and for himself.

The resilience of the Russian army will be put to the test over the current winter and spring, but specialists in the field do not foresee its disintegration. To alter this evaluation, a great deal more backtracking and defeats would be required. As soon as the newly mobilized soldiers are available, the Ukrainians are threatening an attack in the spring. At this point, it is just conjecture as to what Putin's operational goals could be. As soon as he takes office, Russian military commander Sergei Gerasimov will be prepared to confront Ukrainian counteroffensives and work towards a strategic goal (Kyiv, strengthening the land corridor to Crimea, consolidating the Eastern and Southern fronts, and establishing genuine government institutions).

Russia will be much more empowered to continue fighting under the present US and NATO approach

The goal of the West's leaders, including President Biden and his friends, has long been to defang Russia. In addition to the previously mentioned criteria, they engaged in a plethora of unprincipled hypocritical actions both before and during the war. They have solidified their objectives by freezing nearly 300 billion rubles worth of Russian funds. Russia is neither a 'terrorist state' nor an 'imperialist nation,' according to Russians who have access to Western media online. Rallying around the flag is seen as the best course of action by both Russian elites and ordinary Russians. The Russian people's evident will to engage in hostilities with even the last Ukrainian just serves to reinforce their belief that the war will go on indefinitely until Russia is vanquished.

Hints for Success Coming out of Russia

The impact of foreign powers on regional dynamics in the Middle East were isomorphic with the US unipolar international order from the Cold War era to the so-called Arab Spring of 2011. In other words, the USA was the undisputed leader in Middle Eastern affairs throughout this time. But ever since Arab Spring, there have been significant and beneficial shifts in the impact of foreign countries on the Middle East. The trend is now multi-polar, rather than US-centric. This shift is mostly due to the fact that the US' foreign and security policies now prioritize the rivalry between great powers (Ulbertson et al., 2022). Because of this, the USA has deliberately distanced itself from the Middle East, while other rising powers like Russia, China, and India have sought to increase their influence there. The growth of the forces of major extraterritorial powers influencing the Middle East towards a pluralistic balance has been accelerated since the beginning of the Russia-Ukraine war as a result of the intensification of the strategic game between the USA and Russia surrounding Ukraine. As a result, neither side has been able or willing to affect the region strategically.

To begin, the USA is no longer able or willing to exert its hitherto dominant influence in the Middle East. The impacts of foreign powers on regional dynamics in the Middle East were isomorphic with the US unipolar world order from the Cold War's conclusion until the 2008 financial crisis hit. This means that the USA played the role of undisputed leader in Middle Eastern affairs. As a result of the global shift in power and the effects of the war on terror in Iraq and Afghanistan, the USA came to terms with the fact that it had lost some of its national might during the 2008 financial catastrophe (Haass et al., 2008). As a result, the US' worldwide policy has long aimed to withdraw from the Middle East, with a focus on countering the strategic rivalry of big powers rather than fighting terrorism there. Despite clear variations in particular practices, this is a constant strategy shift from the Obama to the Trump and Biden administrations.

The USA is reportedly in a long-term decline and faces the serious threat of losing control of the global financial network, according to TASS, which cites French analyst Emmanuel Todd. As a result, the USA will be pushing for more power in the so-called 'original protectorates' it gained during WWII. It has also made it a priority to limit the development of its rivals, China and Russia.

For Todd, the battle "has become existential even for the USA," which is an intriguing addition. Russia will be the one to break them out of the crisis. They just won't release. Because of this, the battle has no clear endpoint and will inevitably lead to the defeat of one side or the other.

Putin made a solemn pledge on 18 January to keep running his campaign until Russia achieved its objectives. The chief of defence's announcement marked the beginning of military reforms, which included plans to raise the force size from one million to 1.5 million. Among them would be 695,000 contract troops who volunteered. Turkey's preparedness to mediate a solution in the Ukrainian war has been emphasized by TASS and President Erdogan on many occasions.

Important details of the 2022 war as seen via Meduza, a Riga-based independent news outlet, and other sources (including daily coverage by TASS and television networks RT, Moscow, and NTV).

While it's true that the battle narrative might be managed, it's also interesting to note that reports are open about the Russian military's mistakes, defeats, and reverses, which is in line with what the West has to say. Figure 1 shows the major inputs on the war in 2022.

Figure 1: Major Inputs on the War During 2022

Source: Institute for the Study of War (21.00 GMT, 13 November)

The Present Strategy of Russia

Given the harsh Western sanctions that both Russia and Iran are now experiencing, the crisis between Russia and Ukraine has created an ideal environment for a potential alliance between Russia and Iran. Iran reinforced its strategic partnership with Russia and refrained from taking part in the sanctions imposed on Russia as a result of the crisis between Russia and Ukraine. Russia and Iran have steadily increased their collaboration since the war began in many areas, including politics, diplomacy, military, economy, finance, energy, and transportation. They are still in the process of negotiating a long-term collaboration pact, but they have already inked an energy cooperation deal worth around $ 40 billion. Vladimir Putin's visit to Iran in July 2022 demonstrated the significance of Iran to Russia (Tang, 2022).

Now that it has captured territory, Moscow seems to have settled on a basic military goal: to hang on to it. To achieve this goal, you might use two different military tactics. First, use more strategic tactics, like withdrawing from Kharkiv, by erecting tight, thick defences and ensuring that the Ukrainians suffer heavy losses whenever they attempt to reclaim ground. The second strategy involves taking advantage of the weak points in Ukraine's infrastructure, particularly its electrical systems, which will have a negative impact on Ukrainian society, divide the application of force, and increase costs for allies. The possibility of intentional attacks is not eliminated.

In 2023, which side will be more successful?

Because of its entire reliance on the Western powers, Ukraine will have a much more difficult time reclaiming lost territory; parties will increase their mobilization of troops and reduce their ammunition stockpiles. Until sanctions progressively weaken Russia's economic and military might and the West maintains its backing for Ukraine, the latter will retain the upper hand.

Moving Forward When Reasonableness Wins Out

At this time, there are no plans to terminate military operations or enter into negotiations from any side, including the West. The Ukrainian people's desire to reclaim their homeland and dignity is understandable. Some have even suggested retaking Crimea, which would send a strong message to Russia, in the hope of establishing a permanent peace agreement. Meanwhile, Putin and Russia's very survival depend on the war's conclusion. Russia has established a more compact defensive line west of the Dnieper and is therefore more receptive to negotiations than the other side. The discussions seem to be lacking a beginning point. A protracted, grinding war along a line of control that neither party is willing to accept is expected to occur in 2023.

A Schematic Necessitating Diplomacy from All Parties

At this time, no clear geopolitical strategy is in place. The big countries should create a long-term plan that includes neutral India, which can reach out to Russia and Ukraine for support. Given that neither side can win the war or accomplish its strategic goals, the other side has to hear about the dangers of keeping fighting. Russia's economy will continue to decline, and the country will become more reliant on China. Discontent inside Russia is possible as a result of the inevitable decline in the country's CNP and influence.

After a peace deal with Ukraine, the Russian people, oligarchs, and Putin need to know that their country's sovereignty and integrity will be upheld, that the West will not try to change their regime, that sanctions will be lifted, that their frozen reserves will be available, and that important security lines will not be crossed. Offering Russia to be a component of Europe's security architecture other than NATO might be considered, as far-fetched as that may seem.

Getting Ukraine to sit down and negotiate is a wholly different ball game. As vengeance for Ukraine and to coerce Russia into submission, Zelenskyy proposes reclaiming all territories, including Crimea. Since the West's war-fighting reserves and economic troubles are fading, there is no guarantee that they will continue to help Ukraine under such an absolutist attitude, and Ukraine must be forced to realize this. A nuclear holocaust or other unfathomable disaster may result in an assault on Crimea. Leaving a contentious issue for future talks is often the best course of action. Given Russia's longing for global integration, a deal may even inspire its people to overthrow their current government and end the war.

Battle of Attrition Is Likely to Occur!

A road map has been proposed, but given the current state of affairs and geopolitical realities, it seems unlikely that a ceasefire or withdrawal would be achieved via discussions at this time. Everyone must be ready for a protracted war. Even while NATO members are wary of providing powerful, long-range military equipment like Germany's Leopard tanks, the West must maintain its support for Ukraine and make sure there is no geographical escalation, which is now a very real possibility. It is truly a dreadful standoff.

One or both parties will eventually have no choice but to compromise. Russia has experience with frozen wars (in places like Georgia and Moldova as well as Syria and Sudan) and sieges (in places like Stalingrad). Even if a regime transition were to happen, the Russian people would likely see the new leader as being much like the old one—if not worse. It is very possible that World War III is about to break out. The fact that all parties have kept in touch is the only hope.

Conclusion

The war in Ukraine has left no clear victor. It reveals both the greatest and worst aspects of human nature, but in the end, it destroys confidence, teamwork, and the capacity to address global problems. One of the guarantors acts in a way that goes against international law and global standards. The world will have to pay a heavy price for chaos, scarcity, and devastation. No matter what happens, Russia is not going anywhere. Our task now is to reduce losses as much as possible, find common ground without sacrificing our principles, and stop war in a way that benefits everyone.

There are a lot of unknowns and complicated factors that make war predictions in Ukraine difficult. However, everyone involved should be compelled to negotiate a practical compromise after seeing the destabilizing consequences of protracted and very damaging war. Providing stability to Ukraine and hope for Russia's future are two sides of the same coin. It would be more prudent for the West to provide criteria and parameters for starting discussions rather than reacting to recent moves by Moscow and Kyiv or wishing for Putin's impending demise. India seems to be in a prime position to spearhead the peace process, thanks to its strong international profile and outreach to allies like Russia, Ukraine, the USA, and NATO.

REFERENCES

1. Liu Zhongmin. 'Chonggou zhong de zhongdong diqu geju: yinglai heping fazhan "xinqixiang"?' (Reconstructing the Middle East: Ushering in a 'New Climate' of Peaceful Development?), *World Affairs* (2022a), 18:14–19.

2. Zhang Yuan. 'E'wu chongtu yu yilang weichi zhongdong diqu junshi de duiwai xingwei'. (Russia–Ukraine Conflict and Iran's Diplomatic Behaviour of Maintaining the Balance of Power in the Middle East Region), *Arab World Studies* (2022), 5:42–57.
3. Yang Chen. 'Tu'erqi zai e'wu Chongtu de pingheng waijiao: biaoxian, dongyin ji yingxiang'. (Turkey's Balanced Diplomacy in Russia–Ukraine Conflict: Responses, Motivations, and Implications), *Arab World Studies,* (2022), 5:77–94.
4. Wu Shiyao. 'Yiselie jieru e'wu chongtu de dongji, jucuo ji yingxiang'. (Israel's Intervention in Russia–Ukraine Conflict: Motivations, Measures and Impact), *Arab World Studies.* (2022), 5:95–116.
5. She Gangzheng. Xinxing. '"zhongjiandidai": e'wu chongtuzhong de a'labo guojia. (New "Intermediate Zone": Arab Countries Amid the Ukraine War) *Arab World Studies.* (2022); 5:58–76.
6. Dashefsky Arnold & Shekin Ira M., (eds.), *American Jewish Year Book 2020,* New York: Springer Publishing, (2022).
7. Ulbertson Shelly, Shatz Howard J. & Stewart Stephanie. *Renewing U.S. security policy in the Middle East,* Santa Monica: RAND Corporation, (2022).
8. Haass Richard N.; Martin Indyk & Gary Samore. *Restoring the balance: A middle east strategy for the next president,* Brookings Institution Press, (2008).
9. Tang Zhichao. 'Waiyi yu tuwei: wukelan weiji shengji dui zhongdong de yingxiang, (Spill over and Breakthrough: The Impact of the Escalation of Ukraine Crisis on the Middle East), *Russian, East European Camp; Central Asian Studies,* (2022), 5:75.
10. *The Economic Times,* by Nalin Kumar Mohapatra, 1 March 2022.
11. *Bharat Shakti,* by Lt. Gen. P.R. Kumar (retd.), 31 January 2023
12. Zhongmin Liu and Meng Shu. *The Russia–Ukraine conflict and the changing geopolitical landscape in the Middle East,* Springer Nature, (2023), pp. 1-14.

12

Geo-Political, Geo-Strategic, and Geo-Economic Compulsions of the Russia-Ukraine War

Prachi Kushwaha

Introduction

The Russia-Ukraine war is a complex and multifaceted conflict with deep-rooted geo-political, geo-strategic, and geo-economic compulsion. At its core, the conflict revolves around historical, cultural, and territorial factors that have fuelled tensions between the two nations for decades. This article will delve into the key drivers behind the conflict, analyzing the geopolitical ambitions, geostrategic considerations, and geo-economic interests that have contributed to the outbreak and continuation of this war.

Geopolitically, the Russia-Ukraine war can be seen as a manifestation of Russia's desire to reassert its influence over its former Soviet territories. The annexation of Crimea in 2014 demonstrated Moscow's intent to maintain control over regions it perceives as crucial to its security and sphere of influence. The Black Sea region, of which Crimea is a part, holds immense strategic importance due to its proximity to crucial energy transit routes and its potential to provide Russia with a warm-water port for its naval fleet. This geopolitical ambition reflects Russia's aspiration to consolidate power and prevent NATO's expansion into what it considers its traditional sphere of influence.

From a geostrategic standpoint, the conflict is influenced by the broader struggle for regional dominance between Russia and Western powers, particularly the USA and the European Union. Ukraine's efforts to align itself with the West through aspirations for EU and NATO membership have been met with strong opposition from Russia, which views such integration as a direct threat to its strategic interests. The war serves as a battleground for these competing visions of regional order, with both sides seeking to secure allies and weaken adversaries in a bid to shape the political and security landscape of Eastern Europe.

Geo-economic considerations further complicate the conflict. Ukraine holds significance as a transit route for Russian natural gas exports to Europe, which provides Moscow with substantial economic leverage over its neighbours. By disrupting energy supplies through conflict or geopolitical manoeuvring, Russia can exert pressure on European countries heavily dependent on Russian gas imports. Additionally, control over Ukraine's fertile agricultural lands and industrial sectors could bolster Russia's economic strength, further incentivizing its involvement in the conflict.

Moreover, the war created intricate energy dynamics in the region. The annexation of Crimea granted Russia control over offshore oil and gas reserves in the Black Sea, potentially enhancing its energy security and reducing dependence on foreign suppliers. This new-found energy wealth contributes to Russia's overall geo-economic leverage, allowing it to wield influence over both its immediate neighbours and global energy markets. The Russia-Ukraine war is a manifestation of complex and intertwined geopolitical, geostrategic, and geo-economic considerations. Russia's desire to maintain its influence over former Soviet territories, its struggle for regional dominance against Western powers, and its pursuit of economic advantages, all contribute to the conflict's perpetuation. The war serves as a stark reminder of how these interlocking factors can shape the course of international relations and security dynamics. As the conflict continues to evolve, understanding these compulsion factors is crucial for comprehending the broader implications of this protracted and multifaceted struggle.

Geopolitical Dynamics

The Russia-Ukraine conflict has deep historical and geopolitical roots that have shaped its dynamics over time. The origins of the dispute can be traced back to the medieval era, but modern tensions escalated in the aftermath of the Soviet Union's dissolution in 1991. The conflict revolves around issues of sovereignty, ethnic identity, economic interests, and strategic power struggles.

Historical Context (1500-1991): The historical backdrop of the Russia-Ukraine conflict dates back centuries, as both territories were historically intertwined due to their proximity and shared cultural elements. Kyivan Rus, a medieval state centred in present-day Ukraine, played a crucial role in shaping the cultural and linguistic heritage of both nations. However, over the centuries, various empires exerted control over the region, leading to political divisions and ethno- linguistic distinctions.

Post-Soviet Era (1991-2014): The dissolution of the Soviet Union in 1991 marked a turning point, granting Ukraine independence. The newly-formed nation sought to assert its sovereignty and pursue democratic reforms. However, Russia remained influential in Ukrainian affairs, particularly in Crimea and Eastern Ukraine, where Russian-speaking populations were concentrated. The 2004 Orange Revolution and the 2014 Euromaiden protests further highlighted Ukraine's struggle for self-determination and closer ties with the West.

Annexation of Crimea and Eastern Conflict (2014-Present): Tensions escalated dramatically in 2014 when Russia annexed Crimea following a disputed referendum. This move was met with international condemnation and sanctions against Russia. Simultaneously, a pro-Russian separatist movement emerged in Eastern Ukraine, leading to violent clashes. Russia was accused of providing military support to these separatists, which intensified the conflict and finally culminated in the outbreak of war in February 2022.

Geopolitical Factors

1. **Ethnic and Cultural Divides:** Ukraine's diverse population, with ethnic Russians in the east and Ukrainians in the west, plays a crucial role. Russia justifies its actions by asserting its responsibility to protect Russian speakers and ethnic Russians in Ukraine, while Ukraine seeks to maintain its territorial integrity.
2. **Energy Dependency:** The transit of Russian natural gas through

Ukraine gives Russia leverage over its neighbour. Disputes over gas prices and supply have strained their relationship, with Ukraine seeking to reduce its energy dependency on Russia.

3. **NATO and EU Aspirations:** Ukraine's desire to join NATO and the European Union has fuelled tensions. Russia views Western integration as a threat to its sphere of influence and has opposed these aspirations.

4. **Strategic Importance:** The Black Sea region, including Crimea, holds strategic significance due to its naval access and energy resources. Russia's annexation of Crimea bolstered its military presence in the region, alarming neighbouring countries and the international community.

5. **International Response:** The international community, including the USA and European Union, condemned Russia's actions and imposed sanctions. Diplomatic efforts, including the Minsk agreements, aimed to resolve the conflict, but implementation has been challenging due to the ongoing hostilities.

6. **Humanitarian Impact:** The conflict has had a devastating impact on civilians, displacing thousands and causing humanitarian crises. Both sides have been accused of human rights abuses and war crimes.

7. **Path to Resolution:** Resolving the Russia-Ukraine conflict requires a comprehensive approach that addresses the concerns of both nations. Diplomatic negotiations, respect for international law and efforts to rebuild trust are crucial. International mediation and pressure can play a significant role in achieving a peaceful solution.

Geostrategic Imperatives

The Russia-Ukraine conflict is a complex geopolitical issue rooted in historical, cultural and strategic factors. The war's geostrategic imperatives can be summarized in the following key points:

1. **Energy Dependency:** Ukraine's role as a transit country for Russian natural gas pipelines to Europe has provided it with leverage but also made it vulnerable to Russian influence. Russia seeks to maintain control over European energy routes to maintain its dominance in the region.

2. **NATO and EU Expansion:** The potential inclusion of Ukraine in Western alliances, like NATO and the EU, is seen as a threat by Russia. It fears encirclement and the loss of influence over a neighbouring state. The conflict serves as a means to prevent Ukraine's westward integration.
3. **Military and Naval Access:** The war in Ukraine allows Russia to maintain or expand its military presence in Crimea and gain control over key naval facilities in the Black Sea. This enhances Russia's power projection capabilities and bolsters its regional dominance.
4. **Cultural and Linguistic Ties:** Russia emphasizes the shared cultural and linguistic ties between Russians and Ukrainians to justify its intervention. It frames its actions as protecting ethnic Russians in Ukraine, particularly in the eastern regions.
5. **National Identity and Sovereignty:** For Ukraine, the conflict is a struggle to assert its sovereignty and define its national identity separate from Russia. It seeks to strengthen its ties with the West to move away from Russia's sphere of influence.
6. **Buffer Zone and Security:** Russia views Ukraine as a buffer between itself and NATO-aligned countries. A Ukraine under Russian influence would reduce the threat of NATO expansion closer to Russian borders.
7. **Global Standing and Prestige:** The conflict serves as a way for Russia to showcase its military capabilities and assert itself as a global player. It aims to demonstrate its ability to challenge Western powers and protect its perceived interests but after a year of war, Russia has failed to achieve the desired results.
8. **Domestic Politics:** The Russians government uses the conflict to bolster its domestic popularity by tapping into nationalist sentiments and distracting from internal issues. It presents itself as a defender of Russian interests against perceived Western aggression.
9. **Economic Interests:** Control over strategic resources and economic interests in the region, such as access to the Black Sea and agricultural land also contribute to Russia's motivations.

Geo-economic Considerations

The Russia-Ukraine conflict is a complex and multifaceted issue that has significant geo-economic implications. This conflict, which escalated with Russia's annexation of Crimea in 2014 and its subsequent declaration of war in 2022, has far-reaching consequences that extend beyond regional borders. Several geo-economic considerations play a crucial role in understanding this conflict:

1. **Energy Transit Routes:** Russia is a major energy supplier to Europe, providing a significant portion of its natural gas. The conflict has raised concerns about the reliability of energy transit routes, particularly those passing through Ukraine. The diversification of energy sources and transit routes has become a priority for the European Union to reduce dependence on Russian energy, thereby weakening Russia's influence over European economies.
2. **Trade Relations:** Ukraine serves as an important trading partner for both Russia and the European Union. The conflict has disrupted trade flows and created economic instability in the region. The imposition of sanctions by Western countries against Russia and counter-sanctions by Russia has negatively impacted trade relations, affecting economies on both sides.
3. **Economic Sanctions:** The annexation of Crimea and the ongoing conflict in eastern Ukraine prompted Western countries to impose sanctions on Russia. These sanctions targeted key sectors of the Russian economy including finance, energy and defence. The resulting economic pressure has contributed to Russia's economic downturn and prompted discussions about the efficacy of sanctions as a geopolitical tool.
4. **Energy Geopolitics:** The crisis has underscored the strategic importance of energy resources in shaping geopolitics. Russia's control over key energy infrastructure and its ability to use energy as a political tool have heightened concerns about its intensions in the region. This has prompted diversification and investment in renewable energy sources.
5. **Humanitarian Impact:** The conflict's human toll has led to displacement and loss of life, triggering a humanitarian crisis. This crisis has ramifications beyond immediate geo-economic

considerations, as it affects global perceptions of Russia and Ukraine influences international aid efforts and highlights the importance of stability in the region.

6. **Investment Climate:** The conflict has created an uncertain investment climate in both Russia and Ukraine. Foreign direct investment has declined due to political instability and economic sanctions. This affects the long-term economic prospects of both countries and their ability to attract capital for development.
7. **Cyber-security Concerns:** The conflict has seen an escalation in cyber operations, with both sides accusing each other of hacking and online disinformation campaigns. These activities have broader implications for global cyber-security norms and highlight the growing role of cyber tactics in geopolitical conflicts.

Compulsions and Future Prospects

The Russia-Ukraine war is a manifestation of deep-seated compulsions rooted in historical, political and economic factors. While the conflict remains unresolved, the prospect of a negotiated settlement or a lasting ceasefire remains uncertain. The international community's response, through sanctions and diplomatic efforts, underscores the importance of preserving further escalation and finding a peaceful resolution.

The Russia-Ukraine war is a multifaceted conflict driven by intertwined geopolitical, geostrategic and geo-economic considerations. Understanding these complex dynamics is essential for comprehending the motivations behind the actions of Russia and Ukraine, as well as the broader implications for regional and global security.

Geopolitically, the conflict reflects Russia's aspiration to maintain influence over its periphery and prevent NATO's eastward expansion. Ukraine, a former Soviet republic, holds immense symbolic value for Russia, and the fear of encirclement by Western powers has fuelled Moscow's efforts to maintain control over Ukraine or at least its sphere of influence. Conversely, Ukraine seeks to assert its sovereignty and escape Russia's shadow, gravitating towards the European Union and NATO for security and economic partnerships.

Geostrategic considerations further complicate the conflict. The Crimean peninsula's annexation by Russia in 2014 exemplified

Moscow's willingness to use military force to secure strategic assets and buffer zones. Crimea's access to the Black Sea and its significant naval presence are pivotal to Russia's regional power projection. Additionally, the eastern Ukrainian Donbas region, rich in minerals and heavy industry, has economic and strategic importance for both sides. Controlling these areas allows for economic leverage and disrupts the other side's stability.

Geo-economically, the conflict is intertwined with energy dynamics. Russia is a major supplier of natural gas to Europe and Ukraine's key pipelines facilitate this flow. Moscow's influence over Ukraine's energy infrastructure grants it leverage over European energy security. On the other hand, Ukraine seeks to diversify its energy sources and integrate with the European energy market, diminishing its reliance on Russia.

Future prospects are uncertain and multifaceted. A continued war has exacerbated the humanitarian suffering and destabilization of the whole region. Diplomatic efforts, such as the Minsk Agreements, have struggled to bring lasting peace, and the involvement of external actors, like the USA and the European Union adds complexity. Sanctions against Russia have imposed economic costs but have yet to alter Moscow's core objectives significantly. The conflict's outcome could shape the balance of power in Europe and set precedents for international norms. A resolution might involve a compromise granting Ukraine a degree of autonomy while ensuring Russia's security concerns are addressed. The potential for the conflict to spill over into other regions, the Baltics for example, remain a concern.

In conclusion, the Russia-Ukraine conflict embodies a web of interconnected factors, including geopolitical, geostrategic and geo-economic elements. The struggle for influence, security and resources has significant implications for the involved nations, neighbouring countries and the international order. As the conflict's dynamics continue to evolve, finding a peaceful and equitable resolution remains a formidable challenge for global stability and diplomacy.

REFERENCES

1. John J. Mearsheimer. 'The Ukraine Crises and the Resumption of Great- Power Rivalry,' *Foreign Affairs*, 2014.

2. Rajan Menon. 'Geopolitical Implications of the Ukraine Crises,' in *Survival: Goals Politics and Strategy*, 2014.
3. Bobo Lo. *Russia and the New World Disorder,* Yale University Press, 2015).
4. Paul D'Anieri. *Ukraine and Russia: From Civilized Divorce to Uncivil War,* Cambridge University Press, 2019.
5. Stanislav L. Tkachenko and Igor A. Zevelev. *The New Geopolitics of Russia: Understanding Moscow's Strength and Weakness*, Routledge, 2017.
6. Keir Giles. *Russia's War on Everybody: And What It Means For You*, Bloomsbury, 2023.
7. Stanly Johny 'The Past and Present of Russia's War in Ukraine, *The Hindu*, February 2023.
8. Eric Nagourney, Dan Bilefsky and Richard Perez-Pena. 'A Year of War In Ukraine: The Roots of the Crisis," *The New York Times,* February 2023.
9. Steven Pifer. 'The Russia-Ukraine War and Its Ramification for Russia,' Brookings, 2022.

13

Russia-Ukraine War and the Emerging World Order

Jay Maniyar

Introduction

Talk of an emerging world order has become commonplace among intellectual circles these days. The inevitable but slow decline of the West remains on course while traditionally and historically strong nations such as China and India continue to redraw the geopolitical landscape and turn the tide in their favour. This has been the case irrespective of how global conflicts are panning out. The Global South, as it is known, is commanding much more attention and countries such as China and India are dominating several new landscapes such as game-changing new and emerging technologies (for example, artificial intelligence, fifth-generation networks, the Internet of Things, and quantum computing), regional geopolitics, and military strength. The Global South, even led by countries such as China and India, is beginning to headline the world's rule-based order. However, this very order is not just at risk but could instead be entirely overhauled very soon. Just a month ago, in October 2023, US President Joe Biden said that Russian actions in Ukraine and China's manoeuvres over Taiwan have already brought in a new world order.[1]

Further, a country such as Iran is known to complicate the situation for the USA due to its role in Middle Eastern affairs. The stability and security of the Middle Eastern region depends much on Iran and its actions in regard to the West Asian peninsula. Moreover, the region has erupted into conflict following the deadly attacks by the pro-Palestine terrorist group, Hamas, on the state of Israel on 7 October 2023. These events have shaken the foundation of peace, prosperity, and stability in the world.

A new world order may be on the horizon mainly because of the relatively recent ground-breaking development in the world, which is the ongoing Russia-Ukraine conflict (since February 2022 till the present date). There is no doubt that this 'war' has changed the way conflict is perceived in the twenty-first century. Russia launched the war as a 'special military operation' in February 2022 but the disguised intention remains a return-to-the-glory days of the Soviet Union (USSR). Russia intends to capture Ukraine completely, overthrow its government, and then slowly but surely turn its head towards other former Soviet states in the region. Ukraine, on the other hand, is strongly supported by the Western world. Russia and the West are basically at war themselves as far as the mind is concerned. The war in Ukraine is described as the most noticeable geopolitical event since World War II and the 11 September attacks on the USA. The US-led West has poured billions of dollars in aid and military assistance into Ukraine while condemning Russia's actions vehemently. However, Russian president Vladimir Putin continues to dream of a return to the dominant days of the USSR.

This chapter seeks to define this new world order emerging from the conflict in Ukraine and is divided into a few sections. The first briefly looks at what exactly has happened in Eastern Europe and conveys the argument that the war will continue for a long time to come. There is, at present, no end in sight for Ukraine. The second section analyses the emerging world order in the context of the conflict in Ukraine and attempts to decode the geography of regions such as the Indian Ocean and Indo-Pacific regions. The third looks at India's very own role in the Russia-Ukraine conflict as well as its position in the new and emerging world order. Finally, the chapter concludes by emphasising the emerging world order in the context of the immediate future.

The Russia-Ukraine Conflict: It Goes On and On

At the time of writing this chapter, the Russia-Ukraine war had completed 21 months in action. The war began on 24 February 2022 and has continued to persist till date. The reasons given for launching the war by Russia were the 'denazification' and 'demiliarisation' of Ukraine.[2] Following the declaration of war, Ukraine ended diplomatic relations with Russia. There is no sign of the war coming to an end in the immediate future and instead it has entered what can be termed a 'stalemate phase'. The major gains of foreign territory by Russia actually took place in 2014 when Moscow annexed Crimea to the south of Ukraine. There are no significant gains being made by either side on the ground in the current war, but the intensity of the war remains very high. Russian President Vladimir Putin has conveyed no signs of a rapprochement or a withdrawal in the current circumstances. This is evident from his many statements during the conflict. Putin has said that, irrespective of financial failures, Russia's war against Ukraine remains on track.[3] What is worrisome is that the world has been left ravaged because of the Ukraine war. Key supply chains featuring important goods such as food and fertilisers have been impacted and disrupted by the war.[4] This has led to a global crisis wherein countries have called for a cessation of hostilities to ensure that supply chains return to track.

Despite its limited successes on the ground in Ukraine following some quick territorial gains in the early stages of the war, Russia has palpably gone from strength to strength in the war. It has emerged as a pole in the new world order by itself and is aptly implying that multi-polarity is now the status quo. Russia has brought multi-polarity to the fore with its invasion of Ukraine. Russia is not dubbed a superpower despite its large land area, considerable geopolitical influence, and massive stock of nuclear weapons. This is owing to Russia's 'middle' economy and its inability to command influence comparable to the Soviet era. Ukrainian infrastructure such as factories and power plants has been heavily bombed by the Russians. Russia is not alone, though, against a thoroughly well-supported, West-backed Ukraine. Ukraine has received military assistance from its Western allies from almost day one of the war. Kyiv continues to rely on Western supplies to deny Moscow the edge. The Ukrainians have used these weapons to launch very successful counteroffensives against the Russians. These counteroffensives have been launched by Volodymyr Zelenskyy and his government in Kyiv. In fact, the term 'counter-offensive' has become synonymous with Ukraine during the war. These have been undertaken in response to what has been initiated by Russia in Ukraine and are also very localised and effective. Russia itself has received considerable military assistance from partners such as China and Iran is also said to have supplied drones to Moscow.[5] In April this year, the Ukrainians discovered a large number of Chinese components in Russian weapons.[6] China has maintained a conspicuous position in the war. It has been involved in the war through its weapons sales and has also called for peace in Ukraine through 'talks' alone.[7] Even countries such as Pakistan have been accused of aiding the Ukrainians with weapons supplies.

As far as the war itself is concerned, some notable events include the capture of the strategic Mariupol by Russia in May 2022 and the widely condemned Russian referendums in occupied territories of eastern Ukraine in September 2022.[8] The last remaining Ukrainian troops in the city surrendered after being cornered at the Azovstal Iron and Steel Works plant. As far as the latter event is concerned, despite there having been no clarity on the actual occupation of these territories and who controls what, Russia claimed 'victory' in the eastern territories such as Donetsk and Luhansk. Moscow proceeded to hold a referendum after backing separatists in the region. In the same month, Russia mobilised an additional 300,000 troops. The Ukrainians, too, were keen to sign up for military service in large numbers. Also, in September, the Ukranians were able to trigger Russian withdrawal from the Kharkiv Oblast region. Russia bombed the capital, Kyiv, with kamikaze drones in October 2022.[9] In the same month, the Russians were rocked by the bombing of the Crimean bridge, which was called a 'terrorist attack' by Moscow. As per a Brookings article, most Ukrainians these days regard Russia as an enemy.[10]

As per the United Nations Human Rights Council, close to six million people have been internally displaced in Ukraine.[11] As of December 2022, there were 1.3 million Ukrainian refugees in Russia.[12] Come 2023, the war has persisted. Russia has again attempted to invade Kyiv, in northern Ukraine, from Belarus. Belarus, a pro-Russia country, has also been marginally involved in the war and there has been the possibility that Ukraine may invade Belarus. Ukraine has warned Russia not to invade Kyiv from the north again.[13] There seems to be no possibility of the war coming to an end or a ceasefire due to these unfolding events. Indeed, in July, Russian President Putin said that there will be no ceasefire owing to Ukraine's activities in the war.[14] There remains an overarching fear that Russia could be tempted to use tactical nuclear weapons, at the very least, in the war. This could change the scale and scope of the conflict entirely. The USA and the West have heavily sanctioned Russia for its role in the war in Ukraine. As per a report by the National Institute of Economic and Social Research, the major impact of the Russia-Ukraine war on the global economy has been on higher energy prices and loss of confidence in financial markets.[15] The Russian economy has been weakened by sanctions by the USA and the European Union (EU). This has been happening since the conflict in Donbas in the past decade.[16] Another important development in the war has been the role of the North Atlantic Treaty Organisation (NATO). It has considered expansion during the war and new countries such as Finland have joined the cause. Sweden is expected to join NATO soon, too. So far, Russia has fought off the possibility of Ukraine joining NATO.

The Emerging World Order: Placing it in Context

The major equation in the emerging world order borne out of the Russia-Ukraine conflict consists of countries such as China, Iran, and Russia itself against the world's sole superpower in the USA and its Western allies. These perceivably neutral countries on the world's stage have been involved in the war in dubious capacities despite maintaining that war is not the solution to disputes. Other influential countries such as Japan and South Korea have sided with the West, too. This equation is above all and clearly implies that the world is not bipolar (USA versus China) as many are inclined to believe. Instead, it comprises several poles featuring *sui generis* strong points of power, poise, and influence. This multi-polar world order also includes India as a rising South Asian country with the prospective ability to project power well beyond its shores, albeit for peaceful purposes. As a country committed to Gandhian principles, India will always be known for peace and how it propagates peace on the world stage. India has made its direction clear by emerging as a voice of and supporting the global South actively.

While several major countries such as China and India haven't backed Russia directly, their abstention from the cause of the conflict makes certain that there exists a fractured state of affairs. The United Nations Security Council (UNSC) has witnessed a large number of resolutions being sponsored and proposed in regard to the conflict in Ukraine on a very regular basis. To mark the first year of the war in Ukraine, the UN General Assembly (UNGA) again called for an end to the conflict through a new resolution.[17] India has supported only one resolution in favour of Ukraine, that being a procedural vote.[18] India voted in favour of the Ukrainian President Zelenskyy's address to the UNGA. All through the year and now, Russia has been heavily condemned for its actions in Ukraine in the UNGA. Wars, today, have global and far-reaching consequences and the Russia-Ukraine conflict is no different.

US allies such as Japan, South Korea, and Australia have vehemently opposed Russia's 'invasion' of Ukraine. In June 2023, Australia said that it hopes Putin's 'aggression' will come to an end and Ukraine will win decisively.[19] The Chief of the Royal Australian Navy has termed the invasion of Ukraine as the failure of diplomacy and deterrence.[20] An additional point to be mentioned here is that Russian territorial disputes with countries such as Japan could also be threatened with forced solutions thus amplifying the cause of the emerging world order. Russia remains mired in small historical conflicts in East Asia. This is the standout multi-polar region of the world with no superpower (barring American presence in limited numbers) present. The balance of power in this region is the presence of democracies such as Japan and South Korea, backed by the USA, against countries such as North Korea, backed by China. Taiwan is emerging as a small but very, very significant bit of territory owing to the decisive manoeuvres against Taipei by Beijing in a bid to formally annexe the republic and bind it to the mainland for ever. It was widely rumoured that China will seek to annexe Taiwan immediately following the Russian invasion of Ukraine. This, however, has proven untrue.

The Indian Ocean and Indo-Pacific regions are key to a new world order. Much of the geopolitical activities taking place today that may prove to be a cause for conflict, are in these two regions. West Asia, which is in turmoil because of the Israel-Hamas war, is located at the western periphery of the Indo-Pacific region. The Indian Ocean is home to increasing Chinese naval activity that is being dubbed suspicious and unreliable. Chinese spy ships have wreaked havoc in the Indian Ocean.[21] Another proximate area of immense concern is the energy-carrying South China Sea. This crucial water body is home to the greatest number of territorial disputes in the new world order. China is opposed by a number of nations such as Indonesia, the Philippines, and Vietnam (to name a few) over territorial disputes. Territorial affairs have been prickly in this area and the shape of the emerging world order is being tested through the events in this critical sub-region of the Indo-Pacific. The Indo-Pacific, a term being more commonly used nowadays than Asia-Pacific, is now a strategic geography. Recent events include an incident between the Chinese coast guard and a Philippines vessel and a new incident between the Chinese and the Australians in Japan's Exclusive Economic Zone (EEZ).

India's Role in a Conflict-Ridden New World Order

India is an Asian giant in regard to its civilisational history and even its present-day growth and rise. India has been inevitably included in the Russia-Ukraine conflict because of concerns of food security and diplomatic involvement in issues such as the United Nations Security Council (UNSC) resolutions on the conflict as well as its own diplomatic position on the issue. Noted scholar Ashley J. Tellis calls India's involvement in the war 'studied neutrality' towards Russia.[22] Another Indian voice, Happymon Jacob, says that India's position is 'subtly pro-Moscow'.[23] Close Indian strategic partners such as the USA and Japan have been left baffled by India's stance on the issue. The reason behind India's stand on Russia in the wake of the conflict is that India sources a majority of its military equipment from Moscow. New Delhi and Moscow are very closely aligned in the defence realm and the current inventory of Indian forces features at least 60 per cent of Russian-made equipment.

This being said, India has also been a strong voice as far as bringing the conflict to a permanent end is concerned. As far as the humanitarian side of the war is concerned, India has provided Ukraine with plenty of aid on the ground. As of August 2023, India had shipped 14 consignments of aid, especially medicines, to Ukraine.[24] In fact, through its wise actions and agenda, India has reaffirmed its commitment to strategic autonomy. Strategic autonomy in the Indian context means that no greater power will be able to influence or coerce India into adopting positions that run contrary to India's nature as an independent democracy capable of standing alone in the world. Decisions are made at the governmental level after careful deliberations in favour of Indian principles and glorious historical strategic thought. Thus, India has also emerged as a voice of sanity in the conflict. Its many abstentions in the UNGA are actually *not* indicative of proactive support for Russia. If this was indeed the case, India would have voted in favour of Russia. Instead, what India has clearly highlighted is the need for diplomacy, deliberations, and discussions as a means to an end of the war. As far as the direct on-ground impact of the war on India is concerned, there was the loss of one life in March 2022, that of an Indian medical student.[25] The lives of other Indian students were also at peril but Russia offered safe passage to Indians during the early stages of the war. Greece and Azerbaijan have accounted for the most losses of foreign lives in the Russia-Ukraine war.

While Indian Prime Minister Narendra Modi has stated unequivocally that this is 'not an era of war'[26] and has suggested the same to contemporaries such as Vladimir Putin, the world clearly doesn't seem to agree. In fact, a new world order is only emerging from wars and the world would have remained the same or would have only been altered by the US decline and China's rise, had there not been any new conflicts. It can be safely assumed that the world is moving away from uni-polarity and bipolarity to multi-polarity. The USA has been the sole superpower in a single-pole world (post-Cold War and a little beyond) with no opposition whatsoever; the USA and China are competing in a bipolar world (early twenty-first century) and a large number of middle players are staking their claim to becoming more powerful and influential in a multi-polar world (status quo). The USA remains the world's sole superpower, the USA and China continue to compete, and a large number of other nations are slowly but surely asserting their power and influence on the global stage.

Just prior to the Israel-Hamas war, the United States National

Security Advisor (NSA) Jake Sullivan called the Middle Eastern region the 'most peaceful it has ever been'.[27] Much irony is to be gained from the words of these prominent leaders but this does in not any way undermine the fact that two warring parties are more than willing to go into conflict should the need arise, thus justifying the impendency of a new world order. Countries such as China and India remain distant from war themselves but both have been mired in situations such as Taiwan and Kashmir since time immemorial. It has been suggested that China will take Taiwan by force in a few years from now. India, too, remains staunchly opposed to any unusual activity in Kashmir and has routinely criticised initiatives such as the Belt and Road Initiative (BRI) for infringing upon Indian territory. India is not a member of the ambitious Chinese project. India says that the China-Pakistan Economic Corridor (CPEC), a BRI staple, cuts through Indian-claimed territory in Kashmir.

Former US President Barack Obama described India as a country that has already 'risen'.[28] This is a tribute to the hard work being done by New Delhi in all areas of concern. This includes dealing with China and being more assertive and aggressive on the world stage while also maintaining the continuity of and upholding principles of peace and stability. Obama may have also positioned India as a major pole in a multi-polar world with his comments on India's rise. It is also worth mentioning that a new world order is taking birth from new conflicts that are shaking the very foundations of humanity. The term 'world order' is a conspicuous term because of the innumerable ways in which it can take shape. As mentioned earlier, the world has had to contend with all forms of polarity, be it uni-, bi-, or multi-. It is hard to precisely define the new world order despite the decline of the USA clearly suggesting that the world is destined to end up as multi-polar. Multi-polarity is here to stay and the reason is because the USA has begun to announce its withdrawal from the world stage while China, the number two country, doesn't appear to have entirely convinced the world of its own ranking in the system. Both the USA and China have allowed other players to challenge their mantle and this has now become systemic. India is the best example of such a multi-polar world because multi-polarity is being ushered in from the fierce diplomacy of New Delhi. None of the poles ushering in multi-polarity can claim to occupy a uni-

or bi-polar position. Thus, these middle powers will continue to cooperate or compete on the basis of their set of national interests alone. As realism says, states retain primacy in the international system and the new international order is witnessing exactly the same.

Conclusion: A New World Order is Imminent

As this chapter has attempted to summarise, a new world order is clearly imminent. Featuring *n* number of new poles, the multi-polar stage appears to have usurped the unipolar and bipolar ones. Moreover, multilateral organisations such as the Group of Twenty (G20) and BRICS are making a name for themselves in the world of today. The BRICS is in itself the best description of the multi-polar world because of the presence of Russia, India, and China in it. The theory of realism in international relations argues that states are supreme and decide the world order through conflicts with each other in a race for absolute survival. Liberalism, on the other hand, encourages economic cooperation to soothe the world and provide it with an incentive to co-exist happily. Despite the appeals of multilateral groups, platforms such as BRICS have been used by Russia to justify the war in Ukraine as recently as in August 2023.[29] Hence, the conundrum remains as to what sort of a world is it in precise terms.

Even erstwhile important regions are being usurped in a new world order. The term 'Asia-Pacific' is being replaced by 'Indo-Pacific' gradually but surely. These regions will eventually form the staging area for the new world order. Several players such as India, China, Japan, and South Korea (to name a few) find themselves entrenched in Indo-Pacific affairs with a particular focus on the strategic Indian Ocean sub-region. The Indo-Pacific is the foremost geostrategic region and the events taking place in disputed maritime territories such as the South China Sea are a cause for concern. These events are threats to the concept of a free, open, and inclusive Indo-Pacific region as also to free and unimpeded commerce. Freedom of trade and commerce is vital to this region as it is home to the key strategic chokepoints that are responsible for the transit of a bulk of the world's trade. In 2016, an estimated 21 per cent of all global trade passed through the South China Sea.[30] Sixty per cent of all maritime trade passes through Asia, which comprises three-fourths of the Indo-Pacific region.

A new world order will likely be burdened with new responsibilities as the USA weakens and withdraws from the world stage. American withdrawal from countries such as Afghanistan suggests evidence of a new world order because Afghanistan is now in a new power balance by itself as it is controlled by the extremist Afghan Taliban. Further ahead, in the Middle Eastern region, things remain on a delicate precipice owing to the developments in the Israel-Hamas war. The region has been torn apart owing to new developments and the dastardly Hamas attack on Israel has caused mayhem and upheaval in the region. It is becoming abundantly clear that technology-driven and convenient large-scale wars are shaping the new world order and compelling nations that are sitting back to come forward and assume forthright stances in their diplomacy and decision-making. Again, the conflict has inspired a number of resolutions in the UNGA. The Hamas attack has also spotlighted the need to deal with terrorism and terror financing. Terrorism appeared to be on the decline globally but the deaths of over 1,200 people and 200+ hostages have been a shocking new development in the world today.

The Russia-Ukraine war continues to grab world headlines. It is clear that the conflict will continue for some time to come and it remains difficult to assess just when and where it will terminate. Ukraine's dogged opposition of a determined Russia has thrown the war into a stalemate phase. While new attacks are being launched daily, territorial gains have become a thing of the past. As far as India's role in the war is concerned, a lot has been said about India's soft corner for Russia. However, India maintains the unambiguous stance of strategic autonomy and this even applies to its foreign policy decision-making. India abstains from forums such as the UNGA because it is heavily inclined to a call for peace and stability in warring regions and does not support one side against another. However, India has bought heavily discounted Russian oil in keeping with its own interests. India's resoluteness and defiance of an obscure international order is praiseworthy owing to the many factions having resulted in opposing coalitions as can be seen in the Russia-Ukraine war. The West remains committed to what they perceive as Russia's unprovoked aggression while Russia backers have no qualms with Moscow *per se*.

Large-scale conflict has, it can be said, reared its ugly head once again. The Russia-Ukraine war is the clearest example of conflict being used to achieve geostrategic goals. These goals simply cannot be achieved by any other means except war. The Israel-Hamas conflict, nearby, is also an example of the aggressive overtures of terrorism in the world today. What has been witnessed is that the new world order has begun to identify new poles such as Ukraine and Hamas. Ukraine, in particular, has done well to overcome the initial perceptions of it being a lopsided victory in favour of Russia. Kyiv has maintained a defiance of Russia and continues to do so with it now being believed that the stalemate phase of the war will last for a long time to come. While analysts have predicted that the war could go on for two-three more years, it is actually possible that the war might go on for much longer than just a few years. The 'special military operation' has become a permanent military operation. An emerging multi-polar world order has arisen out of the conflict in Ukraine and is likely to stay. While many countries in this new world order are still rising, including even possibly countries such as China and India, they have undoubtedly staked a claim to greater influence and involvement in world affairs. The business end of things, such as weapons assistance and direct sales to both Russia and Ukraine, is on in full swing. A West that can't afford to lose Ukraine to Russia is competing in a world in which Russia aims to announce an interest in its nearby territories. The war in Ukraine has several lessons for a world that is quite accustomed to unprovoked conflict. The greatest hope of mankind remains the prevalence of peace and stability or a return, hitherto, to peace and stability. Whether it will be achieved in the context of the Russia-Ukraine war, remains to be seen.

REFERENCES

1. Wolf, Zachary. 'Biden acknowledges the old world order needs a refresh.' CNN, 19 September 2023 at https://edition.cnn.com/2023/09/19/politics/un-speech-biden-what-matters/index.html
2. PTI. 'Special military operation aimed at 'demilitarisation' and 'denazification' of Ukraine: Putin's televised address.'. *The Hindu*, 24 February 2022 at https://www.thehindu.com/news/international/special-military-operation-aimed-at-demilitarisation-and-denazification-of-ukraine-putins-televised-address/article65080000.ece

3. Gavin, Gabriel. 'Putin claims new world order upon us in rambling Ukraine rant.'. *Politico*, 16 June 2023 at https://www.politico.eu/article/russia-ukraine-war-vladimir-putin-claims-new-world-order-upon-us-in-rambling-rant/
4. Northam, Jackie. 'How the war in Ukraine is affecting the world's supply of fertiliser.' NPR, 28 September 2022 at https://www.npr.org/2022/09/28/1125525861/how-the-war-in-ukraine-is-affecting-the-worlds-supply-of-fertilizer
5. 'China providing parts to Iran drones for Russia invasion, report reveals,' *Middle East Monitor*, 13 June 2023 at https://www.middleeastmonitor.com/20230613-china-providing-parts-to-iran-drones-for-russia-invasion-report-reveals/
6. Williams, Matthias and O'Donnell, John. 'Ukraine says it is finding more Chinese components in Russian weapons.' Reuters, 17 April 2023 at https://www.reuters.com/world/europe/ukraine-says-it-is-finding-more-chinese-components-russian-weapons-2023-04-14/
7. 'China reiterates ceasefire, peace talks 'only way' to end Ukraine war.''. *Al Jazeera* English, 22 September 222023 at https://www.aljazeera.com/news/2023/9/22/china-reiterates-ceasefire-peace-talks-only-way-to-end-ukraine-war
8. 'Understanding Russia's referendums in Ukraine.' *Al Jazeera* English, 20 September 2022 at https://www.aljazeera.com/news/2022/9/20/russia-unfolds-annexation-plan-for-ukraine
9. Mogelson, Luke. 'Russia bombards Kyiv with a crude new weapon.' *The New Yorker*, 17 October 2022 at https://www.newyorker.com/culture/photo-booth/russia-bombards-kyiv-with-a-crude-new-weapon
10. Pifer, Steven. 'The Russia-Ukraine war and its ramifications for Russia.'. Brookings Institution, 8 December 2022 at https://www.brookings.edu/articles/the-russia-ukraine-war-and-its-ramifications-for-russia/
11. 'Ukraine situation'. UNHCR at https://reporting.unhcr.org/operational/situations/ukraine-situation
12. 'Ukrainian refugees by country.', *Statista*, 12 September 2023 at https://www.statista.com/statistics/1312584/ukrainian-refugees-by-country/
13. 'Ukraine says if Russia tries to invade from Belarus again, this time it's ready – "with presents,"', CBS News, 3 March 2023 at https://www.cbsnews.com/news/ukraine-news-russia-war-belarus-invasion-preparation/
14. Folkman, Varg. 'No cease-fire while Ukraine is on the offensive, Putin declares,' *POLITICO*, 30 July 2023 at https://www.politico.eu/article/no-cease-fire-ukraine-russia-war-offensive-vladimir-putin/
15. Liadze, Macchiarelli & Mortimer-Lee, Juanino. 'The Economic Costs of the Russia-Ukraine Conflict,'. National Institute of Economic and Social Research, p. 5., 2 March 2022 at https://www.niesr.ac.uk/wp-content/uploads/2022/03/PP32-Economic-Costs-Russia-Ukraine.pdf
16. Mankoff, Jeffrey. 'Russia's War in Ukraine: Identity, History and Conflict,' Centre for Strategic & International Studies (CSIS), 22 April 2022 at https://www.csis.org/analysis/russias-war-ukraine-identity-history-and-conflict
17. 'UN General Assembly calls for immediate end to war in Ukraine,' United Nations, 23 February 2023 at https://news.un.org/en/story/2023/02/1133847
18. 'For 1st time, India votes against Russia in UNSC on Ukraine,' *The Times of India*, 26 August 2022 at https://timesofindia.indiatimes.com/india/for-1st-time-india-votes-against-russia-in-unsc-on-ukraine/articleshow/93786199.cms

19. 'Australia pledges further support to Ukraine,' Prime Minister of Australia, 26 June 2023 at https://www.pm.gov.au/media/australia-pledges-further-support-ukraine
20. 'Strength at sea is vital to security,' *The Australian*, 7 November 2023 at https://www.theaustralian.com.au/special-reports/strength-at-sea-is-vital-to-security/news-story/e98e23f38b2d5f0b089e95f55fa02032
21. Maniyar, Jay. 'Chinese spy ships in the Indian Ocean – An analysis,' 10 November 2022 at https://timesofindia.indiatimes.com/blogs/voices/chinese-spy-ships-in-the-indian-ocean-an-analysis/
22. Tellis, Ashley. '"What is in our interest": India and the Ukraine War,'. Carnegie Endowment for International Peace, 25 April 2022 at https://carnegieendowment.org/2022/04/25/what-is-in-our-interest-india-and-ukraine-war-pub-86961
23. Jacob, Happymon. 'The anatomy of India's Ukraine dilemma,' *The Hindu*. 28 February 2022 at https://www.thehindu.com/opinion/lead/the-anatomy-of-indias-ukraine-dilemma/article65090424.ece
24. 'India hands over 14th consignment of humanitarian aid comprising essential medicines to Ukraine,' *Economic Times*, 3 August 2023 at https://health.economictimes.indiatimes.com/news/industry/india-hands-over-14th-consignment-of-humanitarian-aid-comprising-essential-medicines-to-ukraine/102395131
25. 'Ukraine invasion: Indian student killed as he tried to buy food,'. BBC News, 1 March 2022 at https://www.bbc.com/news/world-asia-india-60567585
26. Roy, Shubhajit. '"Not an era of war": In US, Modi calls for peaceful resolution of Ukraine conflict,' *Indian Express*, 23 June 2023 at https://indianexpress.com/article/india/narendra-war-speech-us-modi-peaceful-resolution-ukraine-conflict-8681176/
27. Beckerman, Gal. 'The Middle East Region Is Quieter Today Than It Has Been In Two Decades,' *The Atlantic*, 7 October 2023 at https://www.theatlantic.com/international/archive/2023/10/israel-war-middle-east-jake-sullivan/675580/
28. 'Obama charm focuses on 'risen' India,' *The Financial Times*, 7 November 2010 at https://www.ft.com/content/a31165b4-eae7-11df-b28d-00144feab49a
29. 'Putin uses BRICS Summit to justify Russia's war in Ukraine,' Reuters, 23 August 2023 at https://www.reuters.com/world/putin-uses-brics-summit-justify-russias-war-ukraine-2023-08-23/
30. Holt, Sean. 'Five countries, other than China, most dependent on the South China Sea,' CNBC, 17 November 2022 at https://www.cnbc.com/2022/11/18/five-countries-other-than-china-most-dependent-on-the-south-china-sea.html

SECTION III

REGIONAL IMPLICATIONS AND STRATEGIC CONSIDERATIONS OF RUSSIA-UKRAINE WAR

14

Russia-Ukraine War: Lessons Learnt for South and South-East Asia

Abhishek Yadav

"Peaceful coexistence and inclusive growth in neighbourhood are distant dreams but these are compelling realities for India's regional growth in the 21st century."

Introduction

Ukraine and Russia share hundreds of years of cultural, linguistic, and familial links. Many people in Russia and the regions of Ukraine with a Russian ethnic majority view the shared past of the countries as an emotive matter that has been abused for political and military ends. Ukraine was an integral element of the Soviet Union and was the second-most powerful Soviet republic after Russia from a strategic, economic, and cultural standpoint. The ongoing military, political, and economic hostilities between Russia and Ukraine are known as the Russia-Ukraine war. It began in 2014 after the revolution in Ukraine and the overthrow of the pro-Russian president. This set off a chain of occurrences that resulted in the annexation of Crimea by Russia and the escalation of hostilities in Eastern Ukraine, when insurgents with Russian support proclaimed their independence from Ukraine.

Since then, the conflict has intensified into a full-fledged war, which has resulted in thousands of fatalities and numerous displaced populations. Russia's activities have been denounced by the international community, including the United Nations, who have implemented economic penalties as a result. The conflict hasn't been resolved despite numerous rounds of peace talks and other efforts. In addition to affecting Ukraine and Russia, the conflict has had a significant impact on the larger world community. It is a source of constant worry and the focus of diplomatic efforts to find a peaceful resolution because it has heightened tensions between Russia and the West and destabilised the region. The aim of this paper is to bring out the lessons learnt about conventional and unconventional warfare from the Russia-Ukraine war for South and South-East Asia.

Causes of the Conflict

Historical tensions, economic motives, and geopolitical power struggles are just a few of the reasons why Russia and Ukraine are at odds. The historical hostility between Russia and Ukraine, which has been a source of conflict for millennia, is one of the war's main reasons. This has included times when Russia ruled the region and actions taken by Ukraine to defend its independence and fend off Russian influence. Competition for resources, notably natural gas, is another factor. Due to Ukraine's importance as a transit country for Russian gas shipments to Europe, Russia has influence over Ukraine, which exacerbates tensions between the two nations.

Geopolitical power struggles also play a role in the conflict. Russia, which views Ukraine as a crucial buffer against Western dominance, has resisted the Ukrainian government's efforts to ally itself with the West, particularly by seeking stronger connections with the European Union and NATO. The war has also intensified as a result of the 2014 Ukrainian revolution, the overthrow of pro-Russian president Viktor Yanukovych, the annexation of Crimea by Russia, and support for separatist movements in eastern Ukraine. These events have left the region unstable and violent. In essence, a complicated triad of historical conflicts, economic concerns, and geopolitical power struggles underlie the war between Russia and Ukraine. A few reasons which need a mention here are as follows:

(a) **Balance of Power:** Ever since Ukraine split from the Soviet Union, both Russia and the West have vied for greater influence in the country in order to keep the balance of power in the region in their favour.

(b) **Buffer Zone for Western Countries:** For the USA and the European Union, Ukraine is a crucial buffer between Russia and the West. As tensions with Russia rise, the USA and the EU are increasingly determined to keep Ukraine away from Russian control.

(c) **Russian Interest in the Black Sea:** The unique geography of the Black Sea region confers several geopolitical advantages to Russia:

(i) It is an important crossroad and strategic intersection for the entire region.

(ii) Access to the Black Sea is vital for all the littoral and neighbouring states, and greatly enhances the projection of power into several adjacent regions.

(iii) The region is an important transit corridor for goods and energy.

(d) **Protests in Ukraine:**

(i) *Euromaidan Movement:* Euromaidan (European Square) was a wave of demonstrations and civil unrest in Ukraine, which began in November 2013 with public protests in Maidan Nezalezhnosti ('Independence Square') in Kyiv, Ukraine. The protests were sparked by the Ukrainian government's decision to suspend the signing of an association agreement with the European Union, instead choosing closer ties with Russia and the Eurasian Economic Union.

(ii) *Separatist Movement:* The Donbas region (the Donetsk and Luhansk regions) of eastern Ukraine has been facing a pro-Russian separatist movement since 2014. According to the Ukrainian government, the movement is actively supported by the Russian government and Russian paramilitaries make up between 15 to 80 per cent of the separatists fighting against the Ukraine government.

(e) **Invasion of Crimea:**

(i) Russia seized Crimea from Ukraine as the first instance a European country annexed territory from another country since World War II.

(ii) In the wake of the 2014 Ukrainian revolution, and as part of broader turmoil in southern and eastern Ukraine, Russia launched a military intervention in Crimea, which led to the annexation of Crimea from Ukraine. Russia now has a maritime advantage in the region as a result of the invasion and annexation of Crimea.

Ukraine's NATO Membership

NATO has been requested by Ukraine to expedite the process of including it nation in the alliance. A 'red line' has been drawn by Russia, which is concerned about the effects of US-led military alliances moving closer to its borders. Bulgaria, Georgia, Romania, Russia, Turkey, and Ukraine are countries that border the Black Sea. These nations are all members of NATO. The Black Sea is a location of strategic importance and a potential maritime flashpoint as a result of this conflict between NATO nations and Russia.

Current Situation: Russia sought assurances from the USA that Ukraine will not be inducted into NATO. However, the USA did not give any such assurance. This has left the countries in a stand-off, with tens of thousands of Russian troops invading Ukraine. Russia is keeping the tensions high at the Ukraine border in order to get relief from sanctions and other concessions from the West. Any kind of military action by the USA or the EU against Russia would precipitate a major crisis for the whole world, and has so far not been mooted by any of the parties involved.

Concerns with Escalation of Ukrainian Conflict and Different Countries' Stand

The escalation of the conflict in Ukraine has raised several concerns and has drawn multiple international actors, each with their own interests and perspectives and has contributed to the ongoing tensions between Russia and the West.

Russia: Russia's position on the conflict in Ukraine is that it supports the separatist movements in eastern Ukraine and recognizes the annexation of Crimea. Russia has been accused of providing military support to the separatists, including troops and weapons, and of attempting to destabilize Ukraine. For its part, Russia has accused Ukraine of violating the rights of ethnic Russians in Ukraine and of suppressing dissent in eastern Ukraine. Russia has called for a political solution to the conflict and for greater autonomy for separatist regions in eastern Ukraine. Despite international sanctions and criticism, Russia has maintained its support for the separatists in eastern Ukraine and has resisted calls for a return of Crimea to Ukraine. In short, Russia's position on the conflict in Ukraine is one of support for the separatist movements and recognition of the annexation of Crimea, despite international criticism and sanctions. Russia has been actively involved in the conflict, annexing Crimea in 2014 and supporting separatist movements in eastern Ukraine. Russia's actions have been a source of concern for the international community, which has imposed economic sanctions against Russia in response.

Ukraine: Ukraine has been at the centre of the conflict and has expressed concern over Russia's actions, including the annexation of Crimea and support for separatist movements in eastern Ukraine. Ukraine has also expressed interest in moving closer to the West and seeking closer ties with NATO and the European Union.

The European Union: The European Union has expressed concern over the escalation of the conflict in Ukraine and has imposed economic sanctions on Russia in response to its actions. The EU has also provided economic and political support to Ukraine and has encouraged a diplomatic solution to the conflict.

The USA: The USA has expressed concern over the escalation of the conflict in Ukraine and has imposed economic sanctions on Russia in response to its actions. The USA has also provided military and economic support to Ukraine and has called for a diplomatic solution to the conflict.

NATO: NATO has expressed concern over the escalation of the conflict in Ukraine and has increased its presence in the region in response. NATO has also provided military and political support to Ukraine and has reportedly encouraged a diplomatic solution to the conflict.

India: India has maintained a pragmatic approach and maintained a balanced stand in the national interest. Even in the UN Security Council, India refrained from voting against Russia but when Ukraine required humanitarian assistance, India was one of the first to provide wheat and medicines to it.

Lessons Learnt in Unconventional Domain

Urban Warfare: Lack of planning for urban warfare and unconventional operations, and clearing up of areas by Russian forces resulted in slow progress. Ukrainians used heights to attack Russian convoys. Russian infantry was not found securing routes before movement of vehicle convoys which resulted in destruction of tanks. Many times, when Russian convoys tried passing through suburban areas, it provided opportunities for easy ambushes. Lack of contingency planning by Russia facilitated Ukraine's conventional warriors.

Guerrilla Warfare: Under the leadership of President Zelensky, the majority of civilians rose for the national cause. Civilians using anti-tank missiles, AKs and numerous explosives, and IEDs made Russian advances very difficult. Unconventional warfare by the Ukrainians resulted in denying the benefits of a heavy force ratio to the Russians. Moreover, it lowered the morale of Russian troops to prevent casualties from amateur civilians. This boosted Ukrainian morale and strengthened the leadership of President Zelensky.

Information Warfare Campaign: Ukraine support by the Western media and various social media platforms like Facebook, Twitter, etc., influenced the world's perception and boosted images of Ukraine; sympathy garnered additional benefits of modern weapons, equipment, and warlike stores donated by the West to Ukraine. Top attack munitions, Spike launchers, and drones played important precise target roles and gave a tough time to the Russian conventional army.

Intelligence and Information: The power of intelligence and information in a modern-day battlefield is doubly reinforced in this conflict. US intelligence and information operations uncovered almost every move by the Russians well in time. The real-time surprise in Ukrainian information operations, without much fanfare, enabled

President Zelensky communicate with his population and rally them around. His communication ability through social media short clips is something to really learn from.

Misinformation and Human Intelligence (HUMINT). World media support was used by Ukraine for misinformation to demoralize Russian troops and boost the morale of their own populace. Russia lacked HUMINT, that is, boots on the ground, to rectify Ukraine's claim. The Russia-Ukraine war emphasized the importance of HUMINT in the present misinformation campaign led by national and global media. 'A lie repeated many times gradually becomes the truth.'

Language Barrier: The Ukrainians possessed multilingual skills and could decipher English, Russian and local dialects; whereas the Russians were found lacking in knowledge of English.

People's Resistance: Despite being outnumbered, the Ukrainians were contesting the Russian advance along all the thrust lines. Common citizens have joined in the fight with Molotov cocktails and AKs. Ground fighting and air strikes were continuing intermittently.

Recruiting Afghan Commandos: Members of the Afghanistan elite national army commando corps, who were abandoned by the USA and Western allies when the country fell to the Taliban last year, say they are being contacted with offers to join the Russian military to fight in Ukraine.

Ukraine Commandos Attacked Airfields Deep Inside Russia: Ukrainian commandos using small boats have infiltrated the Kinburn Spit, a three-mile finger of sand and scrub curling across the mouth of the Dnipro River west of Kherson, the southern port city that Ukrainians forces liberated from its Russian occupiers.

Danger of Proxy Wars: The conflict in Ukraine serves as a reminder of the dangers of proxy wars, where neighbouring states or international actors use local groups to advance their own interests. Such conflicts can escalate and lead to a large-scale military intervention.

Conventional Lessons at Strategic and National Level

Military Aim: The likely military aim of Russia may have been to capture Kyiv or the line of the Dnieper River and thereby lay down favourable terms. The likely conflict termination at the military level seems to have been misjudged. The selection of the military aim and identification of a correct centre of gravity (CoG) may be a decisive factor in the outcome of the battle.

Importance of Nuclear Deterrence

(a) Ukraine's non-nuclear existence post-1991, based on security guarantees from the West, has indirectly denuded Ukraine of deterrence.

(b) Over-reliance on NATO and the West for national security has left it helpless and fighting a war on its own with limited support.

Grey Zone: Russian IW operations, statements, hostile actions in the cyber/EW domain in the run up to the war were all carefully designed to precipitate war and blame Ukraine for it. There's an urgent need for capability development on India's part to counter grey zone operations by our northern adversary.

Alliances: Overdependence/reliance on alliances, and expecting foreign powers to intervene on one's behalf in a war would prove costly.

Information Warfare

(a) Flow of information has proven to be controlled by the West. We must cultivate friendly assets in the Western media for support for our own information operations.

(b) Future wars will be fought in conditions of high visibility—Tiktok/Twitter, etc. The message to be conveyed must be clear to the lowest echelon and own troops trained to interact with the enemy in a way that supports own information operations.

(c) **Just War:** Russia has largely lost the IW battle as it is seen to be conducting an 'Unjust War.' China would be wary of being accused of starting an 'Unjust War.' It is imperative that own IW narrative be prepared, war gamed and well in advance to be ahead of the news cycle in case of hostilities.

Lack of Surprise and Deception: Lack of surprise and deception by Russia as troops marshalled alongside border for more than three months. The Russian attack was very much eminent. Miscalculated times of attack after massing by Russia gave adequate time. Spring was chosen (24 February 2022) which leads to melting of winter ice making cross-country movement difficult. Perforce Russian 'A' vehicle convoys had to stick to roads providing easy targets for Ukrainian forces. Massing of troops in winter required more maintenance and extra administrative burden on Russia before the attack.

Limited Use of Air Force and SEAD: Limited use of SEAD and DEAD operations by Russia resulted in gainful use of Ukrainian Air Force causing heavy reveres for the Russian Air Force and para campaigns. Also, Russian Air Force and naval assets in the Black Sea were not fully used.

Hardening of Communication—Cyber/Electronic Warfare (EW) Attacks: Russia seems to have bet heavily on hybrid means of waging war as in 2014. However, the same has not borne fruit.

(a) Ukraine carried out EW proofing with US help since 2014 through adoption of OFC for all military communications. Resultantly, their communications/C2 structure has remained intact in the face of the famed Russian EW capability.

(b) Cyber-Attacks have not played a major role once kinetic operations began. Their utility seems to be limited to the grey zone.

Conventional Lessons at Operational and Tactical Level

Economy of Effort: Advancing on multiple axes hampered concentration of forced on any one front and left no reserves to be applied once the battle reached major cities. Almost 110 battle tactical groups (BTG) of Russia were used to invade Ukraine from three sides which amounted to 1,200 tanks and 3,000 AFVs. The area of operations was just 75 × 100 km and included urban territory. Resources used were not commensurate to the expected outcome.

Unity of Command: The absence of theatre commanders to allocate resources and prioritise between various fronts has caused competition between various commanders for obtaining scarce military resources.

Force Structure: The newly-formed battalion/brigade tactical groups (BTG) of Russia (similar to the PLA combined arms brigades) have not been very successful and have reduced flexibility due to lack of central resources.

Firepower: Concentrated employment of firepower (long-range and precision) in the first two days created huge gaps in the Ukrainian fixed defences.

(a) India's fixed defences need to be hardened to a great degree to counter PLA massed firepower. Tunnelling to house logistic echelons is recommended.

(b) Own firepower would prove more effective against PLA moves in the Tibetan plateau due to the relatively open nature of the terrain.

Built-Up Area: Siege tactics to capture cities on the strength of firepower alone has slowed down Russian progress but is cheaper in terms of casualties. A lesson for our Western front where we might get embroiled in city/town battles. Casualty vs. Time be weighed before any such campaign.

Armour: The demonstrated vulnerability of tanks to new–generation equipment (NGE) and poor Russian tank tactics provide the most important lessons for us.

(a) *Emphasis on Javelin and Bayraktar TB2 Drones.* Adoption of these weapon systems on our northern borders could effectively counter PLA armour/APC and nullify the PLA edge.

(b) Russian tanks are proving to be extremely hazardous for the crew due to exposed ammunition, poor vision for drivers and low efficacy of ERA panels.

(c) Russian advances have been restricted to major roads/axes. This has proven very costly as the Ukrainians have easily tracked their movements through CCTV. The PLA too is likely to be road-bound with predictability in movement and thus be easy targets.

(d) Lack of combined arms tactics—Tanks being employed independently without follow-on infantry.

(e) Shoulder-fired SAMs like Stingers have once again proved effective.

Morale: Russian conscripts have displayed low motivation levels and have been reportedly surrendering relatively easily. The PLA too is expected to be weak in this aspect.

Leadership and Military Psyche: The decision-making at all levels requires adequate foresight combined with intellect and measured aggression.

Operational Logistics: Road-bound Russian advance forces ran out of fuel, medical supplies, ammunition, and rations after the first 72 hours. Follow-up logistics, part of the forty-mile long convoy, could not advance due to lack of progress by forward troops. Moreover, the Ukrainians blocked the rear of the logistics convoy exposing a grave weakness in Russian planning processes. Dedicated close logistics support for forward troops is a must.

Way Forward

A practical solution for the situation is to revive the Minsk peace process. Therefore, the West (USA and other Western countries) should persuade both sides to resume talks and live up to their commitments as per the Minsk agreement to restore relative peace on the border. Ending, the conflict in Ukraine between Russia and Ukraine will require a multi-faceted and comprehensive approach. Here are a few possible steps that could be taken to help resolve the conflict:

(a) Diplomatic Engagement: Diplomatic efforts between Russia, Ukraine, and the international community should be stepped up to find a peaceful solution to the conflict. The Minsk agreements, which were signed in 2015, provide a framework for resolving the conflict through political and diplomatic means.

(b) Ceasefire and Withdrawal of Military Forces: A lasting peace in Ukraine will require a ceasefire and the withdrawal of military forces from the conflict zone. This could be facilitated through international monitoring and verification mechanisms.

(c) **Political Dialogue:** Political dialogue between the Ukrainian government and separatist groups in eastern Ukraine should be resumed to find a solution to the conflict. This could include discussions on greater autonomy for separatist regions, constitutional reforms, and protection of minority rights.

(d) **Humanitarian Assistance:** The conflict in Ukraine has resulted in significant humanitarian suffering, and efforts should be made to provide aid to those affected by the conflict.

(e) **Economic Sanctions:** The international community should consider lifting economic sanctions against Russia if it demonstrates a commitment to resolving the conflict and respecting the territorial integrity of Ukraine.

(f) **Addressing Underlying Issues:** The conflict in Ukraine is rooted in historical, cultural, and economic tensions between Russia and Ukraine. Addressing these underlying issues will be critical to finding a lasting peace in the region.

Major Concerns for India and Corollary in its Neighbourhood

India's position on the conflict in Ukraine has been one of non-interference and support for the principles of territorial integrity and sovereignty. India has called for a peaceful resolution of the conflict through diplomatic means and has refrained from taking sides in the dispute. India has maintained its close ties with both Russia and Ukraine and has sought to balance its relationships with both countries. India has also sought to protect its own economic and energy interests in the region and has called for resolution of the conflict in a manner that does not disrupt energy supplies and trade relationships. The conflict in Ukraine and the resulting tensions between Russia and the West have several potential implications for India:

(a) **Energy Security:** India is a major importer of oil and natural gas, and the conflict in Ukraine has raised concerns about the stability of energy supplies from Russia and the impact of international sanctions on energy markets.

(b) **Geopolitical Tensions:** The conflict in Ukraine has contributed to increased tensions between Russia and the West, which could lead to further geopolitical realignments and tensions in other regions, including South Asia.

(c) **Economic Implications:** India has strong economic ties with both Russia and the West, and the conflict in Ukraine and the imposition of economic sanctions could impact trade and investment between India and these countries.

(d) **Security Implications:** The conflict in Ukraine has raised concerns about the stability of Europe and the potential for spill-over into other regions. Almost 70 per cent of the existing inventory in India is of Russian origin. Pending defence contracts worth $ 9 bn to include S-400 air defence systems, and joint production of AK-203 assault rifles are likely to be impacted by sanctions on Russia. Spare parts for IAF and Indian Navy equipment from Ukraine will be significantly affected. Self-reliance in defence production is the need of the hour. A boost to local defence industry is also important.

Corollary in India's Neighbourhood (South and South-East Asia)

Indo-Pakistan Disputes: Major age-old differences between the two nuclear nations could be the tipping of a major conflict in the South Asian region. With the collusion of Pakistan and China, the involvement of international players is obvious. The Russia-Ukraine war actually proves the importance of nuclear weapons as deterrence. In this case, a major war between two nuclear nations seems bleak in the near future.

Indo-Nepal: Nepal is the latest addition to the influence of communism and communist China. With China making roads and railways to connect Tibet and Nepal, the Chinese influence has already made greater inroads in the Nepalese governance and wields a larger influence. Many incidents of ill-treatment of Indians and Tibetan refugees have come in the news reflecting Nepal's changing loyalty and affiliations. Nepal could be a trigger of Indo-Chinese rivalry and may grow into a full-fledged local war. Thus the lessons learnt from the Russia-Ukraine war will be more applicable in this scenario.

Myanmar (Burma): India's eastern neighbour has been neutral since the last seven decades as far as India's activities are concerned. However, minor incidents of ethnic armed group activities across the Indo-Myanmar border have been often noticed. With the military takeover and rule by the State Administrative Council (SAC) since 1 February

2021, Myanmar is in a continuous battle between pro-democracy groups and the military. The internal security situation has deteriorated and many ethnic armed groups have also joined the pro-democracy forces. Seventy-seven-year-old Madam Aung San Suu Kyi is under house arrest and sentenced to 27 years of imprisonment by military courts. Myanmar's troubled future is likely to get worse if international forces converge. China and Russia are unitedly and indirectly supporting the Myanmar military government. Pro-democracy Western countries feel sidelined from South-East Asia. Post the Russia-Ukraine war, the Burmese front could be opened the probability of which is high. In such a situation, India, being a neighbouring nation, will probably get sucked into it. Lessons from the Russia-Ukraine war will be applicable and the same opposing forces—the US-led West and Russia-China—may contest for this strategic country. There are pro-China ethnic groups like Wa state along the borders of China and Myanmar, which could create similar conditions as Donbas in Ukraine. This will facilitate China to capture strategically important territory with the support of a favourable population.

Recommendations and Conclusion

Atmanirbharata

(a) Over-dependence on Russian arms restricts own strategic autonomy India needs diversification and develop a self-reliant defence industry. Ukraine is receiving military equipment from EU nations in the midst of war—we may not find similar ready assistance from our partners. Self-reliance for defence production is important to cut down our import bill and reliance on Russia and the USA.

(b) The changing conflict scenario requires procurement and development of the latest advanced military technology to include unarmed and armed drones and precision weapon systems.

(c) Hybrid warfare will be a challenge for militaries across the world so developing our capability to counter hybrid warfare should include information warfare, cyber-attacks. and perception management.

(d) Early resolution of existing disputed areas should be tried to prevent escalation and false narrative building by our adversary for their own advantage.

Space for conventional conflict exists below the nuclear threshold. We must explore options in this zone on both the western and northern fronts and also appreciate the options available to China in this domain. The conflict in Ukraine highlights the importance of respecting international norms and principles, seeking diplomatic solutions to conflicts, and the need for collective action by the international community to promote peace and stability. The conflict between Russia and Ukraine has several key conclusions that can be drawn upon:

(a) **Territorial Integrity is Crucial:** The conflict in Ukraine has emphasized the importance of respecting the territorial integrity and sovereignty of states. Any efforts to violate these principles can have far-reaching adverse consequences, including military conflict and instability in the region.

(b) **Diplomacy is Necessary:** The conflict in Ukraine has shown that diplomatic efforts are necessary to resolve international conflicts. Military force should be used only as a last resort, and efforts should be made to resolve disputes through diplomatic and political means.

(c) **Economic Sanctions can have Significant Impacts:** The conflict in Ukraine has highlighted the potential impact of economic sanctions on a country's economy and its people. Sanctions should be used carefully and with clear objectives, and the consequences for ordinary citizens should be considered.

(d) **The Role of the International Community:** The conflict in Ukraine has demonstrated the importance of the international community in resolving international conflicts. Collective efforts by the international community can help prevent the escalation of conflicts and promote peace and stability in the region.

(e) **Proxy wars are dangerous.** The conflict in Ukraine serves as a reminder of the dangers of proxy wars, where neighbouring states or international actors use local groups to advance their own interests. Such conflicts can escalate and lead to large-scale military intervention.

15

European Union's Response to the Russia-Ukraine War

Uday Pratap Singh

Introduction

Beginning on 24 February 2022, Russia's military campaign against Ukraine has had a profound impact on Europe's geopolitical, geo-economic, and geostrategic environments. The EU-Russian relationship, which has a long history of political, economic, and energy ties, quickly began to erode as the war escalated. It drew worldwide attention as a result of this conflict.

The conflict in Ukraine is a sobering reminder of the possibilities lost and the various failings at various levels inside the EU to properly engage and manage relations with Russia, particularly eight years after the takeover of Crimea in 2014. The EU and its member-states targeted economic sanctions and diplomatic initiatives against Russia after the takeover of Crimea, but these actions were ineffective in changing the dynamics between the two sides. The EU maintained economic and energy supply ties with Russia in spite of the flagrant violation of international law, with little action taken to address concerns about energy security. This position, in some ways, strengthened Moscow's claims in eastern Ukraine and gave it more authority to reshape relations with the West.

This result is a reflection of the collective European strategy to placate Russia, which puts interest in energy and economic security ahead of Ukraine's territorial integrity. This essay aims to examine how the EU is re-evaluating its security posture in Europe within an interconnected global framework, as well as the effects of the Ukraine war, in which one of the UNSC members is waging territorial aggression against an independent country. In order to achieve this, it focuses on the political, economic, security, and humanitarian aspects of the crisis in Ukraine. The European Union has increased financial aid to Ukraine and intensified sanctions against Russia, targeting sectors like energy, finance, and technology. The EU has also provided advanced weaponry and training to Ukrainian forces. Diplomatic efforts have been persistent, demonstrating the EU's commitment to upholding international law and supporting Ukrainian sovereignty.

Russia-Ukraine Crisis and Its Impact on Security

The EU and Russia's bilateral relationship has been marked by a number of blunders and diplomatic crises, ranging from the annexation of Crimea in 2014 to the start of the conflict in Ukraine in 2022. The EU faced several internal obstacles as a result of the COVID-19 outbreak and the 2015 refugee crisis, which made it more difficult for the organization to deal with Russia's increasing actions in Crimea and along Ukraine's borders. The European security architecture has been severely disturbed by the war in Ukraine, creating new risks and uncertainties for the EU as well as its transatlantic connections with the USA.

Russia's aggressiveness in Ukraine was seen by the Western powers as both an attack on Ukraine and a larger strike on the West. This dispute has brought to light flaws in the diplomatic and security frameworks that now govern conflict resolution, emphasizing the lack of recent defence budget increases, the military's lack of readiness, and the interdependence of the economy. Moscow broke Western principles of peace and security on 24 February 2022, when it invaded Ukraine under the pretence of 'special military operations' and stationed tanks there. The bipolar structure of international relations and the East-West division were terminated with the end of the Cold War in 1990. This period saw the fall of the Soviet Union and a dramatic change in the geopolitical landscape, especially for the countries of Central and Eastern Europe and the newly independent republics that broke away from the Soviet Union.

In stark contrast to the fortification of the European Economic Community into the European Union and the enlargement of NATO was the breakdown of the Warsaw Pact and the Council for Mutual Economic Assistance (Comecon). With the entry of former Soviet states into Western political, economic, and security structures, a new geopolitical environment of collaboration and confrontation with Moscow arose. From a security perspective, the main issue became how to protect Europe as a whole from possible Russian aggression. As the best security actor available to protect Europe and its citizens from Russian threats, NATO has come to be recognized.

NATO's expansion was seen as provocative from the Russian point of view, which helped Moscow justify its actions. Recent decisions by Finland and Sweden to renounce their historical policies of non-alignment and wartime neutrality in reaction to growing Russian aggression represent a significant shift from their long-standing beliefs. After remaining neutral for 80 years, Finland and Sweden decided to apply for membership in NATO because of increased security risks, including the possibility of Russian nuclear action against Ukraine. This choice was supported by a crucial security evaluation that wasn't just political. Neither nation has nuclear weapons, and NATO membership was required due to Moscow's increasing nuclear threat. According to Article 5 of the NATO treaty, such membership offers both collective defence and extended nuclear deterrent.

Geo-economic Dynamics and Security

Although there have always been disputes between the EU and Russia, Moscow's response to Brussels' policies changed significantly once Putin became President. As NATO and the EU expanded at the same time, Moscow's influence waned. From Moscow's perspective, this extension signified the formation of a new fault line separating East and West rather than just a minor geographic shift. Particular difficulties arose with NATO's expansion, as the defence alliance that had been established during the Cold War, re-established itself as a vital player in European and international security, rather than being dismantled. Moscow saw the enlargement of NATO as an immediate danger to its security.

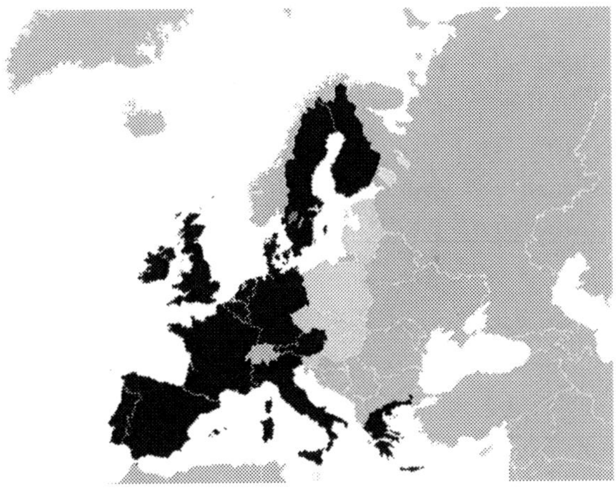

Source: https://www.wikiwand.com/en/2004_enlargement_of_the_European_Union

The European Union had its greatest expansion in 2004 when ten primarily Central and Eastern European nations joined. The objective was to expand the Union's borders eastward and put it closer to Russia. In the light of this, the EU introduced the European Neighbourhood Policy (ENP), which was directed at nations on its eastern and southern borders that were not likely contenders for EU membership. Moscow's sphere of influence intersected the ENP, especially on the eastern flank, and saw the policy as a way to gain political support from its former territories.

Russia's aggressive actions against Ukraine began with the invasion of Crimea in 2014, and they eventually led to Kiev's political allegiance changing from Moscow to Brussels. In spite of this flagrant transgression of international law and Ukraine's territorial integrity, the EU continued to interact with Russia due to concerns about energy and economic security. Asymmetric shocks from the Ukrainian war affected the EU in a number of ways. The Union was forced to diversify its energy sources in order to lessen its reliance on Moscow as a result of the biggest disruption to energy supplies from Russia to Europe. Energy ties between the European Union and Russia were significantly influenced by Russia, which is the world's largest exporter of natural gas and the second largest exporter of oil. But in order to lessen the impact of Moscow's punitive actions, the war compelled the EU to look for alternate energy sources in addition to imposing sanctions on Russia.

Due to the war and the sanctions that followed, exports from Russia and Ukraine decreased, which raised the price of food grains, metals, oil, and gas globally. This increase had a major effect on the economic recovery of Europe, causing rising inflation and stoking recessionary fears. The effects of the war in Ukraine differed among EU members. Poland, Germany, the Czech Republic, Italy, and Spain were the major countries receiving refugee flows. Many of the member-states were significantly dependent on Russian natural gas, crude oil, and solid fossil fuels. Russia continued to be an essential energy partner for the EU despite efforts to diversify its energy sources, especially in terms of cheap natural gas.[1]

The consequences of this dependence were highlighted by the conflict in Ukraine though, as Russia militarized its energy resources and severely hurt the economies of EU members. Rising energy prices as a result of the ensuing energy crisis had a detrimental effect on Europe's economic expansion. As winter approached, the EU and its member-states looked for alternate energy sources to lessen the effects of supply disruptions in response to the crisis. The conflict in Ukraine acted as a wake-up call, emphasizing the pressing need to address reliance on Russian energy supplies and draw lessons from previous attempts to diversify energy sources following the annexation of Crimea in 2014.[2]

European Union Policy of Sanctions

In order to lessen its reliance on Russian energy and stop the flow of money supporting Moscow's war endeavours, the EU was forced to adopt a tough position against Russia amid the worsening humanitarian, economic, and security crises. The following graphic displays the EU's adoption of various actions, including economic sanctions, throughout the course of the last eight months, as the crisis has continued.

The sanctions described above aimed to achieve several goals. They were initially used as a means of denouncing Russia for its invasion of Ukraine. They were then progressively stepped up to put pressure on the Russian government, companies, and certain individuals in an effort to force President Putin to put a stop to the war. Last, but not least, sanctions against Russian energy supplies, imposed as a last resort, highlighted the serious risk presented by the EU's reliance on Russian energy and attempted to gradually untangle it.

The EU enforced a number of industry-specific sanctions after Russia annexed Crimea in 2014 with the intention of punishing Moscow and forcing it to renounce its territorial claims. But these restrictions noticeably excluded important industries like gas, oil, and other commodities, making it impossible for Russia to alter its behaviour. Given Russia's flagrant disregard for international law, the EU's sanctions were seen as weak and lacked the determination to hold Russia accountable and resolve the issue.[3]

Internal disagreements among EU members about the specifics of the economic sanctions imposed on Russia further weakened political cohesion and postponed the settlement of the Ukraine crisis, possibly with more disastrous outcomes down the road. Instead of encouraging a shift in Moscow's political behaviour, the EU's lack of a cogent political endeavour to rebalance its relations with Russia during the previous eight years has strengthened Moscow's regional aspirations. In order to get around the sanctions and continue to participate in international trade, Russia has also established strong economic channels by fortifying ties with other countries.

Economic sanctions have affected Russia and the EU in different ways. Realpolitik has taken precedence over rules and ideals in the EU, as seen by its unwillingness to act decisively in the light of its substantial energy dependence on Russia and divergent political and economic interests with the USA. After Russia annexed Crimea in 2014, the EU has done nothing to diversify its energy sources and lessen its dependency on Russian gas and oil, even though it has articulated norms. Notably, the EU and its member-states prioritized energy security over adherence to international law, as evidenced by the eight years of uninterrupted development of Nordstream II preceding the crisis in Ukraine.

EU Assistance to Ukraine

As of March 2024, the European Union (EU) and its member-states have provided Ukraine with nearly € 81 billion in military, financial, humanitarian, and emergency aid, plus an additional € 17 billion for Ukrainian refugees, bringing the total support to almost € 98 billion. This includes € 47.9 billion in financial, humanitarian, and emergency assistance since 2022, composed of € 11.6 billion from the EU budget in 2022, € 18 billion in loans for 2023, and € 12.2 billion from member-states. In February 2024, the EU approved € 50 billion in new aid for 2024-2027, with € 4.5 billion disbursed in March 2024. Military assistance, managed through the European Peace Facility, totals € 11.1 billion, including a new € 5 billion Ukraine Assistance Fund approved in March 2024, € 3.6 billion for equipment and supplies between February 2022 and February 2023, and € 2 billion for ammunition. Additionally, the EU has set up a training mission for Ukraine's armed forces, and estimates bilateral military support from member-states at around € 22 billion as of March 2024.[4]

European Response to the Ukrainian Crisis

On 16 December 2021, the European Parliament passed a resolution addressing the current military build-up along the Ukrainian border. The resolution stated that this escalation not only poses a threat to peace, stability, and security in Europe, but also acts as a tool for obtaining political concessions from the West at the expense of Ukraine. Regarding Ukraine's desire to join NATO, the resolution opposes Russia's attempts to expand its 'sphere of influence' and dictate its destiny by emphasizing that any nation's choice of alliances should not be contingent on approval from a third party.[5] The resolution also suggests imposing harsh financial and economic sanctions on Russia and asks the High Representative to work with NATO and its partners.[6]

The European Council emphasized after its summit on 16 December 2021 how urgently Russia needs to reduce tensions along its border with Ukraine. It reaffirmed its unwavering support for Ukraine's territorial integrity and sovereignty while threatening serious costs and repercussions for any additional military aggression against the country. The Council demanded that in order to fully implement the Minsk Agreements, diplomatic efforts and support for the Normandy Format be made. Following the summit, the head of the European Commission, Ursula von der Leyen, announced that the EU was ready to apply more sanctions on Russia.[7]

European nations have vowed to stand with Ukraine during this crisis, but they have also made it clear that sending troops there is improbable. Ben Wallace, the Defence Secretary for the United Kingdom, underlined this position in a statement, stressing that it is extremely unlikely that any troops will be sent to Ukraine to confront Russia because it is not a member of NATO.[8] President Biden had similar opinions when he said that the USA was not considering sending soldiers to Ukraine.

A series of phone conversations between President Putin and several European leaders from the UK, France, and Germany revealed active diplomatic efforts to defuse tensions. European leaders voiced their concerns about the state of affairs and emphasized the pressing need for de-escalation through discussion, despite President Putin's constant insistence on starting international negotiations right once in order to provide legally enforceable guarantees.[9] On 22 December 2021, German Foreign Minister Annalena Baerbock urged for communication to diffuse the situation, stressing a return to the negotiation table within the framework of the NATO-Russia Council and the Normandy Format. While NATO allies were open to debate Russia's requests, they would not allow Moscow to impose conditions on the alliance or its partners, stressed Germany's Defence Minister Christine Lambrecht.[10]

Eastern European countries are becoming increasingly alarmed about Russia's actions and demands, especially with regard to legal assurances. The historical experiences of the Baltic states have increased their apprehension of Russia. Moscow's demands for guarantees, which call for the withdrawal of armed forces and weaponry from nations that joined the alliance after 1997 and include most of Eastern Europe, the Baltic states, and the Balkans, would drastically change the security landscape in Europe. With multinational battle groups the size of battalions based there, Poland and the Baltic nations, which joined NATO in 1999 and 2004, respectively, are integral to the alliance's forward presence in both its eastern and northern regions. The alliance's collective defence is strengthened by its advanced presence, which also gives Northern and Eastern Europe crucial confidence and deterrence.[11]

Furthermore, if weapons were to be removed from the boundaries of other European states, NATO would not be able to station missiles in nations like Romania and Poland.[12] These nations see these events as proof of Moscow's attempts to weaken their sovereignty and as an attempt by Russia to re-establish a sphere of influence in the area. The Baltic nations have expressed similar worries, with Gitanas Nauseda, the president of Lithuania, characterizing the current state of affairs as "probably the most dangerous it's been in 30 years."[13]

Russia-Ukraine War and World Order

The way developed countries coordinated their response to Russia's entry into Ukraine is a clear example of how dominant the so-called 'Western' world order is. Countries like Canada, Japan, Australia, South Korea, Singapore, and others offered minimal opposition to the joint efforts of the USA and the EU to impose financial and other sanctions on Russia. Instead, these countries openly backed the sanctions because they knew that if Putin was successful in destroying Ukraine's sovereignty by force, it may inspire other revisionist powers like China and Iran to take similar forceful measures.

For a variety of reasons, many developing nations have spoken very little about Russia's invasion of Ukraine. Some countries like China and North Korea believe that Russia's actions are legitimate, while other countries, like Hungary and Brazil, mainly depend on Russian oil, fertilizers, and resources. Furthermore, a large portion of Africa, Southeast Asia, and the Pacific Islands believe they have no direct stake in the battle. In actuality, the effects of the conflict—such as shortages of food and energy, increased energy costs, and inflation—are entwined with the global power of the system dominated by the West. The dynamics of the international order were already being shaped before the invasion by programs led by the West, including the CPTPP, the Japan-EU Economic Partnership Agreement, the US Indo-Pacific Economic Framework, FOIP, and the Supply Chain Resilience Initiative. Furthermore, cooperative initiatives like AUKUS and the Quad were reinventing concepts of competition, deterrence, and public good provision, especially in fields like artificial intelligence (AI), quantum computing, cyberspace, security, and the digital economy. The rules governing cyberspace, AI, the digital economy, and the role of government in economies and society will ultimately depend on how China and the USA and its allies compete.

Russia's comparative advantages in oil and agriculture, as well as its political and economic advantages, have been severely undermined since the invasion. Russia will be less able to assist China in opposing the Western-led system as a result of its isolation. Russia's aggression has brought the USA closer to its allies and partners, not brought an end to the Western-led system. The USA, the EU, NATO, and its allies have been inspired by Putin's moves to integrate their economies, society, technologies, and energy resources. This geopolitical orientation goes beyond Moscow to include China's endeavours to weaken the Indo-Pacific security architecture spearheaded by the USA.

The possible forcible reunification of Taiwan with the mainland, assertive actions in the South and East China seas, and the effects on international supply lines and sea lanes of communication are among the main causes for concern. Right now, the most important thing is to make sure that international trade stays robust, steady, and operational. The possible forcible reunification of Taiwan with the mainland, assertive actions in the South and East China seas, and the effects on international supply lines and sea lanes of communication are among the main causes for concern. Right now, the most important thing is to make sure that international trade stays robust, steady, and operational. The reaction of developed countries to Russia's invasion of Ukraine, along with worries about China's revisionist tendencies, highlights how the so-called Western international order is changing to compete with and withstand revisionist states that aim to reshape the international order in their favour, rather than signalling the emergence of a post-Western international order.

Conclusion

Europe had its biggest political, economic, and security upheaval since the start of the COVID-19 epidemic as a result of the invasion of Ukraine in February 2022. It also presented a serious threat to one of the EU's most important alliances with Russia. The EU and its member-states were caught off guard by the return of interstate warfare to Europe eight years after the takeover of Crimea. Brussels is adjusting to the new geopolitical environment, which is defined by 'the return of power politics,' as described by the European Council, a key priority. However, the discrepancy between the speed at which policy is being adjusted and the actual ability on the ground has further increased EU uncertainty.

The objective of the war in Ukraine was to replace the current political system in the region with a new one. Before launching military action, Putin may have misjudged two crucial factors: first, the US and EU's unwavering political support for Ukraine, even at great costs like energy decoupling; and second, the resolve of Ukraine's political leadership and people to take on a more powerful foe. The events of the last eight months have forced the EU to take the initiative and create a more coordinated response at the regional level. But the war's after-effects are changing the EU's internal dynamics as well as its exterior relations, which is aggravating security worries and disrupting the economy.

The invasion of Ukraine in 2022 eliminated any last doubts regarding the return of geopolitics since 2014. Europe's return to territorial defence, which has been moving towards political union since 1957, is a challenge to the core tenet of foreign policy: territorial defence. Peace, stability, and security have been replaced by violence, instability, and uncertainty as the EU attempts to navigate a war-torn continent. Renegotiating security in a globalized society presents hitherto unseen issues as the future looks increasingly uncertain.

REFERENCES

1. Eurostat, 2022, From where do we import energy? https://ec.europa.eu/eurostat/cache/infographs/energy/bloc-2c.html
2. Halser, C. and Paraschiv, F. (2022). 'Pathways to Overcoming Natural Gas Dependency on Russia—The German Case,' *Energies*, 15(14): 1-24.
3. Drezner, Daniel. W., (2003) 'How Smart are Smart Sanctions,' *International Studies Review*, 5(1): 107-110.
4. Russia's War Against Ukraine: European Union Responses and U.S. EU Relations (congress.gov)
5. 'Resolution—Situation at the Ukrainian border and in Russian-occupied territories of Ukraine', European Parliament, 16 December 2021, https://www.europarl.europa.eu/doceo/document/TA-9-2021-0515_EN.html, accessed on 29 December 2021.

6. Conclusions, European Council meeting, 16 December 2021, European Council, https://www.consilium.europa.eu/media/53575/20211216-euco-conclusions-en.pdf, accessed on 30 December 2021.
7. Normandy Format—The Normandy Format talks involve the representatives of four countries, Germany, Russia, Ukraine and France, and are aimed to resolve the crisis in Donbas.
8. *BBC*, 18 December 2021, https://www.bbc.com/news/world-europe-59712020, accessed on 30 December 2021.
9. *BBC*, 8 December 2021, https://www.bbc.com/news/world-europe-59582013, accessed on 30 December 2021.
10. *France24*, 22 December 2021, https://www.france24.com/en/europe/20211222-germany-urges-dialogue-with-russia-says-greatly-concerned-by-putin-military-threat, accessed on 30 December 2021.
11. *Politico*, 19 December 2021, https://www.politico.eu/article/russia-cannot-dictate-nato-military-posture-germany-says/, accessed on 30 December 2021.
12. *The Guardian*, 17 December 2021, https://www.theguardian.com/world/2021/dec/17/russia-issues-list-demands-tensions-europe-ukraine-nato, accessed on 30 December 2021.
13. *BBC*, 23 December 2021, https://www.bbc.com/news/world-europe-59766810, accessed on 31 December 2021.

16

The Role of the United Nations Security Council in the Russia-Ukraine War

Manvendra Kumar Verma and Vishal Dixit

Introduction

The conflict between Russia and Ukraine has given rise to a protracted and multifaceted geopolitical crisis which is posing a significant challenge to regional stability and international security. Central to the efforts aimed at resolving this conflict stands the United Nations Security Council (UNSC), the principal agency entrusted with the responsibility of maintaining global peace and security. The Security Council is authorized by UN Charter Chapter VII to implement enforcement actions in order to preserve or re-establish global peace and security.[1] Therefore, the role and effectiveness of the UNSC in addressing the complexities of the Russia-Ukraine war have garnered substantial global attention.

The Russia-Ukraine war is a complex and ongoing dispute primarily centred on geopolitical tensions, territorial disputes, and historical complexities. It gained significant international attention in 2014 following Russia's annexation of Crimea, which was previously part of Ukraine. This move triggered widespread condemnation from the international community, leading to economic sanctions against Russia. The conflict escalated further with the emergence of separatist movements in eastern Ukraine, notably in the Donetsk and Luhansk regions, leading to armed conflict between Ukrainian government forces and pro-Russian separatists. The situation has resulted in a humanitarian crisis, displacing thousands of people and causing casualties on both sides.

The conflict, marked by territorial disputes, military confrontations, and political intricacies, highlights the challenges and limitations of the UNSC's intervention mechanisms in resolving conflicts in contemporary times. The UNSC's involvement in conflicts of such magnitude underscores its critical mandate in responding to and mitigating crises that threaten international peace. However, this conflict offers an avenue to scrutinise the efficacy of multilateral diplomacy and international law in resolving the issues of prolonged territorial disputes. The UNSC's involvement includes issuing resolutions, mediating negotiations, and overseeing efforts to find a diplomatic resolution. Moreover, the UNSC's effectiveness in addressing this conflict has been hampered by divergent interests among its permanent members and challenges related to enforcing resolutions due to veto powers and geopolitical complexities. Russia has been severely impacted by US and EU sanctions; the majority of its banking sector is no longer able to access the dollar-denominated financial system, and default is a real possibility.[2] Nonetheless, the UNSC remains a crucial platform for multilateral dialogue and action in managing conflicts and upholding international peace and security.

This article examines and assesses the extent of the United Nations Security Council's participation and impact on the conflict between Russia and Ukraine by analysing and evaluating existing research, empirical data, and diplomatic papers. This article aims to contribute to the broader discourse on international conflict resolution mechanisms and the effectiveness of the United Nations in addressing contemporary geopolitical crises by exploring historical precedents, analysing the substance and implementation of UNSC resolutions, and outlining the challenges faced by the Council.

Historical Context

The historical context of the Russia-Ukraine conflict is marked by pivotal events that have shaped the dynamics and implications of this protracted dispute.

Annexation of Crimea

In 2014, Russia's annexation of Crimea, a region historically part of Ukraine, triggered a seismic shift in regional geopolitics. The annexation followed a controversial referendum in Crimea, 96.8 per cent of voters in an illegal referendum held on 16 March in the territory of the Autonomous Republic of Crimea and the separate municipality of Sevastopol chose to become subjects of the Russian Federation, with 83.1 per cent of voters casting ballots in favour of the move.[3] Russia's swift incorporation of Crimea into its territory sparked widespread condemnation, challenging established norms of international law regarding territorial integrity. Ukraine faced the loss of significant territory, leading to domestic turmoil and a rupture in bilateral relations with Russia. The move drew condemnation and triggered sanctions from Western nations, altering diplomatic relationships, and fuelling tensions between Russia and the Western powers. The international community swiftly responded to Russia's action. Several countries, particularly the Western powers, condemned the annexation and imposed targeted economic sanctions on Russia.[4] Within the United Nations, the Security Council held discussions regarding the situation in Crimea, highlighting concerns over violations of Ukraine's sovereignty. However, due to Russia's veto power as a permanent member of the UNSC, formal resolutions condemning the annexation were blocked, limiting the Council's ability to take robust action.

Eastern Ukraine Conflict

The annexation of Crimea was followed by a surge in tensions in eastern Ukraine. Pro-Russian separatist movements emerged in the Donetsk and Luhansk regions, leading to armed conflict between Ukrainian government forces and these separatist groups. The situation escalated into a full-fledged conflict characterised by sporadic fighting, ceasefires that were repeatedly violated, and a significant humanitarian toll. The UNSC grappled with addressing the escalating hostilities in eastern Ukraine. Discussions and debates within the Council reflected the deep divisions among its members regarding the conflict. While calls for de-escalation and diplomatic resolutions were reiterated, the Council's ability to intervene effectively was hindered by geopolitical interests and divergent positions among its permanent members, particularly Russia's support for the separatist movements.[5]

UNSC Resolutions on the Russia-Ukraine Conflict

The UNSC resolutions draw upon the foundational principles of the UN Charter in which Articles 39 to 42 outline the UNSC's role in maintaining international peace and security, issuing resolutions, and enforcement mechanisms. The Russia-Ukraine dispute has been the subject of several resolutions in the United Nations Security Council (UNSC) and United Nations General Assembly (UNGA) indicating efforts to address the rising tensions and advance regional peace.

- Resolution 2202 (2015) advocated commitment to the Minsk agreements and reaffirmed support for the sovereignty and territorial integrity of Ukraine. In addition to restating the UNSC's commitment to respecting Ukraine's borders, it emphasized a peaceful resolution of the crisis.[6]
- Resolution 2623 (2022) on convening an emergency special session of the General Assembly on the Russia-Ukraine conflict resolution.[7]
- The UN General Assembly also passed a resolution on 22 February 2023, calling upon Russia to withdraw from Ukraine. Just hours before the war entered its second year, the international body passed a new resolution demanding an end to the fighting.[8]

Notwithstanding, these resolutions emphasised diplomatic solutions and called for adherence to international law, but challenges in implementation persisted. The conflict in eastern Ukraine continued despite ceasefire calls, indicating limitations in enforcing these resolutions on the ground. Impact assessments revealed mixed outcomes with limited success in altering the conflict's trajectory or compelling full cooperation by the involved parties.

Moreover, the recent deliberations of the United Nations Security Council (UNSC) in February 2024 have centred on the humanitarian catastrophe in Ukraine, the execution of the Minsk Agreements,[9, 10] and the legality of acts undertaken by both Russia and Ukraine. Russia has consistently defended its actions by blaming Ukraine for non-compliance with the Minsk agreements and neglecting the protection of Russian-speaking communities in Donbas.[11]

Challenges and Limitations of the UNSC

Veto Power

Role of Veto Power: The veto power wielded by the UNSC's permanent members, notably Russia, has played a significant role in impeding decisive action regarding the Russia-Ukraine conflict. Russia's strategic interests in the region have influenced its stance within the Council, leading to the blockage of resolutions deemed unfavourable to its position. In September 2022, a Security Council resolution denouncing the attempted annexation of areas in Ukraine was vetoed by Russia.[12] The exercise of veto power has hindered the Council's ability to issue unified and enforceable resolutions, impeding diplomatic efforts aimed at conflict resolution.

Impact on Diplomatic Efforts: The use of veto power by a permanent member has resulted in a stalemate within the UNSC, hampering diplomatic initiatives. Conflicting positions among member-states have led to deadlock situations, reducing the Council's effectiveness in issuing resolutions that could facilitate meaningful dialogue or enforce compliance with international norms. The presence of veto power diminishes the prospects of robust action and compromises the Council's ability to address the conflict decisively.

Divergent Interests

Conflicting Interests Among Members: Divergent geopolitical interests among UNSC members, particularly between the Western powers and Russia, have posed significant challenges. Varying perspectives on the Russia-Ukraine conflict, including differing assessments of sovereignty, have hindered cohesive action. It has been stated repeatedly and over again by members of this Council, the General Assembly, and the Secretary-General that Russia's invasion of Ukraine violates both Ukraine's territorial integrity and the UN Charter.[13] However, Disagreements over the issues from the Russian side and supporters have complicated efforts to achieve consensus within the Council.

Hindrance to Coordinated Actions: The presence of divergent interests has hindered the Council's ability to take coordinated actions. Disagreements over the nature of the conflict, preferred approaches to resolution, and diverging strategic priorities among member-states have led to a lack of unity. This lack of consensus has impeded the Council's effectiveness in issuing resolutions that could meaningfully impact the conflict's trajectory.

Enforcement Capabilities

Assessment of Enforcement Capabilities: The UNSC faces limitations in enforcing its resolutions regarding the Russia-Ukraine conflict. The functions and powers of the Security Council under the UN Charter include 'to call on Members to apply economic sanctions and other measures not involving the use of force to prevent or stop aggression and to take military action against an aggressor'[14] but challenges in ensuring compliance on the ground stem from the Council's limited enforcement mechanisms. While resolutions are legally binding, the ability to ensure adherence is constrained by the absence of a standing enforcement force. Reliance on voluntary compliance from involved parties and the absence of robust mechanisms for enforcing sanctions or mandates limit the Council's ability to compel compliance.

Challenges in Ensuring Compliance: The practical challenges of ensuring compliance with UNSC resolutions on the ground pose a significant obstacle. Despite issuing resolutions, the UNSC encounters difficulties in overseeing and enforcing compliance, particularly in conflict zones. Factors such as the lack of monitoring mechanisms, resistance from involved parties, and the absence of a unified approach among member-states hinder effective enforcement and implementation.

Stance of Key UNSC Members

Russia's Position

Within the UNSC, Russia has adopted a prominent and influential stance regarding the Russia-Ukraine conflict. It has consistently defended its actions, including the annexation of Crimea, presenting it as a matter of national interest, and protecting the rights of Russian-speaking populations in Ukraine. Russia has employed its veto power twice to shield itself from Council resolutions condemning its actions, challenging the Council's ability to issue unified responses since the war started.[15]

Moreover, in June 2024, Russian President Vladimir Putin outlined a strategy for achieving victory in Ukraine. According to his theory, Russian forces will be able to make continuous and gradual advances, prevent Ukraine from launching successful counteroffensive operations of strategic importance, and ultimately win a war of attrition against Ukrainian forces.[16]

Examination of Motivations and Strategies

Russia's motivations are multifaceted, combining geopolitical interests, historical ties, and security concerns. Its strategies within the UNSC involve leveraging diplomatic manoeuvres to prevent punitive measures against it and support separatist movements in eastern Ukraine. Russia aims to safeguard its influence in the region and resist what it perceives as Western encroachment in its spheres of influence.

United States and European Powers

Key Western powers, notably the USA and European nations, have staunchly supported Ukraine's territorial integrity and condemned Russia's actions in the conflict. The USA has "provided approximately $ 44.2 billion in military assistance"[17] since the conflict began in February 2022. In June 2024, the US Department of Defence (DoD) declared a security aid package of $ 225 million for Ukraine. Additionally, French President Emmanuel Macron declared that France will supply Ukraine with an undisclosed quantity of Mirage 2000-5 fighter aircraft and will also give training and equipment for a brigade consisting of 4,500 Ukrainian soldiers.[18] The United Kingdom is supplying both lethal and non-lethal armaments, such as tanks, air defence systems, and long-range precision attack missiles.[19] Although the UK has pledged to offer training for Ukrainian fast jet pilots, they will not be supplying combat fighter aircraft. Therefore, the positions of these countries within the UNSC emphasise upholding international law, respect for Ukraine's sovereignty, and the imposition of targeted sanctions against Russia in response to its actions.

Influence on Council Dynamics

The dynamics inside the UNSC regarding the Russia-Ukraine crisis are greatly influenced by the opinions of the USA and European nations.

Their combined position influences the conversation, advocates resolutions denouncing Russia's activities, and emphasises the necessity of diplomatic solutions. But sometimes, different attitudes among the Western powers result in subtle disparities in tactics, which affects the Council's capacity to put forward a united front.

Implications for International Peace and Security

The UNSC's response to the Russia-Ukraine conflict set implications for regional stability with potential spill-over effects on other countries. The conflict also sets precedents for handling similar disputes globally and guides global norms on peace, sovereignty, and international security.

Regional Stability

UNSC's Response and Regional Dynamics

The way the UNSC handles the Russia-Ukraine crisis has a big impact on Eastern Europe's regional stability. The region's geopolitical dynamics are impacted by the conflict's escalation and the UNSC's inability to deliver a definitive settlement. Persistent tensions, military confrontations, and the annexation of Crimea have disrupted stability, fostering an atmosphere of uncertainty and insecurity.

Potential Spill-over Effects

The conflict's effects might extend beyond Ukraine to its neighbours. Concerns regarding spill-over implications include population displacement, the risk of further destabilisation in neighbouring regions, and cross-border security concerns. The refugee crisis, economic turmoil, and security threats are currently posing problems for neighbouring countries.

Global Precedents

Broader Implications for Handling Similar Disputes

The war between Russia and Ukraine establishes parameters for resolving similar problems worldwide. When it comes to handling territorial disputes and abuses of sovereignty, the UNSC's decisions and the international community's strategy serve as models for handling similar situations. Future attempts at settlement are guided by lessons learned from the efficacy of diplomatic interventions and enforcement measures.

Impact on Global Peace and Security Norms

The conflict's effects extend beyond the surrounding areas and have an impact on international standards for security and peace. The UNSC's failure to mediate a durable settlement underscores the difficulties in upholding international law, preserving territorial integrity, and halting unilateral actions that contravene accepted standards. The Russia-Ukraine war functions as a case study for influencing opinions on the effectiveness of international and regional institutions in preserving peace around the world.

Conclusion

Understanding the UNSC's role in the Russia-Ukraine crisis sheds light on several important issues. The annexation of Crimea and the continued hostilities in eastern Ukraine have highlighted the complexity of the conflict and the difficulties in resolving disputes within the framework of the UNSC. Important conclusions highlight the barriers to the Council's ability to resolve the dispute forcefully, including the effects of veto power, competing interests among member-states, and limitations in enforcement instrumentation. The UNSC addressed the Russia-Ukraine conflict in a crucial but constrained manner. Despite the resolutions it issued highlighting Ukraine's sovereignty and territorial integrity, difficulties were encountered in carrying them out and making them legally binding. The difficulties in handling disputes involving strong parties with vested interests are brought to light by the Council's incapacity to see past geopolitical divides and assist in a long-lasting settlement.

A couple of suggestions surface to guide future diplomacy efforts and improve the UNSC's efficacy in comparable disputes. First, to reduce conflicting interests and give global stability precedence over geopolitical rivalry, there is an urgent need for enhanced communication and collaboration among UNSC members. Secondly, initiatives ought to concentrate on fortifying enforcement protocols and devising tactics for fostering agreement within the Council.

Furthermore, placing a strong emphasis on early conflict resolution and preventative diplomacy may help to keep similar problems from getting worse in the future.

REFERENCES

1. United Nations. (2018). *Maintain International Peace and Security*, United Nations. https://www.un.org/en/our-work/maintain-international-peace-and-security
2. Mankoff, J. (2022). Russia's War in Ukraine: Identity, History, and Conflict, www.csis.org. https://www.csis.org/analysis/russias-war-ukraine-identity-history-and-conflict/
3. Olszanski, T. (19 March 2014a). 'The consequences of the annexation of Crimea.' OSW Centre for Eastern Studies. https://www.osw.waw.pl/en/publikacje/analyses/2014-03-19/consequences-annexation-crimea
4. Christie, E. H. (13 July 2015). 'Sanctions after Crimea: Have they worked?' *NATO Review*. https://www.nato.int/docu/review/articles/2015/07/13/sanctions-after-crimea-have-they-worked/index.html
5. Isachenkov, V. (21 February 2022). 'Explainer: The story behind Ukraine's separatist regions,' *AP News*, https://apnews.com/article/russia-ukraine-europe-russia-vladimir-putin-moscow-bcd0c04a2aa146e76b7e757f482f27bb
6. Unanimously Adopting Resolution 2202 (2015). Security Council Calls on Parties to Implement Accords Aimed at Peaceful Settlement in Eastern Ukraine, UN Press. (n.d.), Press.un.org. https://press.un.org/EN/2015/SC11785.DOC.HTM
7. Security Council resolution 2623 (2022). [on convening an emergency special session of the General Assembly on Ukraine]. (2022), Digitallibrary.un.org. https://digitallibrary.un.org/record/3958818?ln=en
8. 'UN General Assembly calls for immediate end to war in Ukraine, *UN News*. (23 February 2023), News.un.org, https://news.un.org/en/story/2023/02/1133847#:~:text=The
9. PA-X: Peace Agreements Database. (n.d.). www.peaceagreements.org. https://www.peaceagreements.org/view/1363
10. Allan, D. (22 May 2020). 'The Minsk-2 agreement, Chatham House – International Affairs Think Tank. https://www.chathamhouse.org/2020/05/minsk-conundrum-western-policy-and-russias-war-eastern-ukraine-0/minsk-2-agreement
11. Meetings Coverage and Press Releases. "Two Years after Russian Federation's Invasion, UN Remains Committed to Ukraine's Sovereignty, Independence, Assistant Secretary-General Tells Security Council," Meetings Coverage and Press Releases, press.un.org, 12 February, 2024, https://press.un.org/en/2024/sc15588.doc.htm.
12. Russia vetoes Security Council resolution condemning attempted annexation of Ukraine regions, *UN News*. (30 September 2022), News.un.org. https://news.un.org/en/story/2022/09/1129102#:~:text=Russia
13. United States Mission to the United Nations. (18 May 2023b). Remarks at a UN Security Council Briefing on Ukraine. United States Mission to the United Nations, https://usun.usmission.gov/remarks-at-a-un-security-council-briefing-on-

ukraine-8/#:~:text=Members

14. United Nations. (2015). Functions and Powers, United Nations Security Council, un.org. https://www.un.org/securitycouncil/content/functions-and-powers
15. Sciboz, J. (2022). Research Guides: Security Council - Quick Links: Vetoes, research.un.org. https://research.un.org/en/docs/sc/quick/veto
16. Bailey, Riley, Christina Harward, Nicole Wolkov, Grace Mappes, and George Barros. 'Russian offensive campaign assessment, June 7, 2024," Institute for the Study of War, 7 June 2024. https://www.understandingwar.org/backgrounder/russian-offensive-campaign-assessment-june-7-2024.
17. U.S. Department of State. (16 September 2022). 'U.S. Security Cooperation With Ukraine.' United States Department of State. https://www.state.gov/u-s-security-cooperation-with-ukraine/
18. Bailey, Riley, Christina Harward, Nicole Wolkov, Grace Mappes, and George Barros. 'Russian offensive campaign assessment, 7 June 2024' Institute for the Study of War, 7 June 2024 https://www.understandingwar.org/backgrounder/russian-offensive-campaign-assessment-june-7-2024
19. Mills, Claire. 'Military Assistance to Ukraine since the Russian Invasion,' commonslibrary.parliament.uk, 2 May 2024. https://researchbriefings.files.parliament.uk/documents/CBP-9477/CBP-9477.pdf.

BIBLIOGRAPHY

- Council on Foreign Relations. (28 February 2023). The UN Security Council.Council on Foreign Relations. https://www.cfr.org/backgrounder/un-security-council
- Dayal, A. & Dunton, C. (1 March 2023). 'The U.N. Security Council Was Designed for Deadlock — Can it Change?' United States Institute of Peace. https://www.usip.org/publications/2023/03/un-security-council-was-designed-for deadlock-can-it-change
- Feltman, J. (28 March 2023). 'War, peace, and the international system after Ukraine.' Brookings, https://www.brookings.edu/articles/war-peace-and-the-international-system-after-ukraine/IJR. (n.d.). UN Security Council Failure to Mediate in the Russia-Ukraine Conflict. IJR. https://www.ijr.org.za/2022/09/30/un-security-council-failure-to-mediate-in-the-russia-ukraine-conflict/
- ОтпарламентаКрымапотребовалипровестиреферендумоботделенииотУкраины | Информационноеагентство "е-Крым." (3 March 2014). Web.archive.org. https://web.archive.org/web/20140303184134/http://www.e-crimea.info/news/ot-parlamenta-kryma-potrebovali-provesti-referendum-ob-otdelenii-ot-ukrainy
- Pszczel, R. (7 July 2022). *NATO Review* - The consequences of Russia's invasion of Ukraine for international security – NATO and beyond. *NATO Review* https://www.nato.int/docu/review/articles/2022/07/07/the-consequences-of-russias-invasion-of-ukraine-for-international-security-nato-and-beyond/index.html
- UN Documents for Ukraine. (2015). Securitycouncilreport.org. https://www.securitycouncilreport.org/un-documents/ukraine/
- United Nations. (2010). 'Role of the Security Council. United Nations

Peacekeeping. https://peacekeeping.un.org/en/role-of-security-council

- United Nations. (15 March 2014). 'UN Security Council action on Crimea referendum blocked.' *UN News*. https://news.un.org/en/story/2014/03/464002-un-security-council-action-crimea-referendum-blocked
- United Nations. (12 January 2023). 'With Invasion of Ukraine, Security Council's 2022 Efforts to Maintain International Peace, Stability Mired by Widening Rifts between Veto-Wielding Members,' UN Press, Press.un.org. https://press.un.org/en/2023/sc15172.doc.htm

17

Russia-Ukraine War: Assessing the Impact on the Gulf States

Sreshtha Chakraborty

Introduction

The Russia-Ukraine war has expedited the East-West split on the international scene and fundamentally changed the continent's security architecture. The Gulf region is one of the areas that have been affected by the geopolitical shocks. Such dynamics provide opportunities and challenges for Gulf Cooperation Council (GCC) members looking to balance their interactions with influential players worldwide. US-Gulf relations date back many years but the alleged 'new cold war' causes issues that need reconfiguring their relationship. The situation demands that Washington and the 'new Gulf' engage in a thorough and severe strategic debate to come to a new understanding. The Gulf-US relationship was evident during the Cold War. The USA persisted in its commitment to preserving the region's security, and the Gulf sided with it and the West. Compared to traditional wars, proxy wars have been fought far more frequently in recent years by the Arab states of the Persian Gulf and the member-states of the Gulf Cooperation Council, which include Saudi Arabia, Bahrain, Qatar, Kuwait, Oman, and the United Arab Emirates. They were, and still are, in a type of competition for supremacy in the Middle East (e.g., proxy wars between Saudi Arabia and Iran in Syria, Iraq, Lebanon, and Yemen),which stresses that the states of the Middle East are hostile, anarchic environments in which war, upheaval, and revolution are always a possibility [Walt, 1987].

Meanwhile, the Ukrainian crisis has constrained the Western ability and desire to strategically influence the Gulf due to the intensification of the geopolitics between the USA and Russia surrounding Ukraine. As a result, the geopolitical competition of the global powers in the region is becoming more complex. In particular, by using the Russia-Ukraine war as a means of consolidating, adjusting, and reorganizing its global ally system, the USA is converting the conflict into a unique platform for upholding and rebuilding American hegemony. Regarding the Russia-Ukraine War, other nations have reacted in various ways to the USA and Russia. The relative decline of the USA and the West in the new geopolitics is primarily reflected in the fact that East, Central Asia, South Asia, and other developing nations and regions neither chose to side with the USA nor follow its lead [Goldberg, 2022].

The Middle East has long been known for conflict and dependency, particularly from the West. Long-lasting conflicts brought on by external intervention and internal conflicts have created an unstable atmosphere detrimental to regional cooperation and development. Even though the Middle East's fundamental traits of dependency and conflict have not entirely changed, there has been a shift in power dynamics since the start of the so-called Arab Uprising in 2011, particularly in the last two years. The Middle East is currently experiencing a more varied and balanced impact from significant powers beyond the region. The Gulf has generally remained neutral (Zhang, 2022; She, 2022; Yang, 2022; Wu, 2022) between the USA and Russia and has not chosen sides. The waning influence of established powers in the Middle East, including the USA, Russia, and Europe, particularly in the light of the USA's strategic retreat from the region and the presence of newer powers like China, has changed the dynamics. However, the conflict between Russia and Ukraine has significantly affected the Middle East. The region has been severely impacted by the spike in energy prices and the food crisis brought on by the Russia-Ukraine war, which has put the region's internal governance and development initiatives to the test [Yahya, 2022].

Reaction of Gulf Countries to the Conflict

In the initial stages of the conflict, it was uncommon for all the Gulf States to oppose or support Russia strongly. Despite appearing to respond differently, most countries in the region remained neutral. The only nations to take firm stances against Russia were Kuwait, which opposed Russia's military action against Ukraine, and Syria, which Russia has recently defended and supported. However, despite the continued operation of the Arab states of the Persian Gulf in an unstable environment, they have not chosen to become directly involved in the hostilities in Ukraine. The Arab states have not aligned themselves with either Russia or Ukraine. Ukraine is supported by the USA and the EU, representing the democratic-liberal perspective, while Russia's stance is seen as undemocratic and anti-liberal (Frolovskyi, 2018).

For a long time, the Gulf's oil monarchies have been viewed as the USA's traditional allies. But the 2022-2023 conflict in Ukraine turned into a spark for Arab-American relations, causing Arab leaders to realize that allying based on a single superpower is a mistake. The Gulf region remains a zone of the American stronghold, and a process of change has been underway that includes the emerging role of China and Russia in the new sub-regional order. It has been evident that presidents Barack Obama (2009-2017) and Joe Biden (2021–) both want to reduce direct US involvement in the Middle East. This is caused, among other things, by East Asia becoming the centre of the global geopolitical competition for hegemony. The Arab countries have enumerated a long list regarding the USA's mismanagement when it comes to their region; mainly, the reasons like the abandonment of US allies (including Hosni Mubarak in Egypt and Ben Ali in Tunisia) during the Arab Uprising, the withdrawal of US troops from Iraq and Afghanistan, the withdrawal of support (especially in the form of arms sales) for Saudi Arabia's war in Yemen, the negotiation of a nuclear deal with Iran, the failure to respond to Bashar al-Assad's use of chemical weapons in Syria, attempts to make Saudi Arabia an international pariah for its involvement in the murder of Saudi journalist Jamal Khashoggi in Istanbul, and much more. This notion among Arabs has contributed to an increase in anti-American sentiment in the Middle East. Still, it also warned the oil monarchies that they needed to form new alliances or become more secure in their own right. China and Russia have decided to capitalize on the US pullout from the Middle East and the growing disenchantment of Arab leaders with US foreign policy. Taking advantage of the US withdrawal from the Middle East, Russia has finalized many trade agreements with GCC nations, like oil supply agreements with Saudi Arabia, military and technical contracts with Qatar, agreements within OPEC+, and a formula for trilateral consultations on Syria. The Gulf Arab states and China are working together more closely, as they share a joint opposition to US hegemony and a desire to alter the prevailing liberal-democratic order. China is using the war as a means of attracting the Arab states, while not openly opposing US hegemony in the Gulf region. However, China has made inroads in the Gulf region by fostering greater international relations and closer economic cooperation. China remains the leading importer of Saudi oil (38%), and the amount of trade between GCC countries and China in 2020 was USD 160 billion [Ministry of Foreign Affairs of the People's Republic of China, 2021]. Xi Jinping's talks with Arab leaders in recent months have concerned, among other things, the inclusion of the Belt and Road Initiative in the vision plan of many Gulf countries.

As the conflict between Russia and Ukraine has developed, the USA has put more and more pressure on Arab nations, particularly its allies, Saudi Arabia and the United Arab Emirates. This comes in direct pressure to take part in confrontation and impose sanctions on Russia, as well as indirect pressure to work with the USA to impose sanctions on Russia in the energy sector. Arab nations did not, however, heedlessly follow US sanctions against Russia, and weighing US and Russian interests has come to dominate Arab foreign policy decisions. Certain nations have participated in geopolitical manoeuvres with the USA, as demonstrated by their defiance of US demands for increased oil production by Saudi Arabia and the United Arab Emirates. The USA has repeatedly urged Saudi Arabia to significantly boost oil production to slow the sharp rise in global oil prices since the start of the Russia-Ukraine war. However, Saudi Arabia has insisted on upholding earlier production agreements with Russia and other significant oil-producing nations. However, as previously noted, the USA continues to be the primary external guarantee of the security of Arab governments, as it holds US military bases in the region and multiple military cooperation agreements between the USA and the GCC member-states [She, 2022].

Reaction of Iran to the Russia-Ukraine War

Achieving consensus on the nuclear agreement has been one of Iran's most pressing demands, as it would enable the country to lift sanctions and alleviate its increasingly dire economic situation. However, the Iran nuclear agreement negotiations have been adversely affected by the Russia-Ukraine war, primarily due to changing perspectives on the region of the USA. The USA, while emphasizing the importance of decoupling sanctions against Russia over the Ukraine issue from the Iran nuclear issue, also maintains the following position: Under a variety of pretexts, Iran's nuclear negotiations are delayed. Due to the severe Western sanctions imposed on both Iran and Russia, the Russia-Ukraine war has provided an impetus for the formation of an alliance between Russia and Iran. About the Russia-Ukraine war, Iran abstained from sanctioning Russia not only in the face of a crisis but also to strengthen its strategic position with Russia. Since the conflict's onset, the collaboration between Russia and Iran has steadily expanded across various domains, including politics, diplomacy, military affairs, economics, finance, energy, transportation, and more. The two countries have entered into an energy collaboration agreement valued at approximately $ 40 billion and are engaged in discussions for a long-term cooperation agreement. In July 2022, Russian President Vladimir Putin visited Iran, emphasizing Russia's significance in Iran [Boltuc, 2021].

Foreign Policy of the Gulf Towards the USA after the Outbreak of the War:

Following the start of the Russia-Ukraine war, US Gulf policy demonstrates internal inconsistencies. The USA has decreased its strategic investment in the Gulf region to reallocate its primary resources towards the strategic rivalry with major global powers. The erosion of trust among the Middle Eastern nations in the USA is becoming increasingly evident. The response of Middle Eastern countries to the Russia-Ukraine war is a direct reaction to the policy of maintaining a balance of power among major nations. Amidst the increasing strategic rivalry between China and the USA, the latter has been cautious in guarding against China's growing influence in the Middle East and has pressured countries in that region. The practices have primarily involved exerting pressure on countries in the Middle East and impeding efforts toward cooperation in the Belt and Road Initiative (BRI). Amidst the escalating tension between China and the USA, the Gulf countries aspire to uphold cooperative relations with both nations. After President Biden's diplomatic trip to the Middle East, specifically Saudi Arabia, Saudi Arabia's Foreign Minister, Adelal-Jubeir, stated that the diplomatic ties between Saudi Arabia and the USA, as well as the United Kingdom, are strong and positive. The oil monarchies have chosen their policy based on their perception of the international environment and power distribution in the international arena. This includes considering the decreasing influence of the USA and the de-hegemonisation process.

The oil monarchies have not complied with the request made by US President Joe Biden to halt the increase in oil prices and instead boost oil production and exports to global markets, spanning from Russia to Europe. Furthermore, Arab leaders decided not to comply with all of Washington's directives. The urgent need for increased revenue from oil sales has arisen due to the pandemic, which has limited this source of income. It is crucial to note that as the oil supply decreases, its price rises, leading to potential gains in the market.

With the onset of the Russia-Ukraine war, the strategic dynamics between the USA and Russia has shifted attention from the Middle East to Ukraine. Consequently, countries in the Middle East have been compelled to make strategic adaptations. In this particular context, the dynamics of international relations in the Middle East have changed. Due to the USA shifting its global focus towards power competition and retracting its strategic presence from the Middle East, certain regions have faced growing pressure to expedite their development and transformation. As previously stated, the participation of Arab states in the conflict in Ukraine has a direct correlation with whether it yields tangible advantages for them, just as Saudi Arabia has done in its mediation with Russia. Prisoners of war captured in Ukraine by Russian soldiers were released, and has provided Ukraine with $ 400 million in humanitarian aid. Saudi Arabia sees the conflict in Ukraine, in which it can determine the outcome, as an opportunity to recover from international isolation. This is in contrast to the USA' accusation of Riyadh in 2018 regarding the assassination of a Saudi journalist employed by *The Washington Post* and other media organizations. Nevertheless, it appears that the oil-producing nations view the energy crisis as a chance to augment their domestic budgets by selling oil and natural gas, given that many of them have entered into agreements to provide the EU and Europe with raw material. The Gulf Arab states adopted a balanced approach towards the Ukraine conflict, refraining from explicitly supporting the USA or Russia while retaining the right to negotiate and enter into a dialogue with either power.

Opportunities and Challenges

The crisis in Ukraine presents the Arab Gulf countries, particularly Saudi Arabia and the United Arab Emirates, with an opportunity to re-establish their relations with the USA during a time when global energy security is at the centre of the situation. This issue has become critical because Gulf countries have strengthened their ties with China and Russia over the past few years. These countries may have a more significant say in the decisions made on a global scale due to the reset and increased oil and gas prices. As a result, the Gulf countries are already responding to the conflict in Ukraine and its aftermath with maturity and pragmatism. As a result, they will probably contemplate the possibility of renewing their bilateral geo-security and strategic relations with the USA while maintaining their growing ties with China and Russia. There is no question in the minds of the Gulf countries that their relationship with the USA is well-established and extensive. The geo-security and strategic relationships between the USA and the Gulf region are deeply ingrained. There is a persistent disregard among Gulf countries for the argument that the USA is withdrawing from the area or has entered a post-US era.

The Gulf states have experienced positive and negative effects due to rising energy prices; however, the precise nature of these effects varies from country to country. Increasing prices have increased revenue and a higher international status for countries that produce energy. This is a positive development. On the other hand, the same circumstances might have a detrimental impact on the economic diversification of those countries over the medium and long term. As a result of the war between Russia and Ukraine, the prices of oil and gas on the international market have been steadily increasing, which has served to the benefit of the Gulf countries. Saudi Arabia and other Gulf countries are increasing their revenues from oil and gas, improving their financial situation, and strengthening their position in society when the international market for energy and even the economy of the entire world is in the doldrums. The depreciation of oil prices and the predicament the conventional oil economy faced in the decade before the conflict between Russia and Ukraine are instances. Consequently, the increase in the cost of oil and gas brought about by the conflict between Russia and Ukraine will unquestionably result in a reduction in the financial pressure on the Gulf countries for a period, which will result in a reduction in the impetus for their economic for a variety of sources.

The incursion by Russia into Ukraine has had a significant impact on agricultural markets, affecting a wide range of regions and posing a threat to the food security of millions of people, both within and beyond the Black Sea area. The conflict has resulted in a decrease in the export of food from Ukraine and Russia, specifically wheat, maize, and sunflower oil. As a result, the prices of these commodities have risen. Additionally, there has been an increased demand for substitute products such as alternative cooking oils. Furthermore, there has been a decline in the export of fertilizers from the Black Sea, which has led to changes in the types and quantities of crops producers intend to cultivate globally. The exorbitant energy expense contributes to the escalation of food and fertilizer prices. Before the conflict, Russia and Ukraine collectively represented over 25 per cent of worldwide wheat exports. The countries most susceptible to the effects of the price hikes caused by the war are those that heavily depend on wheat as a primary source of calories, rely on imports to fulfil their food-security requirements and obtain a substantial portion of their imports from Ukraine and Russia. The worst affected is Yemen, which is facing a twofold impact from the export blockages in the Black Sea region caused by Russia's invasion of Ukraine. Approximately 45 per cent of Yemen's wheat imports come from Russia and Ukraine.

In comparison, an additional 12 per cent is sourced from other countries in the Middle East and the North Africa (MENA) region. In addition, the war has resulted in a significant increase of approximately $ 23 billion per month in the cost of WFP's emergency food aid, which could potentially restrict the extent of WFP's life-saving support in Yemen. The agricultural infrastructure in Yemen is not focused on producing grains, and the expensive fuel prices further raise the production expenses for Yemeni farmers. The Gulf Cooperation Council (GCC) countries rely on imports for up to 90 per cent of their food, including from the Black Sea region. However, they have managed to withstand the effects of Russia's conflict in Ukraine on the agricultural market. Food security in the GCC25 has been strengthened through various measures, such as expanding import sources, implementing advanced technology for food production in dry regions, and controversially acquiring agricultural land in foreign nations. The elevated oil prices have additionally empowered GCC governments to counteract the rise in food prices and shield populations from food insecurity. Despite their relatively secure food situation during the current crisis, analysts advise GCC countries to promote domestic agricultural production, allocate funds to agricultural enterprises, and establish and manage food reserves to mitigate the impact of future crises. The Middle Eastern countries have faced significant challenges in their development due to the simultaneous occurrence of the Arab Uprising and the COVID-19 pandemic crisis. The food crisis, exacerbated by the Russia-Ukraine war, has intensified the economic and social turmoil in the Middle East, particularly in the transitional Arab nations, while also heightening political vulnerabilities.

The Political Divergence

The Russia-Ukraine war commenced in the Arabian Peninsula sub-region of the Middle East, influenced by four contextual factors. The initial event refers to the culmination of the most extensive and profound division ever witnessed in the politics of the Arab Gulf region. Saudi Arabia, Bahrain, the UAE, and Egypt imposed a political and economic blockade on Qatar from June 2017 to January 2021. This action was justified by the claim that Qatar had excessive proximity to Iran and provided support to extremist factions in the area. However, Doha consistently refuted these allegations, which were never verified. The second factor was the repercussions of the disorderly US retreat from

Afghanistan in August 2021, which further solidified the belief in multiple Arab Gulf capitals that the USA is an unreliable security guarantee. The third event refers to the continuous military intervention led by Saudi Arabia in Yemen against the Houthis. This intervention has now reached its eighth year as of 2023. The fourth event was the failure of negotiations. The negotiations between Iranian and P5+1 negotiators to revive the Joint Comprehensive Plan of Action (JCPOA) failed. This resulted from the Trump administration's decision to withdraw from the agreement in 2018 and Iran's subsequent choice to no longer comply with essential terms of the 2015 agreement. The positions that the Arab Gulf states took in response to the invasion that took place in February 2022 fell along a spectrum that ranged from Qatar, which aligned itself most closely with Ukraine (and the position that the USA takes on the war), to Saudi Arabia, Bahrain, and the United Arab Emirates, which lean more closely towards Russia, with Kuwait and Oman being somewhere in the Middle.

Conclusion

The significant increase in oil, commodities, and food prices is a reminder that the Gulf States are not immune to the effects of the war in Ukraine. However, the effects of the war on the economies and societies of the Gulf region will have a secondary impact. Indeed, the restocking of state treasuries and the implementation of long-sought fiscal balance programs will be made possible by the rise in oil prices, which had been on an upward trend for a considerable time before the outbreak of the war. Consequently, the confluence of challenging transitions following the Arab Uprising and the COVID-19 pandemic crisis has posed significant obstacles to development in most Middle Eastern countries. The food crisis, exacerbated by the Russia-Ukraine war, has intensified the economic and social turmoil in the Middle East, particularly in the transitional Arab countries, while also heightening political vulnerabilities. Ultimately, following the commencement of the Russia-Ukraine war, there has been an increase in the number of influential global powers in the Middle East region, leading to heightened competition among these powers.

REFERENCES

1. Bennett Neuhoff. 'Saudi Prisoner Diplomacy During the Ukraine War,' Washington Institute, 20 December 2022, u https://www.washingtoninstitute.org/policy-analysis/saudi-prisoner-diplomacy-during-ukraine-war
2. Caitlin Walsh. The Impact of Russia's Invasion of Ukraine in the Middle East and North Africa, testimony before the House Foreign Affairs Middle East, North Africa, and Global Counterterrorism Subcommittee, 18 May 18 2022, u https:// www.csis.org/analysis/ impact-russias-invasion-Ukraine9-middle-east-and-north-africa
3. Gordon Lubold and Warren Strobel. 'Secret Chinese Port Project in Persian Gulf Rattles US Relations with UAE,' *Wall Street Journal*, 19 November 2021, u https:/ /www. wsj.com/articles/us-china-uae-military-11637274224; and Agnes Helou, 'Chinese and Saudi Firms Create Joint Venture to Make Military Drones in the Kingdom,' *Defence News*, 9 March 2022 u https://www.defensenews.com/ unmanned/2022/03/09/chinese-and-saudi-firms-create-joint-venture-to-make-military-drones-in-the-kingdom
4. Grabowski, Wojciech. (2023). 'Balancing policy of the Arab States of the Persian Gulf in the face of the war in Ukraine,' 10. 192-205.
5. Haass, Richard N., Indyk Martin, and Samore Gary. 2008. *Restoring the balance: A Middle East strategy for the next president*, Brookings Institution Press.
6. Ibid.
7. Jihad Azour, Jeta Menkulasi, and Rodrigo Garcia-Verdu. 'Middle East and North Africa's Commodity Importers Hit by Higher Prices,' International Monetary Fund, I.M.F. Blog, 24 May 24 2022 u https:// www.imf.org/en/Blogs/Articles/ 2022/05/24/blog-mena-commodity-importers-hit-by-higher-prices
8. Kristian Coates Ulrichsen. 'What the Russian Invasion of Ukraine Means for Small States,' *Doha News*, 12 March 2022, u https://dohanews.co/what-the-russian-invasion-of-ukraine-means-forsmall-states
9. Li-Chen Sim. 'The Gulf States: Beneficiaries of the Russia-Europe Energy War?' Middle East Institute, 12 January 2023, u https://www.mei.edu/publications/ gulf-states-beneficiaries-russiaEurope-energy-war
10. Marc Lynch. 'Saudi Oil Cuts and American International Order,' Abu Aardvark's MENA Academy, 9 October 2022, u https://abuaardvark.substack.com/p/saudi-oil-cuts-and-american-international; Qatar hosts the headquarters of the Gas Exporting Countries Forum. See Gas Exporting Countries Forum, "Contact Us" u https://www.gecf.org/contact.aspx
11. Marc Lynch. 'Saudi Oil Cuts and American International Order,' Abu Aardvark's MENA Academy, 9 October 2022 u https://abuaardvark.substack.com/p/saudi-oil-cuts-and-american-international
12. Michaël Tanchum. 'The Russia-Ukraine War Has Turned Egypt's Food Crisis into an Existential Threat to the Economy,' Middle East Institute, 3 March 2022, u https://www. mei.edu/publications/russia-Ukraine-war-has-turned-Egypt's-food-crisis-existential-threateconomy
13. M. Murat Kubilay. 'The Ukraine War Has Upended Turkey's Plans to Stabilize the Economy,' Middle East Institute, 23 March 2022 u https://www.mei.edu/ publications/ Ukraine-war-has-upended-turkeys-plans-stabilize-economy

14. Namgail, Stanzin. (2023). An analysis of Russia-Ukraine war and its impact on global food security.
15. Summer Said et al. 'Saudi Arabia Defied US Warnings Ahead of OPEC+ Production Cut,' *Wall Street Journal*, 11 October 2022 u https://www.wsj.com/articles/saudi-arabia-defied-u-s-warnings-ahead-ofOPEC-production-cut-11665504230
16. Sam Fleming et al. 'West Presses UAE to Clamp Down on Suspected Russia Sanctions Busting,' *Financial Times*, 1 March 2023, https://www.ft.com/ content/fca1878e-9198-4500-b888-24b17043c507
17. Patrick Theros and Dania Thafer. 'What the Al-Ula Summit Has (and Has Not) Accomplished,' Gulf International Forum, 11 January 2021 u https://gulfif.org/what-the-al-ula-gcc-summit-hasand-has-not-accomplished.
18. Perepelytsia, Hryhorii & Novytska, Natalia. (2022). The Influence of Russian Aggression against Ukraine on the Security Situation of the Persian Gulf Countries. Diplomatic Ukraine. 306-314. 10.37837/2707-7683-2022-18.
19. Silvia Boltuc. (2021). 'Iran-Russia cooperation might support Tehran's foreign strategy in Eurasia,' *Geopolitical Report* vol. 12(4), ISSN 2785-2598, Special Eurasia. Link: https://www.specialeurasia.com/2021/10/06/iran-russia-foreign-policy/
20. Silvia Boltuc. (2022). 'The Ukraine conflict can boost Iranian energy exports, *Geopolitical Report* vol. 17 (3), ISSN 2785-2598, Special Eurasia. Link: https://www.specialeurasia.com/2022/03/08/ukraine-iran-energy-export/
21. Steve Holland & Rania el-Gamal. 'Trump Says He Does Not Want War after Attack on Saudi Oil Facilities,' Reuters, 16 September 2019, https://www.reuters.com/article/us-saudi-aramco/trump-says-he-does-not-want-war-after-attack-on-saudi-oil-facilities-idUSKBN1W10X8.
22. The Ukraine Crisis and the Gulf: A Saudi Perspective. Interview with Abdulaziz al Sager, 18 October 2022, available at https://www.institutmontaigne.org/en/analysis/ukraine-crisisand-gulf-saudi-perspective (last access 12 December 2023).
23. Wasser, Becca; Howard J. Shatz, John J. Drennan, Andrew Scobell, Brain G. Carison, and Yvonne K. Crane. 2022. 'Crossroads of competition: China, Russia, and the United States in the Middle East.' Santa Monica, California: RAND Corporation.
24. Yahya, M. (2022). 'The Arab World and the Ukraine conflict: The quest for nonalignment,' Atlantic Council, available at https://www.atlanticcouncil.org.

18

Russia-Ukraine War and Its Impact on the Indo-Pacific Region

Divya Rai and Harikesh Pratap Singh

Introduction

In February 2022, Russia initiated a war against Ukraine, fundamentally altering the global geopolitical landscape and triggering new concerns in the wake of the COVID-19 pandemic. This war, the largest land conflict in Europe since World War II, has resulted in significant loss of life, displacement of millions of Ukrainian citizens, widespread infrastructure damage, food supply shortages, and heightened oil prices. Geopolitically, it has reshaped global energy dynamics, fostered new alliances, bolstered Western cooperation, strained relations with China, and challenged the existing nuclear order. In this context, Russian President Vladimir Putin's recent diplomatic efforts, including his visit to Hanoi on 18 June 2024 following a meeting in North Korea with Kim Jong Un, highlight his strategy to strengthen economic ties with friendly countries like Vietnam. Despite being regarded as a pariah by the West, Putin's engagement with Vietnam underscores Hanoi's delicate balancing act of maintaining relations with major powers such as the USA, China, and Russia. This visit, criticized by the USA, reflects Vietnam's commitment to a diversified and autonomous foreign policy, while also illustrating the broader implications of the Russia-Ukraine war on the Indo-Pacific region's geopolitical dynamics.

Russia-Ukraine War and the Indo-Pacific Region

The Russia-Ukraine war, a complex and enduring conflict, has its roots in the aftermath of the Soviet Union's dissolution in 1991. Ukraine, now an independent state, began seeking closer ties with the European Union in the early 2010s,[1] prompting political and social tensions within the country. The war took a significant turn in February 2014 when Russia annexed Crimea, a region with a substantial Russian-speaking population. This move was met with worldwide condemnation, leading to economic sanctions against Russia.[2] Simultaneously, separatist movements emerged in the Donetsk and Luhansk regions[3] of eastern Ukraine, where pro-Russian factions declared independence. This declaration sparked violent clashes with Ukrainian government forces, ultimately evolving into a full-scale war. The international community swiftly became involved, with Western nations, notably the USA and the European Union, backing Ukraine's territorial integrity.[4] This support included humanitarian aid and military assistance to the Ukrainian government. Throughout the war, multiple ceasefire agreements were attempted, such as the Minsk Protocol in 2014 and the Minsk II agreement in 2015.[5] However, these agreements proved fragile, resulting in persistent violence on the ground. Civilians bore the brunt of the conflict's human cost, with casualties numbering in the thousands and hundreds of thousands displaced. Allegations of human rights violations and potential war crimes were raised by both sides.

Despite various battles and offensives, a military stalemate prevailed, characterized by shifting frontlines and intermittent escalations of violence. The conflict remained unresolved, with self-declared separatist entities established in eastern Ukraine but lacking international recognition. Numerous diplomatic initiatives were undertaken to find a peaceful resolution to the conflict. The Normandy Format, involving Ukraine, Russia, Germany, and France, aimed to facilitate a political settlement. However, progress was slow, and the situation remained precarious.

In the 20th century, Ukraine emerged as the most populous and economically significant republic, boasting advanced agricultural and technological sectors.[6] Its strategic importance for Russia lay in serving as a buffer state between the European Union and Russia, despite ideological differences.[7] The origins of war can be attributed to two main factors.[8] Firstly, territorial disputes between Russia and Ukraine, such as the annexation of Crimea by Russia, aimed at protecting ethnic Russians and fostering division in eastern Ukraine's Donbas region[9] by supporting separatist movements in Donetsk and Luhansk. The second factor was the eastward expansion of the North Atlantic Treaty Organization (NATO), initially established during the Cold War to counteract communist aggression by the USA and European nations. Despite the USSR's dissolution, NATO continued to expand, with 31 member-states and numerous aspiring nations along Russia's borders. NATO's invitation to Finland and Sweden in July 2022, previously neutral states, raised concerns in Russia,[10] as it could potentially allow the deployment of nuclear and military arsenals near its eastern border, constituting a territorial threat. Russia consequently launched an invasion across multiple fronts in Ukraine, including approaches to Kyiv, Kharkiv, and Odessa.[11]

The Indo-Pacific region has emerged as a focal point of global geopolitics, with its significance extending far beyond its geographical boundaries. This expansive area, spanning from the eastern coast of Africa to the western coast of the Americas, encompasses the entire Indian and Pacific oceans. Prime Minister Narendra Modi of India[12] played a pivotal role in shaping the Indo-Pacific concept when he articulated it during the Shangri-La Dialogue in 2018. This geopolitical construct has profound implications for the world's economic, political, and strategic dynamics.

The Indo-Pacific region is notable for several critical features that make it a global centre of attention. Perhaps most prominently, it hosts the world's busiest shipping lanes. These maritime routes are vital for global trade, enabling the transportation of goods, energy resources, and commodities on a massive scale. Key chokepoints within the Indo-Pacific, such as the Strait of Malacca and the South China Sea, play a central role in facilitating these shipping lanes. The Strait of Malacca, in particular, is one of the most significant maritime corridors, connecting the Indian Ocean with the South China Sea and the Pacific Ocean. Energy resources are another fundamental element of the Indo-Pacific's significance. The region contains vast reserves of oil and natural gas, which are essential for the world's energy needs. Several major economies, including the USA, China, India, and Japan, rely on these resources for their energy demands. The accessibility and stability of these energy resources have a direct impact on global energy markets, making developments in the Indo-Pacific of interest to countries worldwide.[13]

The Indo-Pacific: A Region in the Midst of Growing Contention

The Indo-Pacific is also a hub for emerging product and factor markets. With its vast and diverse array of countries, it offers a dynamic environment for trade and investment. As the region's economies continue to grow, opportunities for business and commerce expand. This has led to increased economic engagement, trade agreements, and investment opportunities in the Indo-Pacific. The evolving market dynamics of the region have not only attracted businesses but have also spurred political and strategic interests from major global players. The transition from a unipolar world, characterized by US hegemony after the Cold War, to a multi-polar world,[14] where several major powers coexist, has further enhanced the importance of the Indo-Pacific. In this new multi-polar context, the region is home to several influential global actors. The USA, as the world's largest economy and a military superpower, remains a central player. China, with its rapid economic growth and increasing global influence, is another key presence. India, with its significant demographic and economic potential, Japan as a technological and economic powerhouse, and Australia as a prominent regional actor, all contribute to the region's multi-polarity. The Indo-Pacific encompasses 38 countries, many of which are strategically and economically significant. This diversity is reflected in the sheer scale of the region, with 65 per cent of the world's population residing in these nations. Furthermore, the Indo-Pacific collectively contributes 63 per cent of the world's Gross Domestic Product (GDP). This underscores the vast economic potential and market opportunities that the region represents.

The geopolitical landscape of the Indo-Pacific is marked by a complex interplay of interests, competition, and cooperation among its major players. The USA, while historically a dominant presence in the region, is now navigating a more competitive environment, particularly with China's rise. China's assertive behaviour in asserting territorial claims in the South China Sea and its Belt and Road Initiative, which involves infrastructure development across the region, have raised concerns among Indo-Pacific countries and beyond. These developments have led to a recalibration of US foreign policy[15] and the reinforcement of alliances and partnerships in the region. India, as a key player, is pursuing its Act East policy to enhance economic and strategic engagement with its Indo-Pacific neighbours. Japan, meanwhile, is actively cooperating with various countries to counterbalance China's influence. Australia, situated at the confluence of the Indian and Pacific oceans, has articulated its own Indo-Pacific strategy to safeguard regional stability and security.

The geopolitical implications of the Indo-Pacific are not limited to regional dynamics. Global powers, including European countries, are also recognizing the region's significance. This is exemplified by the European Union's strategy for cooperation in the Indo-Pacific, which emphasizes trade, security, and sustainability. The Indo-Pacific's growing prominence is not merely confined to geopolitical and economic aspects.[16] It also has environmental, cultural, and societal implications. The region is home to diverse ecosystems, and environmental issues such as climate change, marine conservation, and sustainable development are central to the Indo-Pacific's future. The interaction of different cultures, languages, and societies in this region presents opportunities for people-to-people exchanges and cooperation. Indo-Pacific is a multifaceted and dynamic region with far-reaching implications for the global order.[17] Its significance extends beyond traditional geopolitical boundaries to encompass trade, energy, and economic opportunities. The shift from a unipolar world to a multi-polar one has made the region a theatre of competition and cooperation among major global players. The Indo-Pacific's vast population, economic clout, and diverse cultures all contribute to its growing importance on the world stage. As the world continues to evolve in the face of changing power dynamics and global challenges, the Indo-Pacific is likely to remain a central focus of global attention for the foreseeable future.

In recent years, the Indo-Pacific has gained increasing significance for major powers like the USA, the United Kingdom, France, South Korea, and Japan due to shifts in the global economic and political landscape and the rise of China. The region serves as a crucial transit route for global trade and energy, with vital choke points like the Strait of Malacca and the South China Sea. These choke points play a pivotal role in maritime trade, handling over 50 per cent of the world's maritime trade. Any disruption, whether due to security concerns or natural disasters, can have a profound impact on the global economy. Moreover, the Indo-Pacific is home to some of the world's fastest-growing economies, including China, India, and Indonesia, challenging the traditional Western dominance.

The Russia-Ukraine war, which ignited in 2014, has extended its reach far beyond the borders of Eastern Europe, resonating as far as the Indo-Pacific region. While the conflict itself transpires thousands of miles away from the shores of the Indian and Pacific oceans, its impact on the global stage and its indirect implications for the Indo-Pacific are significant and multifaceted. First and foremost, it's essential to understand the distinct features of the Indo-Pacific, a region that has assumed a central role in contemporary geopolitics. This sprawling expanse, stretching from the eastern coast of Africa to the western coast of the Americas, envelops the entirety of the Indian and Pacific oceans.[18] It holds a vital position in the global landscape, characterized by several pivotal attributes. Foremost among these attributes is the role of the Indo-Pacific as the world's principal maritime crossroads. This vast region houses the busiest shipping lanes globally, facilitating the transportation of goods, energy resources, and commodities on an unprecedented scale. Notable chokepoints within the Indo-Pacific, such as the Strait of Malacca and the South China Sea, act as lifelines for global trade, enabling the flow of goods between the Indian Ocean and the South China Sea,[19] and further on to the Pacific Ocean. The significance of these maritime highways cannot be overstated, as they underpin the global supply chain and international trade.

Moreover, the Indo-Pacific boasts an abundance of energy resources, encompassing vast reserves of oil and natural gas. These resources are indispensable for the world's energy needs, providing the lifeblood of industries and economies worldwide. Major global powers, including the USA, China, India, and Japan, rely heavily on the accessibility and stability of these energy resources.[20] The consequences of geopolitical developments in the Indo-Pacific, particularly those affecting energy supplies, can be felt throughout the world. In addition to energy resources, the Indo-Pacific also represents an emerging hub for product and factor markets.[21] Its dynamic environment has generated opportunities for trade, investment, and economic growth. With diverse economies at varying stages of development, the region serves as a fertile ground for business expansion and commerce. Consequently, the Indo-Pacific has become a locus of economic engagement, trade agreements, and investment prospects for countries around the world.

The transition from a unipolar world, which was marked by US hegemony following the Cold War, to a multi-polar world, where several major powers coexist, has further accentuated the importance of the Indo-Pacific. In this new multi-polar context, the region is home to a constellation of influential global actors. The USA, as the world's largest economy and a military superpower, remains a central player. The rise of China, with its rapid economic growth and expanding global influence, has added a new dimension to the regional and global power structure. India, with its significant demographic and economic potential, is on the ascendant, while Japan's technological and economic prowess and Australia's regional influence contribute to the region's multi-polarity.

Spanning across 38 countries, many of which are strategically and economically significant, the Indo-Pacific's diversity is unparalleled. This diversity is not only demographic but also economic, as the region collectively houses 65 per cent of the world's population and contributes 63 per cent of the global Gross Domestic Product (GDP). Such demographics and economic clout make the region an attractive prospect for trade, investment, and global engagement.

The geopolitical ramifications of the Indo-Pacific's rise have not gone unnoticed. As the region becomes an arena of increasing strategic competition and cooperation among major players, it is redefining global power dynamics. The USA, historically the dominant force in the Indo-Pacific, is navigating a more competitive environment, particularly with the ascent of China.[22] This rivalry and Washington's commitment to reassert its influence have led to a revaluation of US foreign policy and the strengthening of alliances and partnerships with regional nations. This pivot is pivotal in recalibrating the regional balance of power. At the same time, India, one of the region's major players, is implementing its 'Act East' policy to bolster its economic and strategic engagement with its Indo-Pacific neighbours. Japan, on the other hand, is actively cooperating with various countries to counterbalance China's increasing influence. Australia, perched at the confluence of the Indian and Pacific oceans, has articulated its own Indo-Pacific strategy,[23] seeking to safeguard regional stability and security. These efforts underline the evolving geopolitical landscape of the Indo-Pacific and the diverse approaches taken by key players.

Echoing Impacts: The Indo-Pacific Region's Response to the Russia-Ukraine War

The geopolitical landscape of the Indo-Pacific is also marked by complex relationships and overlapping interests, as well as territorial disputes and security concerns. The global implications of the Russia-Ukraine war have further accentuated these complexities. In particular, several factors illustrate the ways in which the Russia-Ukraine war indirectly affects the Indo-Pacific.

Geopolitical Implications

The Russia-Ukraine war has raised international concerns about territorial disputes and security issues. The bold actions of Russia, including the annexation of Crimea, have garnered increased attention to similar territorial claims in the Indo-Pacific.[24] China's assertiveness in asserting territorial claims in the South China Sea and its Belt and Road Initiative,[25] which involves infrastructure development across the region, have drawn parallels to Russia's actions in Ukraine. This has led to a revaluation of security concerns in the Indo-Pacific, as regional countries grapple with territorial disputes and navigate the complex geopolitical environment.[26] The echoes of territorial assertions in Ukraine are reverberating in the South China Sea and other parts of the Indo-Pacific.

(a) **Economic Implications:** The Russia-Ukraine war and the subsequent imposition of economic sanctions on Russia have had indirect economic repercussions in the Indo-Pacific. Economic sanctions can disrupt global markets and trade, affecting economies across the Indo-Pacific. For instance, higher oil prices, resulting from sanctions on Russia, can impact energy-dependent countries in the region. The Indo-Pacific's reliance on global trade and energy resources makes it susceptible to disruptions caused by events in other parts of the world, including the Russia-Ukraine war.

(b) **Impact on Global Security:** The Russia-Ukraine war has raised concerns about the stability of the global security order. The use of military force to resolve disputes in Ukraine has created a more fragmented and unstable global security environment. These concerns resonate in the Indo-Pacific, a region marked by territorial disputes and tensions. The war has prompted Indo-Pacific nations to reassess their security strategies and relationships with major powers in response to these evolving global security dynamics. As countries in the Indo-Pacific[27] monitor developments in Ukraine, they must navigate a complex and increasingly uncertain security environment.

(c) **Multilateral Constructs and Divergent Stances:** The Russia-Ukraine war has exposed divisions among nations on the world stage. While G7 countries, including the USA, Canada, France, and the United Kingdom,[28] have condemned the invasion, the G20 nations exhibited differing stances. Similarly, within the Indo-Pacific,[29] countries have shown varying responses to the Russia-Ukraine war. Some nations in the Indo-Pacific have been vocal in their condemnation of the invasion, while others have adopted a more neutral stance, reflective of their geopolitical and economic interests. These divergent positions within the Indo-Pacific underscore the complexity of aligning with global responses to geopolitical crises like the Russia-Ukraine war.

(d) **Implications for Defence Strategies:** The Russia-Ukraine war, particularly the use of advanced drones and anti-ship missiles, has raised concerns about evolving defence strategies in the Indo-Pacific. The war demonstrated the vulnerability of naval forces in highly contested environments. This has prompted

Indo-Pacific nations to reconsider their military capabilities and strategies, recognizing the need for more robust defence measures.[30]

Moreover, the Russia-Ukraine war has significantly disrupted global energy and food security. Russia holds the position of being the world's third-largest producer of petroleum, and Asia, particularly the Indo-Pacific,[31] accounts for a substantial 35 per cent of the global oil consumption. The rupture in the global oil market, exacerbated by the war, has resulted in increased commodity prices, adversely affecting economically vulnerable Southeast Asian countries. India, a net importer of oil, witnessed a widening trade deficit with Russia, impacting its foreign exchange reserves and contributing to the depreciation of the Indian rupee. Singapore, Vietnam, and Thailand,[32] also reliant on these commodities, faced similar economic challenges. The prolonged repercussions of the war can be observed in various dimensions:

(a) **China's Role:** The Russia-Ukraine war has shed light on concerns about security issues in the Indo-Pacific, particularly concerning China's territorial claims in the South China Sea. China's assertive behaviour, including the construction of artificial islands equipped with military facilities, has stirred global unease. As countries in the Indo-Pacific scrutinize these developments, the war serves as a stark reminder of the region's security challenges.[33]

(b) **USA-Taiwan Relations:** The ongoing war could potentially alter the balance of power in the region, influencing Taiwan's security.[34] The USA's stance in the context of the Russia-Ukraine war raises questions, given its strong and unwavering position on Taiwan. The ripple effects of the war are not confined to Europe; they reverberate across the Pacific, affecting key players in Asia.

(c) **Defence Strategy Changes:** The Ukraine war has prompted a re-evaluation of defence strategies, particularly with regard to maritime forces and militaries operating in the Indo-Pacific. The war vividly demonstrated the challenges posed by advanced drones and anti-ship missiles in contested and highly dynamic environments. Consequently, Indo-Pacific navies are compelled to adapt their approach to naval capability development, placing a heightened emphasis on robust defence measures for critical assets like aircraft carriers.[35]

Countries such as Japan and South Korea, that are observing the Russia-Ukraine war with trepidation,[36] are contemplating the possibility of analogous threats emanating from their neighbours, China and North Korea. This has translated into increased defence budgets and significant shifts in their military strategies. Importantly, the unilateral nature of the war in Ukraine, as opposed to Ukraine's non-nuclear status, raises profound concerns about the implications of potential conflicts involving nuclear-armed powers in the Indo-Pacific.[37] The Russia-Ukraine war has also forged stronger ties between Russia and China, altering the dynamics of global geopolitics and contributing to an increased European Union presence in the Indo-Pacific region. Furthermore, the conflict underscores the pressing need for reform within international multilateral organizations, such as the United Nations, which have often been criticized for their ineffectiveness in resolving major conflicts. The inclination towards more focused bilateral and trilateral groupings with clearly defined agendas is gaining momentum as a pragmatic response to the limitations of existing global governance mechanisms.[38]

Conclusion

India's relationship with Russia, deeply intertwined across military, economic, and strategic domains, is notably complex. Russia has consistently served as a key supplier of military hardware to India, and in recent years, it has emerged as a significant source of oil and gas. India's response to the Russia-Ukraine war mirrors this complexity, as it strives to strike a delicate balance between preserving its historical ties with Russia and aligning with shifting geopolitical considerations. The Russia-Ukraine war offers a vivid illustration of the multi-faceted nature of modern warfare, encompassing an array of components, from cyber warfare and influence operations to intricate geopolitical manoeuvring. It underscores the growing prominence of conflicts in the contemporary world and challenges traditional paradigms. The war has not only disrupted existing global norms but has also exposed the inherent limitations of international institutions, particularly the United Nations, in effectively resolving major crises. However, in the midst of these disruptions and challenges, the Russia-Ukraine war has also catalysed the formation of stronger alliances and cooperation among countries. As regional conflicts continue to exert global repercussions, the Indo-Pacific stands out as a focal point of international attention, profoundly shaping the evolving landscape of global affairs. The Indo-Pacific region remains a dynamic and central arena where nations must navigate an ever-evolving geopolitical landscape, driven by the complex interplay of global events and shifting power dynamics.

REFERENCES

1. 'Amid Ukraine War, U.S. Signals the Indo-Pacific is a Vital Priority. (n.d.). United States Institute of Peace, https://www.usip.org/publications/2022/06/amid-ukraine-war-us-signals-indo-pacific-vital-priority
2. Masters, J. (14 February 2023). 'Ukraine: Conflict at the Crossroads of Europe and Russia,' Council on Foreign Relations. https://www.cfr.org/backgrounder/ukraine-conflict-crossroads-europe-and-russia
3. Masters, J. (14 February 2023). 'Ukraine: Conflict at the Crossroads of Europe and Russia,' Council on Foreign Relations, https://www.cfr.org/backgrounder/ukraine-conflict-crossroads-europe-and-russia
4. Ibid.
5. Mankoff, J. (13 October 2022). 'Russia's War in Ukraine: Identity, History, and Conflict,' https://www.csis.org/analysis/russias-war-ukraine-identity-history-and-conflict
6. Ibid.
7. Leonard, T. G. A. I. K. M. (1 March 2023). 'United West, divided from the rest: Global public opinion one year into Russia's war on Ukraine,' ECFR. https://ecfr.eu/publication/united-west-divided-from-the-rest-global-public-opinion-one-year-into-russias-war-on-ukraine/
8. Madhav, R. (25 March 2023). 'Tension in Indo-Pacific and Russia-Ukraine conflict are symptoms of an emerging global disorder,' *The Indian Express*, https://indianexpress.com/article/opinion/columns/cold-war-us-china-tensions-over-south-china-sea-pm-modi-donald-trump-fumio-kishida-japans-indo-pacific-strategy-russia-ukraine-war-8517498/
9. Mankoff, J. (13 October 2022). 'Russia's War in Ukraine: Identity, History, and Conflict.' https://www.csis.org/analysis/russias-war-ukraine-identity-history-and-conflict
10. IDC. 'The Initial Consequences of the Russia-Ukraine War on Asia/Pacific ICT Vendors and Technology Buyers. (n.d.).' IDC: The Premier Global Market Intelligence Company, https://www.idc.com/ap/supply-chain/assets/blog-detail?id=40877fdb510c9de83b4a
11. Ibid.

12. Bhattacherjee, K. (17 June 2023). 'Ukraine war and the Indo-Pacific situation to figure in Modi-Biden talks,' *The Hindu*, https://www.thehindu.com/news/national/narendra-modi-joe-biden-talks/article66977469.ece
13. Gerstl, M. I. A. A. (23 April 2023). 'Mixed reactions to the Russian war ýagainst Ukraine in the Indo-Pacific: Views of governments and civil society. CEIAS. https://ceias.eu/indopacific-views-of-russian-aggression/
14. Johnson, R. & Johnson, R. (14 June 2023). 'How the war in Ukraine is impacting security in the Indo-Pacific,' Breaking Defence. https://breakingdefense.com/2023/06/how-the-war-in-ukraine-impacts-asian-security/
15. 'Amid Ukraine War, U.S. Signals the Indo-Pacific is a Vital Priority,' (n.d.), United States Institute of Peace, https://www.usip.org/publications/2022/06/amid-ukraine-war-us-signals-indo-pacific-vital-priority
16. Chinoy, S. & Chinoy, S. (7 March 2022). 'How Russia-Ukraine conflict will have a major fallout on Indo-Pacific.' *Firstpost*, https://www.firstpost.com/world/how-russia-ukraine-conflict-will-have-a-major-fallout-on-indo-pacific-10436521.html
17. 'Lessons from Ukraine for the Indo-Pacific. (11 March 2022). *Internationale Politik Quarterly*, https://ip-quarterly.com/en/lessons-ukraine-indo-pacific
18. What are Indo-Pacific powers learning from the war in Ukraine?' (20 January 2023). DIIS, https://www.diis.dk/en/research/what-are-indo-pacific-powers-learning-from-the-war-in-ukraine
19. Ibid.
20. Ibid.
21. IDC. 'The Initial Consequences of the Russia-Ukraine War on Asia/Pacific ICT Vendors and Technology Buyers, (n.d.), IDC: The Premier Global Market Intelligence Company, https://www.idc.com/ap/supply-chain/assets/blog-detail?id=40877fdb510c9de83b4a
22. Bhattacherjee, K. (17 June 2023). 'Ukraine war and the Indo-Pacific situation to figure in Modi-Biden talks,' *The Hindu*, https://www.thehindu.com/news/national/narendra-modi-joe-biden-talks/article66977469.ece
23. 'War in Ukraine: Impact on the Indo-Pacific.' (2 July 2022). India Foundation, https://indiafoundation.in/articles-and-commentaries/war-in-ukraine-impact-on-the-indo-pacific/
24. Cooperation and Conflict in the Indo-Pacific | Proceedings - May 2023, vol. 149/5/1,443. (30 April 2023), U.S. Naval Institute, https://www.usni.org/magazines/proceedings/2023/may/cooperation-and-conflict-indo-pacific
25. Gerstl, M. I. A. A. (23 April 2023). 'Mixed reactions to the Russian war ýagainst Ukraine in the Indo-Pacific: Views of governments and civil society, ,EIAS. https://ceias.eu/indopacific-views-of-russian-aggression/
26. Saha, P. (11 March 2023). 'The ongoing Russia-Ukraine conflict: Impact on Southeast Asia,' ORF, https://www.orfonline.org/expert-speak/the-ongoing-russia-ukraine-conflict-impact-on-southeast-asia/
27. 'The impact of Russia-Ukraine conflict on the security environment in the Indo-Pacific region. (n.d.). FRS, https://www.frstrategie.org/en/programs/japan-program/impact-russia-ukraine-conflict-security-environment-indo-pacific-region-2023
28. 'What are Indo-Pacific powers learning from the war in Ukraine?' (20 January 2023). DIIS, https://www.diis.dk/en/research/what-are-indo-pacific-powers-

learning-from-the-war-in-ukraine

29. Strategic Brief no. 33 - 2022 - War in Ukraine: Strategic Dilemmas in the Indo-Pacific. (n.d.). https://www.irsem.fr/publications-de-l-irsem/breves-strategiques/strategic-brief-no-33-2022-war-in-ukraine-strategic-dilemmas-in-the-indo-pacific.html
30. Wishnick, E. (30 January 2023). 'Ukraine's Ripple Effect on Russia's Indo-Pacific Horizon,' CNA, https://www.cna.org/our-media/indepth/2023/01/ukraines-ripple-effect-on-russias-indo-pacific-horizon
31. Pietrobon, E. (n.d.). Analytics. Valdai Club. https://valdaiclub.com/a/highlights/the-indo-pacific-in-the-wake-of-the-ukraine/
32. Ibid.
33. Ibid.
34. 'The impact of Russia-Ukraine conflict on the security environment in the Indo-Pacific region. (n.d.). FRS, https://www.frstrategie.org/en/programs/japan-program/impact-russia-ukraine-conflict-security-environment-indo-pacific-region-2023
35. 'The Ukraine War: Impact on Indo-Pacific Regional Dynamics. (n.d.). Delhi Policy Group, https://www.delhipolicygroup.org/publication/policy-briefs/the-ukraine-war-impact-on-indo-pacific-regional-dynamics.html
36. Harris, H. B. (10 November 2022). 'The Impact of the War in Ukraine on the Indo-Pacific Region. RAND, https://www.rand.org/pubs/conf_proceedings/CFA2070-3.html#the-impact-of-the-war-in-ukraine-on-the-indopacific-region-keynote-presentation
37. 'The lessons of the Ukraine war for the Indo-Pacific Region: a preview of, rather than a change in, what we will face in 10-15 years, (n.d.). https://www.jiia.or.jp/en/ajiss_commentary/the-lessons-of-the-ukraine-war-for-the-indo-pacific-region.html
38. Ibid.

19

Russia's Invasion of Ukraine: An Analysis of European Union Policies

Tanvir Ahmed

Introduction

Russia's invasion of Ukraine has opened up a new rivalry between the European Union (EU) and Russia. It has been looked upon by the international community as a geopolitical competition involving the EU along with Russia. Moreover, Ukraine and Russia have not had a smooth journey since their separation from the dissolution of the USSR. Russia re-emerged as an active player in global politics, whereas Ukraine was reduced to a political pawn by Western powers. Ukraine has over the years failed to integrate the two separate forces of Ukrainian nationalists and pro-Russian separatists, which has impacted its project of nation-building. Russia's invasion of Ukraine has also deeply impacted the societies of the two neighbours as it has divided families and communities. Since the start of this invasion, Ukraine has experienced subsequent uprisings in its southern and eastern regions, loss of its territory, which took away many lives and tightening of its economy. Moreover, recently, leaders from around the world gathered in Switzerland on 15-16 June 2024 to put pressure on Russia to put an end to the conflict in Ukraine and to embrace the 10-point peace proposal proposed by Ukrainian President Volodymyr Zelenskyy. He viewed the large turnout as a success and expressed optimism that the accords reached during the negotiations will influence the course of peace negotiations.

It is also argued that "the Ukrainian crisis that started with the Euromaidan protests in November 2013 and has culminated thus far in Russia's annexation of Crimea represents the biggest geopolitical shock to the European security system since the end of the Cold War."[1] It massively impacted the relationship between the EU and Russia. The Western leaders reacted strongly and unanimously condemned Russia. They interpreted it as aggression and invasion of a foreign territory. To them, it was an act of annexation. Then US Secretary of State, John Kerry described "Moscow's intervention in Crimea as an incredible act of aggression' and the EU leadership called it an unprovoked violation of Ukraine's sovereignty and territorial integrity.[2] To them, by taking control over Crimea, Russia has violated many international laws such as Article 2(4) of the UN Charter, which explains that 'all members shall refrain from the threat or use of force against the territorial integrity of any state'. The 'Declaration on Principles of International Law' (1971) adopted by the UN General Assembly, declared that illegal and territorial acquisition resulting from the risk or use of force, principles 1-V of the CSCE Helsinki Final Act (1975), to the Treaty of Friendship and cooperation between Russia and Ukraine (1997) and also few other mutual interstate treaties and understandings which confirmed and assured Ukraine's independence and territorial integrity.[3]

EU-Russia Relations

The European Union-Russia relations have gone through different phases. But the recent Ukraine conflict along with earlier problems has deteriorated the relationship. In the initial phase of the relationship, following the disintegration of the Soviet Union, the member-states of what was then called the European community saw an opportunity to include some post-Soviet states under the European sphere of influence. Immediately, following the disintegration of the Soviet Union, the EU and some Western countries were more worried about the survival of these newly-democratic countries rather than the EU expansion policy. By the early 1990s, Russia and most of the post-Soviet states were facing many economic and political challenges. Russia was looking for a partner who could provide stability in their country. Europe got an opportunity to cooperate with Russia. The first Russian President, Boris Yeltsin, saw this as a huge opportunity to transit Russia into a democracy and also towards the West. Yeltsin immediately started a discussion for a partnership with Europe. In the negotiation process, the EU wanted Russia to follow EU laws and regulations and wanted Russia to act like Europeans. The Agreement is known as Partnership and Cooperation Agreement (PCA) which set out the working relationship between the two parties and set benchmarks for Russia to meet on issues such as human rights, economics, and political participation. The Agreement also expected future bilateral and political relations. However, in reality, the agreement faces many difficulties. Some of the important issues like NATO expansion, first Chechen war, and war in Yugoslavia have derailed the EU-Russia relationship. On 31 December 1999 Yeltsin resigned.

In the second phase of the EU-Russia relationship, a new hope emerged with the coming of Vladimir Putin as the new President. Many observers imagined a positive development in the relationship. But immediately, things quickly changed as the EU expanded it expansion policy towards the post-Soviet states. As the EU reached the border of Russia, the situation became tense. As tension intensified, Russia by 2002, raised concerns over many issues like its citizens in Kaliningrad, the Oblast and naval base separated from the rest of the country by Poland and Lithuania, both of whom were about to enter the EU, and also over the treatment of Russian-speaking minorities in Estonia and Latvia, both new members, both with policies designed to isolate and potentially discriminate against Russian speakers. The EU had a discussion on this issue with its new members who joined it on1 May 2004. All the important points that were included in the PCA agreement between the EU and Russia will be implemented by the new members also. Russia was no longer seen as a weak economy since the time the PCA was agreed to along with the EU expansion policy. In fact, Russia has expanded its natural gas production and now it is seen as a global power. Now, the EU-Russia relationship cannot be seen from Russia's weak position. The main conflict in EU-Russia relations started when Russia was again seen through the lens of the global powers' perspectives and the EU from the Eastern expansion policy. The conflict escalated further when the EU developed the European Neighbourhood Policy (ENP) for its eastern and southern neighbours with the aim "to attain the closest possible political association and the maximum possible measures of economic integration."[4] At the same time, Russia questioned the EU how it could think that Russia would be placed under the same policy along with the small post-Soviet states. Russia didn't want to join the group, as the PCA agreement was still going on. As the EU was supposed to renew the PCA agreement as it was coming to an end, Russia declined to sign the earlier PCA point. Instead of European Neighbourhood Policy (ENP), the EU and Russia signed the Common Space Agreement (CSA).

The third phase of EU-Russia relations is marked as an important period as it faces many challenges. The world was facing global recession in 2008. The economic recession had a serious impact on the economy of EU countries. Greece was the worst sufferer along with a few other EU countries. This year is also known for the conflict between Russia and Georgia. This conflict had a serious impact on the EU-Russia relationship. Things began to improve a little when Dmitry Medvedev came to power, as he wanted to continue the interaction process irrespective of the difference and confrontation. In fact, both the EU and Russia had different opinions on world affairs. Some of the important issues like the Syrian crisis, and independent status of Kosovo has further worsened the relationship.

The fourth phase of EU-Russia relationship includes the Ukrainian conflict which has completely deteriorated the relationship. Both the EU and Russia blame each other for the Ukrainian conflict. Moreover, many observers believe that there is a distrust and lack of cooperation which has also worsened the relationship.

European Union Enlargement Policy

The biggest extension of the European Union took place on 1 May 2004. During the enlargement process "10 European countries which include Cyprus, the Czech Republic, Estonia, Hungary, Latvia, Lithuania, Malta, Poland, Slovakia, and Slovenia became full members of the European Union."[5] After the entry of these new countries into the Union, the EU moved further to the east and the south. To integrate these states, the EU required a specific policy to include these 'New abroad' states. The ENP was proposed by the EU in 2003 to include these new states. It covers Southern Mediterranean and also Ukraine, Moldova and Belarus.

The ENP was formally declared by the EU in 2004. The plan was expanded further towards the countries of South Caucasus which include Georgia, Armenia, and Azerbaijan. The main purpose of the ENP "is to share the benefits of the EU's 2004 enlargement with neighbouring countries in strengthening stability, security, and well being for all concerned."[6] It also provides opportunities for these new states to cooperate with the European Union on issues of security, political, economic, etc.

Since the formation of the ENP, the EU has faced the challenges of having a specific policy for its eastern and southern neighbours, as these states have different culture, behaviour, and aspirations in comparison to other EU neighbouring countries. Hence, the Polish and the Swedish initiated a difference within the ENP and also established a new Eastern Partnership (EaP) plan which will help "to address specific challenges near the EU's Eastern borders."[7] The main purpose of this policy "is to create a relationship with the post-Soviet states."[8] It also aims to differentiate between the eastern and southern neighbours, and seeks closer ties with the EU for each member. The EaP was officially launched on 2009 at the Prague Summit. Russia criticized this policy and saw as a direct threat to it. The Russian Minister of Foreign Affairs, Sergei Lavrov, when addressing the Brussels Forum in 2009, said that "we are accused of having spheres of influence, but what is the Eastern Partnership, if not an attempt to extend the EU's sphere of influence, including to Belarus."[9] It offered EU relationship with Armenia, Azerbaijan, Belarus, Georgia, Moldova, and Ukraine. Moreover, it offered a two dimensional approach—bilateral and multi lateral. In the bilateral approach, individual member-states would have a direct relation with the EU. It mainly discusses the Association Agreement which contains the deep and comprehensive free trade agreement (DCFTA), along with social, economic, and energy sector development along with other issues. It also offers financial support to each member state during the negotiation process of the Association Agreement. On the other hand, the multilateral approach provides 'important information' regarding security, transit to democracy, how to make reforms, etc. The multilateral approach is divided into three parts: political, technical, and nongovernmental. In relation to the political aspect, all the foreign ministers of member-states met in the annual meeting of the EaP summit to discuss political issues. In relation to the technical aspect, it involves working groups to discuss particular topics or issues. In relation to the nongovernmental aspect, it includes civil society which will help it to create an EaP civil society forum. The EaP also provided a platform for discussion on the issues of democracy, rule of law, good governance, etc. Thus, the EaP is seen by the EU as close economic and political cooperation with the Eastern European countries, while, on the other hand, Russia views the EaP policy from the geopolitical perspectives.

Geopolitical Context of the Conflict

Ukraine was part of Russia for centuries and both countries were closely aligned during the Soviet period.[10] Russia and Ukraine together formed the Kievan Rus, the first eastern Slavic state, with its capital being Kiev and fraternal relations of Russia and Ukraine dates back to the ninth century. Russia and Ukraine have a long standing cultural and historical connection. The conflict between Russia and Ukraine has been looked upon by the international community as a geopolitical competition between the EU and Russia. Apart from Ukraine and Russia, some of the important international actors involved in this conflict are: European Union, OSCE, UN, NATO, USA, Germany, Turkey, and France, among others. Moreover, the failure to achieve a possible solution in the post-Cold War arrangement has also worsened the correlation between the West and Russia. The two major geopolitical trends that emerged out of the Ukrainian conflict can be that "the insensitivity of the West to Russian security concerns after the Cold War, as demonstrated by the decision to expand NATO and Western missile defence systems into Eastern Europe, and also Russian attempts to maintain global influence similar to its levels at the height of the Soviet Union."[11] These two reasons had a huge impact on the relationship between the West and Russia.

Moreover, Ukraine is geographically connected to both Russia and NATO member-countries like Poland, Slovakia, Hungary, and Romania. Russia is more interested in Ukraine because it is geographically much closer to Russia, historically connected to it and also has many ethnic Russians living in Eastern and Southern Ukraine. Ukraine is geopolitically very important for Russia and the USA in the New World order because of its strategic location. It is the second biggest country in Europe; it shares a border with Russia; the Russian Black Sea fleet is located in Crimea, the eastern and southern regions of Ukraine are economically very prosperous; it has a nuclear power reactor, and it is also the main transit point for Russia's natural gas and oil pipelines that goes to other EU countries. Russian leaders have many times questioned Ukraine's plan to join the EU Association Agreement which would have benefitted Ukraine to improve its political and economic conditions, and also have access to EU markets. In fact, Russia has directly opposed Ukraine joining the NATO. Russia's aggression on Crimea, along with the escalation of the conflict to the southern and eastern regions turns out to be a 'hot' war between Ukraine (supported by the USA and the EU countries) and Russia. The situation resembles the 'Cold War' period. In fact many observers believe that the situation is turning out to be a 'New Cold War' between the EU and Russia. Also, the UN General Assembly passed a declaration on Ukraine's territorial integrity and condemned the takeover of Crimea, stated the referendum 'non-valid', appealed to the global community not to recognise the significant change that took place in Crimea. It isn't a single narrative of annexation of part of a sovereign state. There is also a parallel narrative. According to Mearsheimer, "the reasons behind the troubled relationship between West and Russia is NATO enlargement, the central element of a larger strategy to move Ukraine out of Russia's orbit and integrate it into the West, the EU's eastward expansion and the continuous West backing of the pro-democracy movement in Ukraine."[12] He also believed that the West was equally responsible for the crisis as it continued its EU and NATO enlargement in the Eastern European countries in spite of the warning from Russia which provoked Putin. In fact, Mearsheimer believed that a 'misguided strategy' by the USA and NATO has been to a large extent responsible for the crisis. On 18 March 2014, President Putin clearly declared that it was "the geopolitical rationale for the 'reunification' with Crimea."[13] Moreover, NATO's presence on the Russian border also disturbs Putin. The future option of Ukraine's membership in NATO has been viewed by Putin "as an acute threat to the security of Southern Russia."[14] Towards a considerable level, Crimea's takeover by Russia was an outcome of the US government under George W. Bush proposing

Ukraine's and Georgia's NATO membership at the Bucharest Summit in 2008. By this argument, it can be analysed that the Russian war in Georgia in 2008 and the Russian aggression in Crimea in 2014 is not a surprise.

The EU and most of its allies put the blame for the Ukrainian conflict squarely on Russia. But from Russian perspectives it is not wholly responsible for it. It was the clash of geopolitical control and expansion. From the Russian perspectives its security was threatened by the growing presence of NATO on its border.

Russia's Invasion of Ukraine

Russia's invasion of Ukraine on 24 February 2022 marked the beginning of one of the worst armed conflicts in Europe in years. Most of the Western powers have imposed sanctions on Russia for its offensive actions in Ukraine. Prior to the invasion, "Russia had mobilized between 150,000 and 190,000 personnel and 120 battalion tactical groups (BTGs) on its border with Ukraine, in Belarus, and in Ukraine's occupied Crimea region, according to the US government estimates."[15] On 21 February 2022, President Putin announced that Russia would support the autonomy of the Donetsk and Luhansk regions. Immediately after 21 February 2022, President Putin declared that Russia would send 'peacekeepers' into Donetsk and Luhansk by claiming that it has to be defended against Ukrainian offensive actions in the region. On 24 February 2022 following a month of warnings by the USA, European allies, and NATO, Russia invaded Ukraine. Putin announced that it will conduct a "Special Military Operation to protect its people and to 'demilitarize' and 'de-nazify' Ukraine."[16] Many analysts believed that it was Putin deliberate tactic to overthrow the elected government in Ukraine. Shortly, after Putin's announcement on television about Russia's 'Special Military Operation', Russia attacked key targets with missiles. Immediately, Russian forces made quick gains in key targets. Along with this, a few defence analysts believe that despite the Russian forces gaining in key targets, Russian forces underperformed in the first phase of the invasion. In addition, many observers were impressed by the Ukrainian resistance. They were also amazed by the guerrilla warfare and counterattack tactics used by the Ukrainian forces. Moreover, Russia was accused by Ukraine, the Biden Administration and non-government organizations for it repeated war crimes in Ukraine.

European Union's Response to the Invasion

The ruthless war of aggression waged by Russia against Ukraine and the illegitimate annexation of its Donetsk, Luhansk, Zaporizhzhia, and Kherson regions are both fiercely condemned by the European Union and its member-states. They also condemn Belarus' participation in the Russian military aggression. In order to discuss the situation in Ukraine from various perspectives, the European Council and the Council of the European Union have been meeting on a regular basis since February 2022. The EU has significantly increased sanctions against Russia in response to the military aggression, adding a large number of individuals and entities to the sanctions list and by adopting unprecedented restrictive measures. Some of them are:

- "Freezing the assets of 207 entities (including key banks) and 1,473 individuals (primarily Russian officials and elites), to whom travel bans also apply.
- Imposing debt and equity restrictions on certain banks and companies.
- Restricting transactions with Russia's central bank and blocking access to its reserve holdings.
- Banning transactions with certain Russian state-owned military-industrial enterprises.
- Disconnecting 10 leading Russian financial institutions—including Sberbank, Russia's largest bank—from SWIFT (the world's dominant international financial messaging system).
- Broadening export controls on dual-use goods and technologies.
- Banning certain exports in the aviation, maritime, and technology sectors (e.g., semiconductors) and the export of drone engines and luxury goods to Russia.
- Closing EU airspace, seaports, and roads to Russian aircraft, ships, and freight operators, respectively.
- Suspending broadcasting activities of nine Russian state-owned media outlets (including subsidiaries).

- Banning EU exports of oil refining technologies.
- Prohibiting Russian coal imports."[17]

Conclusion

Russia's invasion of Ukraine is the outcome of a larger failure to establish a post-Cold War settlement in world affairs. Also, Russia's invasion of Ukraine has directly threatened European security and has worsened the Russian-West relationship. Moreover, it was a conflict of geopolitical control and expansion on Ukrainian land. Both the West and the Russians are highly interested in Ukraine because of its strategic location. On one hand, the Western leaders wanted to continue NATO expansion by including post-Soviet states. On the other, Russia believed that its security was threatened with the growing presence of NATO on its borders. Also, the European Union Expansion Policy is not supported by Russia. However, for its part, the West doesn't want to see the same level of domination of Russia over the post-Soviet countries. The United Nations Security Council has highly condemned Russia's action in Ukraine. The continuous EU and NATO ambitious policies and Russia's security and territorial fears have escalated the conflict between both the sides. It is a competition between the EU and Russia to control their respective spheres of influence. Overall, it can be said that the geopolitical competition between the EU and Russia has posed a serious threat to the entire Eurasian region.

REFERENCES

1. Henrik Boesen Lindbo Arsen. *Great Power Politics and the Ukrainian Crisis: NATO, EU and Russia after 2014*, Denmark: Lone RavnkildeogVikiRachlitz, 2014, p. 10.
2. Elizabeth A. Wood, William E. Pomeranz, E. Wayne Merry, and Maxim Trudolyubov. *Roots of Russia's War in Ukraine*, New York: Columbia University Press, 2016, p. 66.
3. Anton Bebler. 'The Russian-Ukrainian Conflict over Crimea,' Teorija in Praksa, (Slovenia), vol. 52, no.1, March 2015, p. 208.
4. J.L. Black and Michael Johns (eds.). *The Return of the Cold War: Ukraine, the West and Russia*, New York: Routledge, 2016, p. 56.
5. Pabrick, Artis and Andis Kudors (eds.). *The war in Ukraine: Lessons for Europe*, Riga: University of Latvia Press, 2015, p. 146.
6. Ibid., p. 147.
7. Ibid., p. 147.
8. Wilczewska and R. Sakwa. *Ukraine and Russia: People, Politics, Propaganda and*

Perspectives, Bristol (UK): *E-International Relations Publishing,* 2015, p. 135.

9. Pabrick, Artis and Andis Kudors (eds.). *The war in Ukraine Lessons for Europe,* Riga: *University of Latvia Press,* 2015, p. 146.
10. Mcmahon, R. 'From Ukraine in Crisis,' Council on Foreign Relations, 2014, pp. 11-13.
11. Anthony Ramicone. 'The Ukrainian Crisis: A Disputed Past and Present,' IOP Policy Program, Institute of Politics, Harvard Kennedy School, Harvard, May 2014, p. 11.
12. John J. Mearsheimer. 'Why the Ukraine Crisis is the West's Fault: The Liberal Delusion that Provoked Putin,' *Foreign Affairs,* New York, October 2014, p. 8.
13. Anton Bebler. 'The Russian-Ukrainian Conflict over Crimea,' Teorija in Praksa, vol. 52, no. 1, March 2015, p. 214.
14. Ibid., p. 214.
15. Andrew S. Brown. 'Russia's War in Ukraine: Military and Intelligence Aspects.'
16. Congressional Research Service (CRS), Washington, D.C. 27 April 2022, p. 1.
17. Ibid., p. 3.

Index